A PASSION FOR
MOUNTAINS

A PASSION FOR MOUNTAINS

Edited by
Hannah Burrows-Smith

ROBERT HALE • LONDON

© Hannah Burrows-Smith 2014

Additional material © (2014) Adrian Burgess, Adrian Nelhams, Alan Hinkes, Alun Richardson, Andy Perkins, Bruce Goodlad, Cain Olson, Chris Dale, Chris Parkin, Iain Peter, John Barry, Jonathan Preston, Libby Peter, Mal Creasey, Mark Seaton, Mark Walker, Martin Burrows-Smith, Martin Moran, Mike Pescod, Ric Potter, Richard Peart, Richard McHardy, Rob Collister, Robin Andrews, Rocio Siemens, Ron James, Rowland Edwards, Smiler Cuthbertson, Tania Noakes, Tim Neill, Victor Saunders

First published in Great Britain 2014

ISBN 978-0-7198-0719-0

Robert Hale Limited
Clerkenwell House
Clerkenwell Green
London EC1R 0HT

www.halebooks.com

2 4 6 8 10 9 7 5 3 1

Designed by Eurodesign
Printed in China

To the memory of Roger Payne, British Mountain Guide,
who died on Mont Blanc in July 2012

'Being in the mountains with Roger was FUN.
Alpine starts, gritstone bouldering, untracked slopes, sunsets to be photographed,
beers to be drunk: all these and more had to be shared with his friends
in the knowledge that life is really very good indeed.'

Andy Perkins

CONTENTS

ACKNOWLEDGEMENTS

Many thanks to all the British Mountain Guides who volunteered their support, not just those who wrote the articles themselves but everyone I chatted to about the book and who thought about having a go at writing, even if it was to no avail.

In particular, I am grateful to the following guides for their help in many ways: Robin Andrews, John Barry, Tim Blakemore, John Brailsford, Adrian Burgess, Martin Burrows-Smith, Julie-Ann Clyma, Rob Collister, Mal Creasey, Smiler Cuthbertson, Rowland Edwards, Graham Frost, Bruce Goodlad, K.C. Gordon, Alan Hinkes, Ron James, Rob Jarvis, Tim Jepson, Nick Kekus, Alan Kimber, Bob Lewis, Steve Long, John Lyall, Martin Moran, Kathy Murphy, Steve Long, Richard McHardy, Tim Neill, Adrian Nelhams, Tania Noakes, Cain Olson, Chris Parkin, Dick Peart, Mike Pescod, Iain Peter, Libby Peter, Ric Potter, Jonathon Preston, George Reid, Alun Richardson, Owen Samuels, Mark Seaton, Rocio Siemens, Mick Tighe, Ewen Todd, Mark Walker and Tim Walker. Particular thanks go to Andy Perkins for his words of dedication to Roger Payne.

Thanks go to the following people for contributing photographs and further advice: Keith Ball, John Farrar, Janine Frost, Pete Harrison, Walter Laserer, Mike Lates, Rory McLean, Mike Mortimer, Simon Panton, Charles Sherwood, Stuart Stanley and David Stone at the Scottish Mountaineering Club. I am also grateful to the parents of Chris Dale – Bernard and Eileen Dale – and to his brother Jon for allowing me to include one of Chris's many stories in this book.

Many thanks go to my parents, Marian and Martin, and to my sister Katie and her husband Kirk for being there on countless occasions to bounce ideas off.

Finally, I would like to thank the editorial and design teams at our publishers Robert Hale for keeping this book on track, with a small amount of pressure and patience.

ABOUT THE IFMGA

The IFMGA: an Association at an International Level

The IFMGA, founded in 1965 by guides from Austria, France, Switzerland and Italy, is currently a body of mountain guide associations from more than twenty countries in Europe, Asia, the Americas and Oceania, representing a total of almost 6,000 guides.

The aim of the association is to maintain close ties between all mountain guides; to harmonize the work regulations that govern the profession; to ensure better safety conditions for clients; and to facilitate the ability of mountain guides to work abroad, on mountains all over the globe. This last point manifests itself in the solidarity that exists between all guides, no matter what their country of origin, and the spontaneous assistance they provide to one another.

Highly Competent Guides with a High Level of Training

The highest training level in existence is required in four different disciplines in order to become a certified IFMGA mountain guide: rock-climbing, ice-climbing, mountaineering and ski mountaineering. IFMGA training gives a guide the ability to work on any mountain range, whether they already know the mountain or not. It takes five to ten years to become a mountain guide, from the moment a potential guide starts serious mountaineering to the moment when he or she receives his or her guide diploma.

Proper Training Guarantees an International Standard

The Technical Commission of the IFMGA looks to its permanent working group to study the evolution of techniques and how to improve the level of guide training. This Commission, made up of national technical directors, meets twice a year.

Guides are trained by the training schemes managed or run by their national associations, sometimes in collaboration with an organization such as a school or university.

Becoming a Member of the IFMGA

Becoming a member involves a long process of integration that must be backed up by national legislation. To be accepted into the IFMGA can take a new country from five to 15 years, which is until the criteria required are fulfilled (notably in the capacity of the country's association to train guides to the required level).

Experience shows that the harmonious development in mountain guide activity, necessary for the safety of the public, is provided for by legal status or clear regulations. Indeed, to obtain a valid IFMGA diploma requires a very long and very intensive investment on the part of the guide. Inversely, in the absence of rigorous guidelines, few guides would put themselves through sufficiently high levels of training, giving the entire profession a confused image that would not help its development or protect the public interest on safety matters. It is therefore sometimes difficult for the public to distinguish between the highly competent IFMGA guides and the lesser competent guides who have few qualifications, or none.

EDITOR'S NOTE

What is the journey for a climber that begins with their own passion to lead climbs; to go first, to be on the sharp end of a climbing rope, to seek out adventure amongst the many cliffs and mountains of the world? Learning by one's own experience and from that of others, to work out moves and solve the puzzles that rock and ice challenge us with. Working out difficult terrain and making key decisions that get the team into tricky places, and back out again.

To then want to lead others in the same environments, for *their* own pleasure and not our own, to make holidays for people in the mountains and to make a career out of it – that might be seen as a different avenue to take. Simply as climbers, we can perhaps focus entirely on ourselves whilst concentrating on the moves of a climb, all else in life forgotten for a moment. But being a mountaineer is to be a decision-maker in the mountains and in that role we have to look outside ourselves to share our climbing, our mountains, our skiing, in order to make a journey into a wild mountainous environment work for others.

A mountaineer has to have an understanding of route choice (including conditions of the route) and of the weather, together with an understanding of, and empathy with, their companions' abilities – and also a realistic view of their own. Many people take to being leaders in mountain environments, using their own experience and taking further training to gain awards and qualifications. On aspiring to become an International Mountain Guide a candidate has to have gained experience at a high standard as a mountaineer, as a climber and as a skier. They are then trained and assessed at an equally high standard, and gain much experience working alongside other guides. On qualification they can operate all over the world.

The opportunity of having a collection of articles entirely written by guides was presented to the British Mountain Guides by Alexander Stilwell at Hale Books. Initially Rob Jarvis started the project and got the ball rolling, searching for ideas amongst the membership as to what could be written. However, he soon became busy with new paternal duties, so I took over as project manager and editor, and started to work out how the book might be presented.

I hoped that a book could be produced to represent all the mountain activities that British guides thrive on, in a manner that hopefully represents us as a group of people and shows the depth of climbing and mountaineering experience that we have. The idea was to bring together a variety of tales from across the board; of the membership, of mountaineering and climbing activity, of locations in the UK and around the world, and of varied writing styles and approaches to what each author thought would make a good story.

I was keen to include stories that represented skiing as a mountaineering activity. The world of back-country skiing and ski-touring is not really represented in this book, even though it is from this diverse activity that many working guides earn their living for half of the year – and, indeed, to be an IFMGA Mountain Guide is to be an accomplished back-country skier and ski-tourer. Could we have a book on the climbing and mountaineering accomplishments of guides and not include a few tales that may have involved skis at some point? So a handful of skiing-related stories have been included, even though they do suggest a small family and Continental bias … I hope that they add something to the nature of the book.

Once I had decided that this book would be a collection of stories that guides wanted to write about – what would these bring to the whole? To have a relative freedom to write about anything that was indeed a story, an account of a personal experience, might include quite naturally some classic climbs, but would hopefully also involve mention of some of the more random, wilder places in which we often find ourselves.

One thing would soon become apparent from such a collection of stories; they all happened to people prior to becoming, or whilst being, a guide and perhaps something can be learnt from each of us about how we manage ourselves and relate to our companions whilst operating in the varied and challenging mountain environments in which we work and play.

Initially brought together through the year 2012, this book has, at times, had the feeling of pulling teeth! Where were the stories going to come from – plenty of contenders out there, but who would write them down? Within a guide's working year there's not always a lot of free time, with varied work commitments and precious time to be spent with other halves, families and, of course, on holidays ourselves. A handful of great story-tellers in spoken word would not put them to paper for anything! Yet steadily throughout the year, amongst the messages of apology and support for the book, the stories themselves did start to appear …

FOREWORD

A *Passion for Mountains* gives a very good insight into the world of the British Mountain Guides. We are a small organization of professional mountaineers and skiers. We come from a range of backgrounds and professions (there are doctors, carpenters, engineers, teachers, lecturers, builders, architects and soldiers amongst our members) but we all have one thing in common – an absolute commitment to and love for climbing and mountaineering and the mountaineer's way of life.

It isn't easy to become a guide. You must pass many technical assessments of the various climbing and skiing skills but, more importantly, before you even get to the assessment stage, you need to amass a huge amount of mountaineering experience. This book gives an insight into the climbing adventures that contribute to a guide's experience. It shows, sometimes in fascinating detail, the difficulties that even some of the world's most experienced mountaineers encounter when making decisions in the mountains. It gives us a unique perspective into what motivates and drives climbers; where we find fulfilment and reward and, at the same time, how we deal with failure.

As I browsed through the list of contributors and looked at the mountains and routes climbed and skied I found myself being constantly distracted. I was drawn back to my own memories of days spent in the hills with some of the authors and to my own ascents of the routes and mountains that they describe. I was transported back into their company and reminded of their passion and enthusiasm for the hills. Their accounts vividly reminded me of the pleasure and fun, the fear, tension and hard work that are the very essence of climbing and mountaineering. I was catapulted back to sun-kissed granite, to cold bivouacs and to stressful days at high altitude and reminded anew of the overwhelming beauty of the mountain environment. Sometimes, it is their guiding exploits that are being described and sometimes it is personal climbing with friends, but always, on every climb, it is the sheer enthusiasm and passion for the hills that shines through.

Mountaineers possess a restless spirit; they are hard to satisfy and rarely content. Always there is another climb, a better route, a different descent, a better challenge. This comes across strongly in *A Passion for Mountains*. However, from time to time, we also get a glimpse of the comforting glow that comes from a successful and well-planned ascent and of the deep pleasure that comes from simply being in the mountains with good companions.

Mountain guides are great people to share time in the mountains with. Their experience, passion and knowledge can make the mountains accessible to all. This book gives a taste of the endless possibilities that exist. It is full of temptation and enticement. Above all, it is a reminder that time is short and there are many routes waiting to be climbed. It is time to dust off those often discussed plans and to begin to turn them from dreams into reality.

Iain Peter

The eminent Victorians who turned the Alps into *The Playground of Europe* (as Leslie Stephen's famous book was titled) also created the profession of mountain guide. The gentlemen, often dons or clergymen, provided the inspiration and the financial means, while peasants from the Alpine valleys lent the muscle and the mountain-craft. 'You had only to say *what* was to be done, and *how* it was to be done, and the work *was* done, if it was possible. Such men are not common, and when they are known, they are valued', wrote Edward Whymper of his great guide, Michel Croz. The best guides and their regular clients established a rapport based on mutual respect and affection. They were, on the mountain at least, partners.

By Robin Andrews, with an update on recent developments contributed by Rob Collister and Libby Peter.

In British upland areas, guides have been operating for as long as visitors have wished to climb mountains, in other words from the early nineteenth century (although botanists were employing local guides to take them into the hills as early as the seventeenth century). Robin Hughes, aged fifty-two, of Capel Curig, is

On the west ridge of Sgurr nan Gillian, Skye Cuillin. John Mackenzie is first on the left

Courtesy of SMC image archive

On Knight's Peak;
John Mackenzie with
Thomas Meares

described as 'guide to the Snowdonia Hills' in the census of 1861. Around the same time, William Roberts, the original Snowdon ranger, was reputed to have made over two thousand ascents of Snowdon. But the modest, now unglaciated hills of Britain could never support a body of professional climbing guides on the scale of the Alps. Besides, the work was strictly seasonal and only botanists ever wanted to leave the beaten track.

When, in the early 1900s, the Wasdale Head Hotel did take on a climbing guide for the benefit of its patrons, he was a Frenchman, one of the Gaspard clan from the Écrins. To quote the publicity material of the time: 'A FIRST CLASS DAUPHINE GUIDE AND CLIMBER … who will conduct climbers on the various Climbs in the District at a moderate charge.' A part of his duties was to clean all the boots each night. (Similarly, Mattias Zurbriggen, who was employed as a guide on Martin Conway's expedition to the Karakoram in 1892, spent more of his time shooting chamois for the pot and mending boots than cutting steps.)

The first native-born, true mountain guide in Britain was probably John Mackenzie, whose career in the Cuillin of Skye spanned fifty years. With Norman Collie he made one of the greatest of the early climbing partnerships. In 1896 they ascended Sgurr Coir' an Lochain, the last unclimbed summit in Britain and in 1906 were the first to find and climb the remarkable Cioch on Sron na Ciche. Collie and Mackenzie are buried side by side in Struan churchyard and in the Cuillin they are commemorated as Sgurr Thormaid and Sgurr MhicChoinnich. Ben Humble described a meeting in 1930: 'Later that evening we had the good fortune to fall in with John Mackenzie.… He is the most famous mountain guide in Britain; a man among men, ruddy-complexioned and clear of eye.… What a grand life Mackenzie has had!'

However, the first full-time professional British guide, who chose his career for a reason which resonates with modern guides, seems to have been Jerry Wright who wrote: 'The magic of the mountains captivated me when I was a boy and I have remained enthralled ever since. When I was a young man I had no means to climb regularly in the 1920s, so I became a professional mountain guide.'

He was based in Borrowdale, and towards the end of his life estimated that he had spent 3,500 days guiding on British crags. He climbed Napes Needle over six hundred times and claimed the fastest ascent in a race with Fred Balcombe. He eked out a frugal living, but suffered considerable hostility from club climbers for making money from climbing. In the post-war years he founded the Mountaineering

Association, which, until its demise in the late 1960s, made a huge and still under-rated contribution to mountain training.

Other part-time professional guides of this era were Jim Birkett, Jim Cameron, Chuck Hudson, Charlie Wilson, Joe Williams and Len Muscroft in the Lake District and George 'Scotty' Dwyer and Evan Roberts in Wales. Hudson was probably the first to guide Central Buttress on Scafell, his party of three men and a woman clambering over Wilson, belayed in slings at the Chock-stone.

The eccentric Millican Dalton, self-styled 'Professor of Adventure', would emerge from his comfortably appointed cave on Castle Crag to lead his clients in the Borrowdale Valley, or on rafting expeditions on Derwent Water. Looking back in 1972, John Baxter remembered that even in those days guides used to squabble about an appropriate daily rate: 'The Lakes' guides suggested £2.50 a day, £5 for exceptionally difficult courses.... The cautious Welshmen felt that these charges were too high and that "sensation-seeking novices might pester guides with their fivers".'

In 1944 the British Mountaineering Council was formed and began to develop a registration scheme for professional guides. This was launched in 1947, with Charlie Wilson the proud owner of certificate number 1. So-called BMC guides were registered for a specific mountain area as either 'mountain' or 'rock-climbing' guides, with an additional endorsement for Scottish climbing, administered by the Association of Scottish Climbing Clubs (the ASCC). Tickets were renewable every five years.

J.E.B. Wright in Seatoller, Lake District, 1932

Douglas Milner

Numbers increased in a trickle through the 1950s and 1960s and included some well-known names of the time: George Fisher, Bill Peascod, Bob Downes, Johnny Lees of RAF Mountain Rescue, Ron James (who was to become Treasurer and then President of BMG in the 1990s, and was rewarded with an MBE for services to mountaineering), Don Roscoe (still a regular at the Beacon climbing wall in North Wales in 2012) and the first female guide, Gwen Moffat. The competence of aspirants was tested by a day on the crag with a selected elder statesman or two. Colin Firth recalls a cryptic note from A.B.

Millican Dalton, photo taken in the Lakes in 1930

George Dalton

Medusa Wall on Esk Buttress, Lake District, 1964. Richard McHardy climbing, belayed by Martin Boysen

Tut Braithwaite and Richard McHardy on the Pinnacle Girdle on Clogwyn Du'r Arddu, 1968

Hargreaves: 'Meet on Green Ledge at 10 a.m.' He and Nev Collighan correctly identified this as being on Pillar Rock, and were on time to meet A.B.H. and Eric Arnison. When offered belay gloves, A.B.H. politely declined, saying his hands were quite warm. As the afternoon drew on, Arnison, who sang in a church choir, said he would have to be going, as he mustn't be late for evensong.

At one point the BMC Guides seemed to be stagnating, challenged by the Mountaineering Association, which at its height provided both British and Alpine training on a large scale. (Many MA instructors also became guides with the BMC, for example Geoff Arkless who, bearded and wiry, had the great advantage of looking like everyone's idea of an Alpine guide.) Then, in the 1960s, the Mountain Leader Training Board began accrediting leaders for the rapidly expanding outdoor education sector, which had experienced a number of high-profile accidents, and guides found a new role.

The route into the Alpine mainstream began for British guides in 1972, the year of Britain's entry into the European Union (then called the EEC), when the BMC Guides Sub-committee was formed. The Guides became a largely autonomous body and the assessment procedure was formalized and considerably stiffened. John Cunningham and Bill March devised an additional, mandatory winter assessment, introduced in 1976. Minimum standards for personal climbing were raised to HVS 5a on rock, grade IV on ice (see Climbing Grades at the end of this book), reflecting current trends (an inevitable and continuing process) and existing guides were given

Mal Creasey

until 1980 to catch up, after which formal carnets were issued for life. Fred Harper submitted himself and his Glenmore Lodge staff *en masse* for the new assessment.

Approaching the summit of Mont Blanc

There now began a prolonged courtship by the British Mountain Guides of the body representing the guides' associations of the Alpine countries (the UIAGM), a process fraught with difficulties and, in some quarters, outright hostility. Two major obstacles stood in the way. The first was structural.

To join the UIAGM, BMG needed to be a totally independent yet officially recognized body. The second was a question of standards of training and assessment, particularly in the realms of alpinism and skiing. The agenda was pushed along tirelessly by a visionary and committed group of guides, who realized that there was everything to gain from *rapprochement*. The Francophile John Brailsford played a crucial role, as did Geneva-based Bob Lewis, first Secretary of the new Association of British Mountain Guides, and Colin Firth, who succeeded him in 1975. Peter Boardman, National Officer of the BMC and an internationally recognized figure after his success on the south-west face of Everest, proved an invaluable ally. Lewis remembers that Fred Harper played a major role in facilitating the merger of English and Scottish interests and the final amicable break with the BMC and the ASCC, which was accomplished in 1975. At this time there were fewer than fifty British guides.

In June 1977 a formal application to join the UIAGM was rejected. *The Times* ran the story under the headline: 'Competence of Britain's mountain guides

Martin Burrows-Smith

A BMG guides ski test being held on the Great Slab of Coire an Lochain, featuring (l-r) Steve Boyden, Peter Cliff, Steve Hartland and Alastair 'Cube' Cain

queried.' British guides were distinctly piqued. In a letter to the editor, Pete Boardman complained about 'stagnant vested interest', while for the BMC Bob Pettigrew offered a bouquet of sour grapes, writing: 'Our guides have been mercifully spared the tedium of interminable glacier plods, or the equivalent of queue jumping on the Matterhorn, the bread and butter work of most continental guides.' It was felt that some of the Europeans had failed to grasp a crucial difference between their own training schemes and the British one: continentals typically entered into guiding relatively young and inexperienced, usually still in their teens, while British applicants were required to show a much greater depth and breadth of experience before being accepted for assessment. On the other hand, it has to be admitted that the training component of the British scheme at that time left a lot to be desired.

With the encouragement of Anderl Heckmair (first to ascend the Eiger's north face and a hugely respected figure both as climber and guide) among others, Britain submitted a fresh application and sent a delegation to the next meeting in November 1977 at Aosta. Colin Firth, John Brailsford and Peter Boardman drove out and entered the lions' den. Firth remembers they had a whip round at a committee meeting before setting off to cover their petrol money. It was a hard-fought occasion, at which the French were supportive but Heckmair had to harangue the Swiss and Austrian representatives with the immortal words: 'We are mountain guides, not ski instructors!' Finally, BMG was accepted, but with the proviso that ski and avalanche training be taken much more seriously.

A few British guides were already excellent skiers (Martin Burrows-Smith standing out) but most were not. Many a head-plant was to ensue over the coming years as hard-bitten climbers of the highest calibre submitted themselves to the indignities of mastering the slippery art. Bob Lewis relates that he had two very well-known qualified guides as 'trainee assistants' on the Haute Route: 'The clients were impressed with their history but not by their skiing!' It was a common story at the time, but in-service ski technique courses run by BASI (the British Association of Snowsport Instructors) trainers were introduced in the early 1990s to speed up the process.

Ron James

A lifetime of guides' badges and carnets

The hard work has paid off for many and skiing is now an integral part of the guides' scheme. Today, it is probably fair to say that for most guides, with a few notable exceptions, ski-touring and off-piste skiing are a more important aspect of their work than Scottish winter climbing.

Avalanche training relevant to the Alps rather than Scotland took a while to get off the ground but, in 1992, at the instigation of Rob Collister, Canadian guide Phil Hein was invited to the UK to run a train-the-trainers course and establish a template for the week-long course with which guides now start their Alpine training. Meanwhile, in 1978, shortly after the British Mountain Guides were accepted into the international body, the UIAGM president attended the BMG Summer Test as an observer. The course was being run in the Lakes that year and involved climbing on Dow Crag and Castle Rock. The following February a delegation from the UIAGM Technical Commission attended an in-service training course at Glenmore Lodge, superbly hosted by Fred Harper. The course addressed skiing, ski-mountaineering and short-roping with clients. The weather was miraculous: Cairngorm and the Northern Corries plastered with perfect *névé* under a blue sky! The event became a lively exchange of ideas, and the delegates were satisfied with what they saw. They went on to observe the Winter Test on Ben Nevis which, crucially, was convened throughout this evolutionary period by Alan Kimber and Klaus Schwarz based on Loch Eil Outward Bound centre. The holding of the UIAGM general meeting at Plas y Brenin in 1984 cemented Britain's position as a full and active member and made a fitting close to a decade of change.

Thirty-five years on from that seminal meeting in Aosta, the number of qualified guides has risen to over 180, of whom seven are women. The membership, as one

Roger Payne ski-
mountaineering on the
Truex Tours, above his
home town of Leysin

would expect, comprises rugged indi-
vidualists from widely differing
backgrounds. It includes some of the
best-known figures in British climbing,
and some who would hesitate to claim
'household name' status in their own
home, but all operate under the same
professional code; all are products of the
same stringent selection process. Their
work is enormously diverse. You will
find guides leading clients on 8,000-
metre peaks, conducting ski-tours in
Antarctica, operating at extreme technical levels on rock and ice, appearing
as expert witnesses, acting as safety
back-up for film crews, delivering
lectures, chairing meetings, writing
books and, above all, giving people days
out in the mountains they will never
forget.

Some guides run their own busi-
nesses, employing others; some work
freelance; some work in centres or in
the administration of mountain
training. All are now accepted into the
Alpine scene, and many live in France
or Switzerland. Fred Harper was an
important pioneer in this respect, one of
the first to base himself abroad. His
professionalism and charisma did much
to establish the reputation and respect
that British guides now enjoy in Europe.

The UIAGM has expanded to
include many more countries outside of both the Alpine zone and Europe and,
reflecting that, has become the IFMGA (International Federation of Mountain
Guides' Associations), with English the official language. Training Officers of the
BMG have become increasingly involved in the work of the IFMGA's Technical
Commission, monitoring standards, trying to ensure consistency in training and
assessment schemes, and addressing issues arising from new areas of work such as
canyoning and high altitude expeditions. Roger Payne, in particular, during his Pres-
idency, invested a huge amount of energy in the deliberations of the IFMGA and
was held in such high esteem that he was made an honorary member, the first British
guide to be so recognized. Sadly this had to be announced posthumously at the
General Assembly held in Aviemore in December 2012, following Roger's death in
an avalanche on Mont Maudit earlier that year. Over the same period the IFMGA
climbing championship was held at Ratho, near Edinburgh, with ninety-nine guides
from ten different countries competing.

Tim Blakemore

The BMG has become a limited company to protect its officers, who nowadays each receive an honorarium in recognition of the amount of time and work put in voluntarily to the running of the association. Office space and a secretary are shared with the MLTB (Mountain Leader Training Board) in Capel Curig. The introduction of a newsletter, *News from the Mountains*, by Nigel Shepherd in the 1990s was a valuable development, as was the creation of a website by Chris Ayres a few years later (subsequently renewed and expanded by Bruce Goodlad). Training and assessment courses and standards continue to evolve, as do procedures for dealing with accidents and complaints, an area in which David Hopkins, Tim Jepson and Peter Cliff have all played an important part over the years.

Guides work in some of the most dangerous environments on Earth. Tragically but inevitably there have been accidents, each one causing guides collectively and individually to take stock, scrutinize their working practices and reaffirm the values of honesty, with oneself and others, personal responsibility and acceptance of risk, which are at the heart of mountaineering.

Today, there seems to be no shortage of talented and dedicated young men and women aspiring to adopt the 'grand life' of a guide or, as John Brailsford was fond of putting it: '*le métier du guide*'.

Candidates at the end of their BMG ski test. Back row (l-r): Tim Blakemore, Matt Hellikar, Rob Jarvis, Mark Thomas, Neil Johnson and Richard Mansfield (BMG training officer at the time). Front row: Hannah Burrows-Smith and Jon Bracey (second assessor)

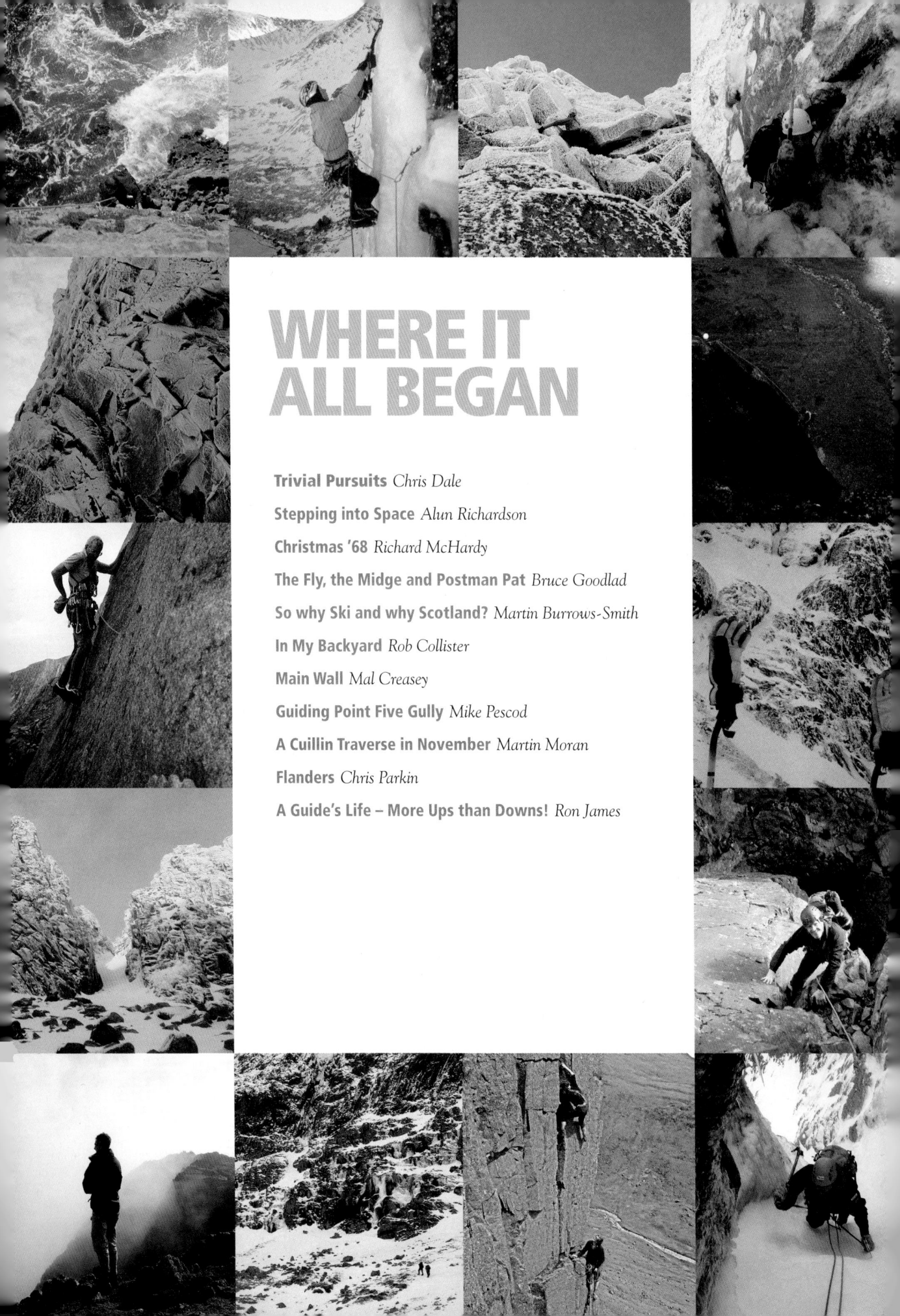

WHERE IT ALL BEGAN

TRIVIAL PURSUITS

Chris Dale

'Ye can stick yer grade six up yer arse, ye wee English – – – –.'

Those immortal words were inscribed one March evening in the Gelder hut book. Big and bold for all to chunder over and, let's face it, Ewen probably did. Ewen, like me, was in his early twenties, but here any comparison ends, as he already had silver hair and a rather gaunt, etched, expressive face, that spoke of a tough past. I had instantly warmed to his self-deprecating wit whilst on a recent international climbing meet – it was impossible to take oneself too seriously when in his presence. We had both plunged to new depths of humiliation when we had found ourselves, trapped by honour, in the futility of an eating contest. The Yugoslavians had, with diplomacy, opted out, leaving us to savour the question-

Back in the mid-1980s, when mixed climbing was developing on Scotland's winter mountains, Chris Dale and Ewen Todd found themselves on the snowed-up cliffs of Lochnagar. With the prospect of a new route on testing winter terrain, how does one climber or a climbing team work out the balance between personal achievement and self-preservation? What keeps a climber going in tricky places, on unknown, unclimbed rock faces, or informs the decision to keep going or to back off?

able delights of pint glasses of curry powder, salt, milk, strawberry jam, cooking oil and cigarette butts. We both finished our respective beverages, without regurgitation; a draw was given and a lifelong friendship had begun.

It all started a few weeks earlier, when Willie (his older, baldy brother) and I had placed a route, shame on us, in the esoteric order of grade VI (in Coire An Lochain and probably still requiring a second ascent). Now I won't say that life was unbearable since then, in fact things had been generally pretty good – you know, aqua-blue skies, squeaky *névé* – all that sort of thing. No, life wasn't unbearable, but Ewen was!

'Och, there's nae such thing as grade VI, we've had grade Vs in Scotland fae ovur thurty years, an I don't see why we should change nu.'

'But, Ewen, Jerry Smith talked of grade VI on Parallel Buttress way back in '56 … Johnny Cunningham was looking for a VI when he found The Chancer … Everybody knows it was only a matter of time until it was introduced, just like the old VS system. When the … '

Hannah Burrows-Smith

The Lochnagar cliffs as you first see them on arrival at the corrie

'Aye, that's another thing I'd like tae get strate we ye ...' And so it went on.

The moon was full and blue, the stars clear and bright, the Milky Way a cream ribbon spanning the sky, a veritable stairway to heaven.

'Hey, Ewen – fancy doing a climb tonight?'

'*Climb, Kruss?* No it's party time tha nu, luke ur's "Wee Charlie" wiya carryout.'

The night drunk and laughed itself away, the south-east face aid route on the bothy had a peg eliminated, Wee Charlie's primmy blew up and Ewen even asked me if I wanted to go climbing ... just before collapsing into a snow drift ...

'Just for a wee rest, ye know.'

Much, much later ... the bothy was empty.

'Well, Ewen, looks as though you've survived another death bivouac.'

'Aye ... I dinnae ken how they kun call thus a sleeping bag. A'm sure I could sue them under thae Trade Descriptions Act.... Thae original weight withute warumth pit!'

I staggered to the door, nursing a rather delicate drunkard's head.

'*Oh no!*'

'What's the matter, Kruss?'

'It looks like it's going to be another one of those gorgeous days .... Oh Gawd – why couldn't it rain just for *one* day?'

Unable to muster a convincing ploy to satisfy our consciences, we made the long plod up to the 'icy crucible' of Lochnagar. The last four years of drinking and bodily abuse seemed to be finally taking their toll. Head throbbing and lolling, every pore oozing, I leadenly ploughed an iridescent trail, snail-like, through the virginal snows – a testament to a wasted youth.

'Hey, Ewen, this can't be winter climbing – look, I'm getting a tan.'

'Aye, but just remember, laddie, it can change from this, to this, just like that' (with a click of his fingers). He continued with a wry, distant look in his eyes: 'Aye,

The cliffs surrounding Black Spout Gully catching the morning sunshine; the Pinnacle Face is to its left

it's *toooo* quiet by half, before ye know ut we cud bae plunged intae the depths uv a "blizzard nightmare".... Aye, lad, wa're doomed, arl doomed.'

But, the apocalypse didn't arrive and we were soon sitting on a favourite boulder, gazing into the corrie. The cliffs were damp with silence, the air still and sleepy, the highest rocks were only now being caught by the sun, glittering and resplendent, clad in icy armour; the veritable frozen fantasy fortress …

'Hey yuuu, Get offa ma root!' A cardinal sin had been committed. 'It's nae un wunter cundution.' Some unfortunate soul was currently trespassing on the first pitch of Ewen's route for the day.

'Av ye got yer EEEeeee BBBBBBbbbb's [EB boots]?'

'Well, Ewen, looks as though Crypt's out for today … what about Eagle Ridge? You said that it was a great route and that you would do it again.'

'Aye, but I just dud ut u week ago an a'm nut dane ut agin tuday.'

'So it can't be that good after all.'

'Look … Ut's fukin brulient, but a'm nut duwinut agun tuday.'

Defeated, I compromised: 'Well, I just did Parallel Buttress and Parallel B the other weekend, so how about Pinnacle Face?'

'Aye, why not?'

That day in The Crucible was a truly great one. I can't remember laughing so much whilst winter climbing. One disillusioned leader, after failing on the initial groove of Eagle Ridge, returned down his steps to his second and uttered the unforgettable line: 'I say, Cecil, the snow doesn't seem to be sticking to the rock today.'

Another kept on body-printing off the first pitch of Parallel A, and quite impressive they were too – his dogged optimism and remarkable survivals were quite humbling. Body-printing, for the uninitiated, is an ancient and growing activity, in which one finds the tallest structure (it doesn't matter what) one can pluck up the courage to leap off, legs and arms spread-eagled. Marks are given for depth and

Tim Neill climbing the first pitch of the Link Face Direct. This first pitch is commonly done these days by those repeating Argonaut itself

definition of the print, the height and trajectory of the dive and the originality and sincerity of the accompanied manic scream. Taking all things into account, our lad, on and off the blue water ice of Parallel A, was without doubt stupefying – we were indeed in the hallowed presence of a Master.

Sorry, I digress (not for the first time). Oh yes – Pinnacle Face, outmanoeuvred again! Some friends had been hiding in the moat that abuts the face and had sneaked up the first pitch whilst we were getting ready for battle.

What now? We found ourselves strolling carefree, up the even slopes of The Black Spout, with no particular wish or whim.

'Fancy holding my ropes on this?' I had found a groove, to God knows where, but it looked hard enough to keep us interested for a while and even seemed to offer a few runners (oh, the naïvety of youth).

And so the contest began … well, that's what I foolishly thought anyway. After several minutes of hooking on tiny nothings, I had completely exhausted my repertoire of heel hooks and knee bars and had made all of 3 metres of vertical progress. Unwilling to reappear cartwheeling down the gully in front of our friends on Pinnacle Face, I resorted to cowardly depths; placed a friend and lowered to the ground. This was ridiculous; I was already completely goosed. If only I could get a long enough run up, I could beat my high point, with a single leap …. Maybe that was the answer!

It wasn't.

I did swap my tools over, however, and now with 'Barracuda' in my right hand, I could cam its adze in a rather neat slot and mantel on to the smooth and steeply sloping slab of the chock-stone above.

The continuation groove was thinly glazed on its left wall; however, reassuring decoy clods of frozen moss and the occasional sod lured me merrily on.

At roughly 35 metres above the ground, unable to down climb and without the requisite protection to avoid a ground fall, the trap was sprung. At this point, the right wall overhung, forcing an exit on to the high-angled slabs that formed the smooth left wall of the groove. I tried my hardest to find something worthy of being called a runner and failed – miserably – I guess it was still winter climbing even though the sun was shining.

I finally plucked up the courage to commit to the moves, easing myself up the smooth slab on throwaway pick placements, under the controlled detachment of the soloist, without notion of failure or success; a slave to the moment. Thank God, a foothold was unearthed and I reviewed the situation.

'Oh my God, what have I done?'

Before mere panic had chance to escalate into uncontrollable gibbering spasms, I managed to squeeze a peg into a hidden horizontal break. It protruded obscenely and had to be tied off. With limited options, I then chose to imagine that this sole talisman was adequate to contemplate my escape.

I edged across the smooth slab leftward; the ice was much too thin, just a hoary spittle encasing all in its gossamer shell. Suddenly my front points broke the seal and I was left, feet slide-scrabbling, on the bare rock slab, tools miraculously still hooked. It was now time for some quick improvisation and, with a few sturdy requests, I frantically tension-traversed from my 'little friend' for about 5 metres, before landing on a short snow arête, which led quickly to a belay.

By the time Ewen had rejoined me (he did manage to second the pitch free, admittedly with a very snug rope), I had almost finished my sixth cigarette. (This confirmed the difficulty of the pitch; that is six ciggies for a VI, five for a V etc, etc. It's obviously not an infallible method of grading, but it is as accurate as any I have found.)

Bathing in the fool's fleeting glow of survival, I found myself busy admiring the fine set of tracks, criss-crossing the frozen loch. Clearly etched deep in the pile of the recent carpet of pristine powder, their lines, straight and true, appeared as the first intersecting tangents of some unfathomable creation by an unknown draughtsman, the only flaw in his design being a long, sinuous curve punctuated by a few yellow smudges.

'Look, Ewen, have you seen those tracks?' It was a while before it slowly dawned on me that they led to our sacks.

'Aye, luke thare mine; oh gawd a'm still blazing, Kruss.'

Until then, I hadn't realized how drunk he still was. I had initially thought that we might have been engineering a new start to Route 1, but now I could see the Springboard well below us. What now? All that effort for nothing? Well, it was Ewen's pitch next anyway.

There seemed to be an all-too-blatant line above us, but there were an awful lot of unfriendly looking bits, not to mention that band of overhangs. I tried not to laugh when I showed him 'the line'.

The going was hard straight from the belay, which focused my attention, as I was pinned below twenty-four of Chouinard's sharpest points. After some pick camming and deft footwork Ewen shook his way leftward in his normal, worryingly effective

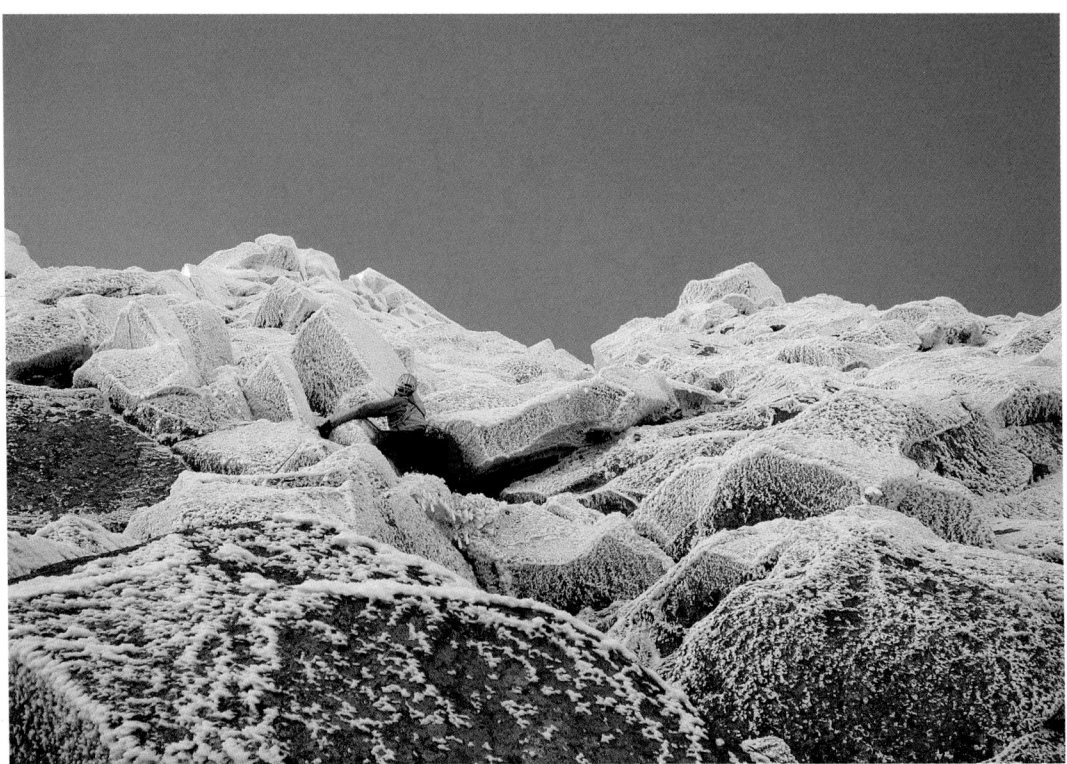

Moving on to the steep second pitch of the Link Face Direct

style. After a short but heart-stopping slide, he had climbed the corner and had made an awkward rightward traverse under a huge overhang. It was at this point that a *mauvais pas* was reached.

'Och, a think thar'll bae tae much drag uf a go roond tha corner, Kruss ... a'll bring yer up tae ere.'

The sly dog!

The pitch proved harder than it looked and the exposure was sobering, which was just as well, since it was hard enough understanding Ewen when he was sober, let alone half-cut.

The next pitch also proved deceptively hard, starting with a few back and footing moves up an overhanging V-groove and a pull over an overhang. From here, an easy left-slanting groove begged an escape (we were later to discover that this was the line taken by Jon Anderson's and Andy Nisbet's 1979 Winter Link Face and then, much later, Chris Cartwright's and Simon Richardson's 1998 Link Face Direct). However, our line was all too obvious; a rightward exit gaining a fine, steep square-cut corner with an off-width at its back. The left wall was very steep; the right a little less so, being covered by a thin film of verglas and sugared with a fine dusting of powder. Progress was gained with the dubious aid of a 5-centimetre thick, intermittent tongue of snow ice resting on the outer edge of the crack. Unfortunately, we had no big cams and progress had to be boldly won.

At anxiety's edge, the left wall unsportingly overhung but offered the gift of a welcome small 'rock' which was soon welded into a diagonal crack. A few moves later I found myself weightless, easing myself on to the absolute tip of my axe in the same diagonal crease. The following moves remain an adrenaline-soaked blur; they did, however, bridge the gap to the next stance, where the end-of-season blues finally caught up with me.

'I guess it had been quite an intense season. What a ridiculous sport this is', I mused. 'Here we are, freezing and scaring ourselves stupid. And look down there; two couples happily strolling and chatting their way up The Spout. Contented, well-adjusted types, socially acceptable ... the crag has no power over them.'

'The line' continued but was still blatantly hard, with a steep wall guarding the next pitch. Ewen successfully managed to get both feet off the ledge a couple of times, before collapsing back onto the belay. We reversed roles but I only managed a few paltry feet higher before popping off. Running on vapours, I dug deep and, with the aid of a few facefuls of powder, some hyperventilation and a serious talk with myself, I momentarily tricked the logical self and was up.

The next 15 metres still proved worrying; mostly pick camming and shallow ice placements, with a high rock-over midway. I eventually exited via a V-chimney and belayed below a rather inhospitable crack.

The day had, as so often happens, suddenly passed us by. The corrie was empty and the moon had almost risen as Ewen rejoined me at the belay; it was just becoming really dark. Expecting an easier day, we had stupidly left our head-torches in our sacks by the loch, so a hasty abseil retreat was made down the initial pitch of Route 2. Still coiling the ropes, we had already thought of a name; The Argonaut.

That was the easy part.

'Well, Ewen, what grade do you think it was then? ... What's that, Ewen? – I can't hear.'

After idly stomping and kicking the snow for a short while, head bowed, all he could muster to utter was that: 'A may ave bun wrong.'

'So it was a grade VI.'

'Aye, a guess ut must ave bun.'

We both laughed and yodelled our way back to the sacks....The world had been turned upside down – Ewen believes in grade VI!

We stopped briefly, close to the bottom of our route, and I traced a line up an even more improbable wall.

'Hey, Ewen, see this line, *now that* would be grade VII.'

'Och, thar's nae such thang us u grade VII, we've ad grade VIs un Scotland fae ovur u duzen yurs ...'

※ ※ ※ ※ ※

The route The Argonaut (VII 8) on Lochnagar had its first ascent on 1 March 1984 by Chris Dale and Ewen Todd. The second ascent was by Tom Bridgeland and Andy Sharp in 2000.

The Link Face Direct was climbed by Simon Richardson and Chris Cartwright on 1 Feb 1998. Pitch 1 is just left of The Argonaut and, according to the new Cairngorm guidebook, any repeats of The Argonaut have taken the first Link pitch, so perhaps no one has repeated The Argonaut – possibly put off by the need for ice and a pendulum ...

Chris Dale at home amid the steep and wild wintry terrain of the Darkness Beckons, on Sail Mhor crag, Beinn Eighe

Martin Moran

It was on 19 February in the winter of 2011 that we lost Chris Dale to cancer. He had been a keen writer about his many climbing adventures in Scotland and the Alps and this chapter 'Trivial Pursuits' comes with the appreciated permission of his family, via Ewen Todd.

STEPPING INTO SPACE

Alun Richardson

During the 1930s the brilliant climber Colin Kirkus remarked to his close friend, Alf Bridges, that 'Going to the right place, at the right time, with the right people is all that matters; what one does is purely incidental.' I have often pondered this statement as I have battled with driving rain on a mountainside, sat on a belay shivering in the cold or coped with disappointment when a rock climb hasn't quite lived up to the guidebook writer's enthusiasm. Climbing in good company is important to me and many a miserable situation has been turned into a fun one with the

Just going climbing with a friend is one of the simplest pleasures we are lucky to enjoy on British crags and mountain cliffs. Memories of the early days flood back from an era in your life when nothing else seemed to matter but the next route and the friends we shared those routes with, as Alun Richardson remembers well.

right people, but surely, when all things are equal, the route matters ... doesn't it?

My home is in Pembrokeshire, a quiet and beautiful corner of south-west Wales that has miles and miles of pale-coloured limestone rising steeply from the Irish Sea. Storms, huge waves and giant tides have battered the coast, carving the soft rock into a plethora of sea caves, steep walls and deep zawns. The striking cliffs are home to some of the UK's rarest sea birds such as puffins, razorbills and choughs, but what brought me to live here are the 5,000 world-class rock climbs sprinkled along the entire coast and, with not a single bolt in sight, they are truly adventurous. The most wonderful thing about climbing here is that twenty minutes after leaving the car park one can be totally committed to getting to the top of a climb, where retreat is difficult and the outcome is not certain. This adventurous quality means that the history of climbing here is riddled with the names of some of the UK's best adventure climbers – Pat Littlejohn, Ben Wintringham, Richard Harrison, Martin Crocker, Crispin Waddy, Paul Donnithorne, Emma Alsford, John Dunne, Tim Emmett, Ben Bransby, to name just a few.

The cliffs of Pembrokeshire have given me plenty of opportunity to test Colin Kirkus's statement and attempt to answer the question about whether the route really matters, or whether it all comes down to simply who you are with.

I had only been climbing for a few years on my first visit; Alan and I were quietly pushing the grades from the ignorance of our own experiences – not always a quick way to learn, with forgotten ropes or inadequate equipment, but definitely a quick

The cliffs of Mother Carey's Kitchen catching the late afternoon sun, with a climber on the top pitch of Wraith E2 5b

way to have adventures! It was possibly our ignorance that led us to climb a route that was so brilliant that we abseiled back down and did it again immediately afterwards. Pembroke climbs are not big, but what they lack in height, they more than make up for in steepness and exposure. Like most Pembrokeshire climbs this route can be done in one long pitch, but that would miss out on the joy and excitement of a hanging belay over a deep turquoise sea.

The route we had our sights on is found at Mother Carey's Kitchen, a small cove close to the popular seaside town of Tenby. It is a beautiful place to climb, steep but peppered with good holds and protection, but does have a reputation for the tide literally chasing some climbers up the cliff! The crag is named after the 'Mother Careys' or kittiwakes that glide, stiff-winged, like paper aeroplanes past the climbers clinging to the steep faces. It is often referred to as Mother Scarey's because of the gravity-defying 'Space Face' and the effect it has on climbers when they first visit.

Like many of the truly adventurous routes in Pembrokeshire this climb is gained from an exciting cliff-top abseil from a large block at the top of the east side of the south face. I can still see the rope fluttering into the unknown as I threw it off the edge of the cliff. I knew the rope was long enough, but I had no idea whether the ends were in the sea and, to reduce the chances of the ropes becoming jammed around boulders under the sea, I hadn't tied knots in the ends. Having to abseil to reach routes makes Pembrokeshire climbing spectacularly committing, especially when you can't get back to the rope after starting your route. I remember one climb where I let go of the abseil rope only to watch it spiral away and hang 10 metres out from the cliff and 3 metres above the sea. It certainly focused our mind on getting to the top of the route, that's for sure! Nowadays I always take a pair of jumars with me and leave them attached to the abseil rope!

Kath Murphy

Julian Fincham
seconding Star Gate,
E3 5c – Deep Space
tackles the great cleft
to its left

Our route didn't start from the bottom of the abseil; it climbed the landward side of a deep cleft where the wall starts to curve round into the wildly overhanging Space Face. The cleft is actually a small through-sea-cave situated behind the South Face that you have just abseiled down. The start of a climb can bring a variety of emotions to the surface; anxiety, excitement, nervousness, laughter, calmness – and sometimes all of them. On this day Alan and I were full of confidence and the sounds of banter echoed around the rock that surrounded us. We uncoiled the ropes carefully to avoid the pools of water and tried not to look too intently upward at the series of short cracks and pockets that led almost all the way to a belay in a small cave below the roof.

The first few moves up a groove and wall felt tricky and my feet tried to find the drier sections of rock that had lost their veneer of dampness left by the receding tide. I was soon climbing the line of pockets via sustained 'juggy' moves; the compact rock, large holds and perfect gear more than compensated for my nervousness. You could probably protect the whole of the first pitch on threads, but some are a little more difficult to place than wires and friends because your hand or arm is holding on to them! Soon my way forward was barred by a large overlap, or roof, so a little below it I started a tricky blind move out over the sea. I scuttled back the first time, too aware of the space below my feet and the prospect of a backward pendulum. I placed another piece of gear to add to the already immaculate protection I had. A blind grope for a good hold and the moves were over quickly and the security of a small cave and an exposed hanging belay could be enjoyed.

I watched Alan getting ready to climb and took a few moments to absorb the vista around me. I could see small fish weaving amongst the kelp in the clear waters below and gannets were dislocating their wings just as they entered the water after a dive from over 50 metres. I scanned the horizon for another UK sea cliff climbing paradise – the small island of Lundy. I am sure the island moves, on a weekly basis, to a new place along the coast; it never seems to be in the same place where I last saw it, that's for sure.

Alan climbed confidently to meet me, which was reassuring as he had the second pitch; a brutal, but short-lived start over a daunting roof and then some fine wall-climbing and bridging. We swopped gear and had the usual friendly banter that two climbers exchange when hanging in an exposed situation with a big roof above them. From the hanging belay, I watched as he traversed slightly leftward on holds that were like grabbing large frisbees. Selecting the best ones to use can prove problematical and more than one climber has floundered trying to find the combination of holds that make the pitch 5a and not 5b. Once the holds over the roof had been grasped, Alan quickly scuttled his feet up and over so the handholds became his footholds, and breathed a sigh of relief. His mood changed from one of being unsure of his abilities to one of 'well, that was easier than it looked'. The last time I had heard him say that he had fallen from the top of a VS when soloing and broke both ankles, so I held the ropes tightly.

At this point on the climb, the exposure is now huge for the leader and I know of one climber who felt sick when looking down between their feet at the drop below. You can make the exposure even greater by traversing rightward to the Fresh Air Finish that follows the right edge of the wall. I couldn't see Alan now but could just hear his echoed mumblings about good gear or nice moves. The standard route continues up the wall to reach a chimney and then a finishing corner. As I seconded the pitch I found it quite sustained until I realized that the back of the cave was close enough to bridge across. It is a ridiculous position to be in – looking down between your legs at the sea lapping the boulders you have recently left. Once you are established over the roof you won't fail as the climbing is a little easier, but spare a thought for climbers on harder routes where, if it gets *too* hard, it is either a case of lowering into the sea and swimming, or getting to the top any way you can.

The final escape from the shaded chimney/corner brings welcome sunlight and a soft grass slope to lie on. We hugged in a manly-blokey sort of way and smiled. We had climbed a great route together and had a lot of fun – so much in fact that we decided to go and do it again, but swop the pitches.

Vicci Chelton on the top pitch of Brazen Buttress E2 5b, Mother Carey's Kitchen

Did the route matter? I doubt that we would have laughed and smiled as much if the route hadn't been of such a high quality, but maybe Colin Kirkus is right; the experience of having an adventure with a close friend is all that really matters. Whether I would have enjoyed the experience as much with someone I didn't know is something I can only ponder, as I can never repeat the experience of climbing this route for the first time again.

Pembrokeshire is certainly the right place; whether it's the right time with the right people will depend on your choice of climbing partners. I will let you decide if the route matters as you lie in the grass and bask in the warm glow of an ascent of a great route and, if you have anything left in the tank, go back and do it again just for the joy of it.

The route Deep Space E2 5b, 5a was first climbed in 1975 by one of the star sea-cliff climbers of the 1970s and 1980s, Pat Littlejohn, with D. Garner. Alun Richardson climbed it with Alan Dance in 1982.

CHRISTMAS '68

Richard McHardy

A normally straightforward climb in Snowdonia seemed to be a good idea, although one may disagree given the conditions and the time of day.... Richard McHardy gives an account of a memorable day out where a number of factors contributed to the discovery that luck was on his side that day.

This story is about how a walk in the park can become a nightmare experience.

You could say that it started in late November with a squad of Irish shuttering joiners. They had cocked-up their job, having concreted over a plywood shutter which completely blocked the chimney they were making. I abseiled down with a sledgehammer and removed it. Along with my wife Barbara, a friend Geoff Douglas and his girlfriend 'Little Pat' Taylor, I had arranged to go to Wales on the Christmas Eve as soon as we could get away. The Irish had other ideas. The foreman had an enforcer; he was about as tall as Chris Dale, immensely strong and more than a bit thick. I was unable to breathe as, with his arms locked around my chest, I was bundled into a grotty van. I was being taken to an Irish social club by way of thanks for the abseil job. The whole squad was along the bar with a double whiskey in one hand and a pint of Guinness in the other; their arms never stopped – dram, Guinness, dram, Guinness. After two hours of this I was seriously scared; not being a big drinker, I could have died. The front door was locked but in the bogs there was a little transom window. With the toilet door locked I got my head through the window, but with nothing to pull or push against, my body became stuck. Hogarth could not have conceived the sight; half out, half in with the contents of my stomach emptying over my arms and terrified of the paddies breaking the door down. Eventually gravity helped and I fell to the floor outside. I was not popular; even Dougy would not sympathize with my plight; they obviously thought I was a willing participant.

The weather in Wales was cloudy and cold, with a good snow covering on the hills. On Boxing Day, after the pub, we got an invitation to a party at Mo and Jackie Antoine's (two larger-than-life characters on the Welsh scene in the sixties). Late on in the evening we had a game of rugby, during which some bad-tempered bloke picked me up; according to Joe Brown, 'above the bloke's head', and threw me into a pile of bricks. This broke a knuckle; the one that secures the little finger to the hand. Years previously, the only finger that I could beat the legendary female guide

Brede Arkless with, in a finger-pulling contest, was my little finger. Holding a piton hammer or pulling on jugs was going to be hard.

Early the next afternoon we felt well enough to go to Ogwen. By the time we arrived in Cwm Idwal there was less than an hour of daylight left. The snow must have fallen in still air as it covered the Idwal Slabs in an even mask, disguising any features. There was no wind and, with no other people about, only silence.

We had no crampons or ice tools but this did not seem to be a problem; there was no ice, or none that we could see. The cloud and snow and the failing light made the place seem on the one hand benign and on the other hand, creepy. The Ordinary Route on the Idwal Slabs is a 150-metre Diff and at first follows a funnel. 'This shouldn't take long, Doug, don't let us bother with two ropes.'

The climbing was easy enough, but clearing deep snow to find runners was the only thing to delay progress. Before the last pitch I took a belay on a poor nut. It was now dark but the cloud had started to lift. To abseil down with only one rope would have meant losing too much gear. Some 3 metres below was a good runner, so Doug took a belay there. It was my idea that got us there, so Doug was happy for me to continue leading. On the previous pitch I had run out of gear so now I had none; the climbing had been straightforward so I didn't bother to let down a loop of rope so I could get the runners off Doug. I climbed past several good runner placements and did wonder whether this would come back to haunt me. The cloud had now gone, leaving the slabs in bright moonlight. My last runner was the poor nut 3 metres above Doug, a good 20 metres below.

Above me was a dark corner, hidden from any moonlight and choked with ice; seepage from the easy ground above. This corner appeared to be the only line of weakness. There were only two options, the first being to down climb, which without ever being able to see my feet and with a total lack of runners would be difficult and dangerous. The other option, which made absolutely no sense, was to make a long step across the bottom of the icy groove to the slabs on the right. I chose the latter, which brought me to a foothold where I could stand on both feet. I was stuck – completely and utterly stuck.

To my right was a slab, covered in smooth powder snow, devoid of any features and stretching over to a climb called Charity and beyond. Reversing the move was impossible; it would entail a long step across the ice-filled groove which was dark and out of the moonlight. The least I would fall was about 40 metres and that was assuming Doug's belay were to hold. Normally, when you go off-route or grind to a frightened halt leading or soloing, somewhere there is a way ahead; it is about thinking a way through and keeping fear under control. The difference now was my total lack of escape. Above my feet was a smaller foothold; if I could stand with my left foot on this I could reach over to my right, but the trouble was that the lace on my left foot was loose and trapped under my right foot. This should not have been a big problem, but the loose lace had glued to the icy foothold. After a lot of scratching with my right foot the lace became free. Over to the right I uncovered a jug big enough for two hands, enabling a move to the right. This meant leaving the safety of the footholds and hanging by my arms, with my knees trying to get some purchase on the snow-covered rock. If I could manage this I could then take more weight on my left arm as the broken knuckle on my right hand was weakening my right grip.

Any further progress seemed impossible: I was suspended on my arms; my knees getting very little purchase on the snow-covered slab. This slab appeared to continue in a smooth, unbroken surface to the right. Above was a steep wall. Finding the jug that I was now hanging on had been a pleasant surprise; however, no matter what I tried doing with this hold, it seemed as if there was no chance of it getting me anywhere. I had to accept the horrible truth – the snow on the ground at the bottom of the slabs was not deep enough to cushion a fall and I would probably take Doug with me. It would be true to say that I had absolutely no chance.

Then I reached and poked the finger of my right hand in the snow, expecting to hit rock. It seemed inconceivable that there should be any features hidden under the snow, but my hand disappeared. There was a shallow groove totally hidden under the snow and, after a lot of painful effort, I had shifted enough snow to make a move into this groove. Every move up, I had to excavate more of the deep powder, all the time thinking that there would be a sting in the tail. There never was.

After Doug got up the pitch we had to scramble up a considerable distance of easy ground below the grassy terrace. Going down the descent gully was going to be dodgy as it was totally out of any moonlight, so we plumped for an abseil off a small tree. If we were just to the left of the gully we were probably okay, but if we were above Suicide Wall, our single rope would not be long enough. Luck was with us. By now it was quite late and Barbara and Pat had gone down to the car park near Ogwen Cottage. Barbara knew the script – it happened a lot; I would often spend half the day drinking tea and talking, then go climbing and finish in the dark. Nothing unusual in that. Little Pat, on the other hand, had picked up the vibes; her Doug might be in the mire. They rang the Padarn Lake Hotel in Llanberis. Joe answered the phone: 'The boys are playing darts. Ring up after midnight if they have not appeared!' He also knew the script; drinking tea and talking too much is a Manchester vice.

THE FLY, THE MIDGE AND POSTMAN PAT

Bruce Goodlad

Creag Meagaidh is one of those mysterious mountains; famous but hidden from view, it sits on the east-west divide about halfway between Ben Nevis and the Cairngorms, above Loch Laggan. Its mighty cliffs are hidden deep in Coire Ardair, and during the summer, the cliffs are dripping wet and covered in moss and turf, and offer no interest to the climber. In winter everything changes; the turf freezes and the big drainage lines freeze to form some of the most compelling winter climbs in the UK.

Finding perfect ice amongst the vast cliffs of Creag Meagaidh: is it down to good fortune, to constant trying and exploration, or down to knowing the right people? We all have a little luck some of the time, but the rest is earned by keeping getting out on the mountain, as Bruce Goodlad discovers.

The first ascent list on Creag Meagaidh reads like a who's who of Scottish winter climbing: Patey, Marshall, Lang and Fowler to name but a few. The classic routes have strong lines and were picked off first by those hardy men cutting steps. As climbers moved to using front points and two ice tools, a new style of route moved on to these cliffs – initially climbing the thin ice streaks then, as techniques and difficulties have advanced, on to hard mixed terrain.

It is a difficult mountain to get into condition as the base of the climbs is pretty low. Ideally you'd want a wet autumn, so the cliffs become wet and the vegetation is really soggy. Then you need a load of snow followed by some melt-freeze to bring the ice into condition, then a low freeze to set everything nice and solid. Once you have woken up from your dream and realized that your picks are once again in semi-frozen mud you realize just how difficult a mountain it is to get into condition!

Having climbed on Meagaidh dozens of times there are three stand-out routes for me: The Fly, The Midge and Postman Pat. Harder routes have been climbed here, but to me these climbs epitomize everything that I love about the mountain.

Back in the early 1990s I was studying geography at Glasgow University, at a time when student loans had just been introduced. I took advantage of the government's generous offer and took as much cash as they would give me and headed to the Alps at the first opportunity to try this icefall thing everyone was raving about. I had hardly done any winter climbing at this point but under the expert (sort of)

The iced-up cliffs of Creag Meagaidh. The Pinnacle Face is the blacker buttress half in shadow on the left.

tutelage of messieurs Clothier, McEwan, Blyth and Marshall I was soon bashing my way up Scottish grade V style routes, albeit on great-quality Alpine ice.

I couldn't wait to try my newfound skills on the Scottish hills and my opportunity soon came. Snow and a good freeze had given the Highlands some decent conditions, so James Turner and I headed for the Ben. We didn't have a car, so it was the train to Balloch to get out of the city, then a walk to the roundabout on the A82 at the south end of Loch Lomond. Here there was a big lay-by just after the roundabout so, if you positioned yourself well with a rope draped over your rucksack and your thumb out, it was pretty easy to head north. Getting back at the end of a weekend was never so easy, but that's another story.

We had heard on the grapevine that Minus Two Gully on Ben Nevis was in condition and being a *Cold Climbs* tick we had to give it a go. Not having a car was pretty normal for students back then, as was having very little money, so we had become experts at all the places where we could doss for free all over the Highlands. The greenkeeper's hut on the golf course outside Fort William was a favourite. Not many people play golf in the winter climbing season so it seemed pretty safe to leave kit there and we were right at the start of the walk-in, and close to the road.

We headed up the Ben the following morning to find the route in perfect condition; squeaky ice, good ice screws, perfect! My first grade V was in the bag. The plan for the following day was a bit more complicated. A good friend of ours, Graeme Ettle, had been climbing on Creag Meagaidh and had walked under The Fly Direct. This stunning ice line drops the length of Pinnacle Face following the line of a shallow gully; it is one of the most compelling ice lines I have climbed and doesn't come into condition very often.

Graeme had been on the phone to Robin Clothier and said he thought it looked in condition … Robin and I had arranged to climb together on the Sunday but Robin had a dinner party on the Saturday night that he couldn't get out of – however, he did have a plan. He didn't drink at the party, dropped his wife off at home, then headed north. I was pretty sure he wouldn't turn up or, if he did, it wouldn't be until we had had a good night's sleep. Curled up in our sleeping bags I just about had a heart attack when the door to the shed burst open at 2 a.m.: 'Right, off we go' and off we went.

We drove round to the Meagaidh car park and walked straight in. Arriving at the loch it was still dark but, as we approached Pinnacle Buttress, the cliffs began to appear in the first glimmers of dawn. Although we wanted to climb The Fly we were drawn to a streak of ice to its right which we were sure was a potential new route. We had to give it a go, but alas our attempt ended at about 30 metres where the ice got too thin for my bottle and I lowered back to the ground. Andy Perkins was later to make the first ascent, naming it White Knuckle Ride (after a high-speed descent he and a partner made of Centre Post later the same day).

We soon reorganized and Robin set off on the first pitch of The Fly. At this

Dave Green setting off on the big pitch of The Fly

point the first other climbers were beginning to arrive into the corrie. Chris Forrest and Wilson Moir made a bee-line for our route, only to find Robin struggling with damp, soft ice and considering jumping off from 10 metres up. Slow, upward progress with some bold moves on to the slab on the right from Robin discouraged the boys and they headed off instead for '59 Face Route.

As we gained height the ice improved. It was continuously thin, with very little protection but with good belays. Some of them were too far apart for our 60-metre ropes so there was a bit of moving together on grade V+ ground. That's what Scottish ice-climbing is all about. With not many runners to put in or take out the route went surprisingly quickly and we were on our way back to Glasgow long before January's darkness enveloped us.

The thinly-iced nature of the climbing becomes clear

The huge wall to the right of The Fly has a number of routes on it. Most wander about on ledges joining the best bits of ice. Conditions have seldom been good enough to create a route that took the main face in a direct line. Back in 1983 the prolific Andy Nisbet had accepted the challenge of the wall and created The Midge. Andy's route was a fine line, but he did have to traverse about a bit to find the best ice.

Scottish winter climbing in the 1990s was pre-internet so there were no blogs, no forums, just good judgement, a canny eye on the weather and a network of spies dotted around the Highlands who could be phoned for up-to-date weather and conditions. The word was out that The Fly was in, so Robin and I headed for Meagaidh again, hoping that if The Fly was still in then so would The Midge be.

Looking at Pinnacle Buttress from the loch we could see a continuous line of white that linked all the key features of the original route, running into the top icefall on The Fly. We had to give it a go, and we were in luck as the ice, though thin, was *good* and thin and was reinforced with some decent underlying turf and moss. As on The Fly, we got pretty good belays but not much in the way of other protection. The situations were amazing, being strapped on to the thin ice with the Coire Ardair laid out below us. The mountain was busy; we could hear teams on all the big routes. Andy Perkins was on his White Knuckle Ride and we could hear Kath Murphy and Dave Green on The Fly.

We managed to keep true to our intended line, keeping the route arrow straight all the way to where we joined Dave and Kath for the final section of steep ice to the summit. In the new grading system The Fly is now given VII 6. The climbing on our direct 'Super Midge' was easier, but it was every bit as serious so we felt the grade VII 5 was appropriate.

We headed north that night and climbed Gully of the Gods on Beinn Bhan the next day to round off one of the best weekend's climbing I have ever had.

Over the next few years I slowly picked off the other Meagaidh classics: Pumpkin,

Wand, Diadem, Last Post. My success rate slowly improved and we always had a great adventure. I will always remember the sight of John Taylor, who was up to his knees in mud and was beating the ground with his ski stick and cursing all things Scottish when he fell off the 'railway sleeper' footpath on our way home.

Winter in the year 2000 was a big year for me as I had been accepted on to the guide's training scheme and had made it as far as the Scottish winter test. The winter test is often referred to as the filter; most people who can pass this test of mountaineering skill and guiding judgement go on to become mountain guides.

I was living in Aviemore at the time and had been over on the west coast doing a training course, then working for Alan Kimber. Alan gave me a client who wanted to try winter climbing, so first we climbed Golden Oldie on the west face of Aonach Mor and then we did Crowberry Gully on the Buachaille. Both were in perfect condition; we sat on both summits wearing sunglasses, looking out on a pristine white Scotland. At the end of the weekend I suggested to the client that he should never go winter climbing again as we had just had two of the best days I could remember and it was unlikely ever to get any better.

Robin Clothier on the Super Midge

I got home that night and had started to get my kit sorted when Graeme Ettle, with whom I was sharing a house, came in and said 'We are off to Meagaidh tomorrow', which meant I was driving him to Meagaidh since, at that time, Graeme didn't have a car or a driving licence.

'What's the rush,' I grumbled, 'could I not have a day off?' Although I knew how rarely certain routes come into condition, I was feeling pretty knackered.

'Postman Pat is in condition, Stork did it today; we have to go.' So off we went. When Postman Pat was first climbed by Mal Duff and Andy Perkins back in 1991 they climbed a steep ice pillar, then had some pretty wild mixed climbing through steep mixed ground and then moved on to the easier upper gully. We arrived in the corrie to find the route in amazing condition; the steep mixed section was just a second pillar of perfect blue ice.

Graeme Ettle climbing the icicle pitch of Postman Pat, VII 7

The climbing was amazing; the ice was every bit as good as European cascade ice but with a Scottish-style backdrop – perfection! Two steep ice pitches led us over the mixed ground into the upper shallow gully. The terrain is still grade V but it felt pretty straightforward after what we'd climbed below. The route has a ramp running up to its right, which makes it perfect for taking photographs back at the route. Andy Clark made the long walk to be rewarded with a cover shot for the Ben Nevis guidebook.

Hanging the kit up that night I thought I would finally get a day off, but Rick Marchant arrived at the door, asking 'Are you up for Sticil Face tomorrow?' and with a good forecast I had to go. We had an awesome day out on one of the Cairngorms' finest routes. When I woke to the patter of rain against the window the following morning I could pull the duvet back over my head with some satisfaction.

Returning back down the mountain at the end of the day

SO WHY SKI AND WHY SCOTLAND?

Martin Burrows-Smith

Well, these days, the first question is easily answered as your typical full-time, Alps-based guide will be earning as much, if not more, on skis in winter and spring as on foot in the summer. It was not always the case, and certainly not in the 1960s when I first went climbing. Unless you were brought up in an Alpine village, skiing was for the motivated wealthy, the privileged, those lucky enough to go on a school trip, or whatever …

My introduction to the mountains, for sure, was not on skis. I can't remember why but the tradition of a south-coast family holiday was broken

Making tracks in Scottish gullies, Martin Burrows-Smith, a keen climber and skier, has explored the full potential of Scotland's winter environment on skis, where the skills of mountaineer and of steep skier are brought together for the best effect. Yet here, a second element becomes apparent, that of discovering a new passion that the mountains will fulfil for many years.

with a trip to Appin in the Scottish Highlands. We explored and walked all over and I was hooked. Aged fifteen, and in those days with no parental concern, I persuaded a friend on a hostelling/cycling/hiking trip from London through the Peaks, Lakes and North Wales with the intention of climbing the highest hills in each area. Kinder, Gable, Scafell, Tryfan and Snowdon all succumbed and not without a good drenching on the way. While cycling down the Llanberis Pass we stopped below the Cromlech. High above, climbers seemed to be impossibly moving on the rock and at the same time a motorbike angled over the bridge. The guy on the back had a rope draped over his shoulders. I had to do this – go rock-climbing and own a bike!

I first touched rock and rope the following Easter (1963) and shortly afterwards owned a £20 motorbike. Despite being keen and reasonably skilled at all ball games, I could now see a future elsewhere and a focus for spare time and life itself. This meant a choice of a northern university, Manchester, and a progressively poor academic career being taken over by rock, snow and ice. However, there was certainly no thought of any skiing on the horizon, let alone earning any money from the sport.

A weekend wasted was anathema and so every Friday night or Saturday morning it was away to the Peaks, Wales or the Lakes; Scotland in the winter and the Alps

About to set off
down Hayfork Gully,
An Teallach

in the summer. The Padarn, Moon, Golden Rule, Clachaig and National became just as important as Cloggy, Stanage, Scafell, the Buchaille and the Dru. No big deal this, as all one's climbing friends did exactly the same.

After a brief career in the packaging industry, I drifted into instructing. You could do that in those days – I'd met Rowland Edwards in the Padarn and he told me the Brenin had an advanced rock course starting the following week and he was the only one who could climb above Hard Severe! Would I like a job? That was it ...

By the following autumn I'd moved on to Ullswater's Outward Bound School, a wonderful place to be and gain experience, with great staff. When the snow came I had my first outing on skis. This involved a hike up Raise and then a ski over and round the Dodds to our local pub at Dockray. All the others were very competent but gave me no instruction – they just laughed and my girlfriend and wife-to-be skied rings round me. I just schussed, traversed and fell – a lot!

A year later I landed a job at Glenmore Lodge. It's hard to believe it now, but in those days there were a dozen or so ski schools in the Spey Valley and even at the Lodge all instructors had to ski, as many winter weeks were devoted to the teaching of piste skiing.

Technical progress was rapid and absorbing, and along with the canoeing, new ways of adventuring were opening up. But somehow with the skiing, something was missing. Perfecting and demonstrating a compression turn for a BASI Assessor or trying to keep up with Keith Geddes on the White Lady bumps was all very well, but I needed more. This was soon rectified when I first put on touring skins and lifting cable bindings. Immediately I could see a future as a mountaineer, but on skis.

At a morning staff meeting, Fred Harper had asked if any of us (the Lodge instructors) were interested in becoming involved in ski-touring instruction and

Martin Burrows-Smith

only two hands went up – Ben Beattie's and mine. Within a couple of seasons I was the expert, not because I was any good but because I was one of the few who actually *did* it. All the best skiers in Scotland were racers or ex-racers from Highland villages. They'd been skiing since early school and had better things to do than plod up a mountain in search of adventure.

In 1976, I became a mountain guide. This was at a time when skiing (and indeed Alpine climbing) was not yet part of the BMG Training/Assessment syllabus. This was all due to change progressively – and quite rightly, as more and more opportunities were opening up in the Alpine areas and the British Mountain Guides were becoming integrated in the international set-up, the IFMGA. For several seasons I organized and ran the guides' ski mountaineering courses in the Cairngorms.

With easy access and generally useful snow cover, the 'Gorms were ideal for touring with long skins and skates across the plateaux and exciting descents to lochs and coires. Inevitably interest and involvement in the steeper ground began to take hold. In Coire an t-Sneachda, Aladdin's Couloir had experienced some traffic once its ice pitch was covered. It was not particularly steep, but serious and impressive enough, with the exposure at the top and steep side walls further down. There was talk of skiing Aladdin's Mirror to its right but no one could commit, me included. Then, early one season an occluded front sat over the Highlands for a couple of weeks and, when the weather cleared, magically, everything was covered. It was time for action.

The plan was to do the Couloir first as a warm-up and then, with the fantastic snow cover, it would be easy to ski out and round to the ski-tows in Coire Cas, and go back up and across to the top of Sneachda for the Mirror itself. After a few turns at the top of the Couloir, impatience set in as I realized conditions were perfect; I

The Carn Mor Dearg Arête leading the eye to the summit cliffs of Ben Nevis

The author skiing
Crotched Gully,
Northern Corries of the
Cairngorms

was warmed up and should just go for it. It was steep and committing enough to start with and no place to fail or fall, then an awkward traverse across a rocky rib led to wide, easier slopes and within minutes I was in the floor of the coire. What next? With no particular plan I made two more round trips to the top of Sneachda and skied Jacob's Ladder and Central Gully.

That evening I was buzzing; I'd found a new and exciting way of spending days in the Scottish hills. I was, I guess, a half-decent winter climber (you had to be at the Lodge) but did I really enjoy it? I loved the climbing itself, particularly when there was continuous movement, as on a long solo, but the early starts, long walk-ins and freezing stances were not my cup of tea. Now I could be moving non-stop all day with plenty of challenge, adventure and excitement thrown in – and weren't the Highlands, just covered in worthy and dramatic grade I and II and even well-filled grade III gullies, waiting for the steely edge of ski?

First, I explored deeper into the Cairngorms, but soon wanted to go further afield. Meagaidh seemed a good bet and the obvious lines were soon dispatched. Particularly memorable was a day of atrocious weather on Cinderella in the inner corrie. By now I'd wised up with the long, easy-angle approaches and created a gradually rising track direct to the foot of the gully. On the climb up I found it ice-free and at the top I poked my head above the cornice-free exit to be confronted by a westerly hurricane. Skis were put on awkwardly just below and a dramatic descent was enjoyed, followed by an easy wind-assisted cruise down the tracks of my ascent.

Inevitably, Ben Nevis was next on the list. It became an obsession to ski every skiable line, even though often the quality wasn't up to much as it was a popular hill and the easy gullies had a lot of traffic up and down, wrecking the pristine nature of the snow. Highlights were Tower, No. 2/Garadh and the two Castle gullies. A very firm Tower Gully seemed serious at the top and on its traverse under Gardyloo Buttress, and while No. 2 needed a rope to get in, Garadh itself was well filled and surprisingly straightforward.

On another day, I arrived at the top of South Castle Gully, having traversed the edge of the northern face all the way from the summit looking for something to do. It's a long way to go to the top of the Ben and come away with nothing and on this occasion I'd just been confronted with a series of monstrous cornices with no way in. But South Castle surprised me with a much smaller affair that could be outflanked at its side and a great and characterful descent, followed by a couple of wee hops over short, icy steps.

Perhaps my best day on the Ben was on its quieter and more remote side. There was snow everywhere and a tricky drive up to the Steal car park allowed a long skin and climb up by the waterslide into Coire Eoghainn and on to the arête up to the Ben. I was looking for a way into Cresta on the Little Brenva Face but no way! A short descent back down the arête and the cornice relented above Bob Run. An easy, if committing, slide-in found great snow and no ice. Orgasmic turns down this and then a traversing re-ascent to the top of the abseil posts. From here I could follow my line of ascent on perfect snow all the way back to the car. This must be the biggest vertical drop in Scotland and unlike the other sides of the Ben it is blissfully quiet and track free.

I took my skis all over – Ben Lui's Central Gully in a white-out, route-finding technicalities in Glencoe, the immaculate couloirs of An Teallach and Seana Bhraigh and wonderful link-ups in the Fannichs and Beinn Dearg above the Ullapool road. Increasingly, I tried to connect all the descents into a worthwhile, rhythmic and logical tour – far more satisfying. But this usually meant skiing the descents without the prior knowledge of having climbed them first. This inspection process, although at times seeming essential, could also feel soulless, as if the 'tick' of the descent was all-important and the appeal and purity of a quality round trip was lost.

My first visit to An Teallach highlighted the difference between these two approaches. An unlikely hill for skiing perhaps, but a superb magazine photo of the soaring line of Lord's Gully suggested otherwise. Access from the top looked problematical to say the least, so I was going to have to climb it first to check the conditions and best line. It was a great day for ski-touring, with extravagant snow cover, blue sky and no wind. Having parked the car near Dundonnell House, I was soon skinning in earnest and within the hour I was curving round above Loch Toll an Lochain with a breathtaking view of one of the Highlands' classic corries. Round the back of the corrie there was a typical change in snow quality from the wind-blown hard pack of the south side of Glas Mheall Liath to the deep soft slab of the lee slopes leading up to the gully. I worked my way carefully up the gully's left side,

Martin Burrows-Smith

Looking up at the Castle Gullies on Ben Nevis

Martin Burrows-Smith

The northern corrie of
An Teallach, Coire
a'Ghlas Thuill (l-r): the
Prongs (1-4), the Alley
and Hayfork Gully

continually checking the suspect snow conditions and eventually convincing myself
it was safe: i.e. spooky to climb but great to ski! The gully was wide, curving, seduc-
tive – there was adventure here, I'd have a wee look …

Halfway up was a narrows – wide enough for a ski? Just, I thought. A steep, wind-
blown edge led up to the left then the slope broadened, steepening again to its apex
under the hanging diamond-shaped rock of Lord Berkeley's Seat. I cut a big stance,
dumped the gear and traversed out right, looking for a link with the summit of Sgurr
Fiona. Rock, ice, horrendous exposure – no way! I scuttled back to my stance, happy
to make a descent of the gully itself. Awkwardly on with the skis, tighten the sack,
warm up the legs, grip the poles, adjust to the 2 metres of metal edge, then don't
delay – GO!

A few bouncing, side-slipping jumps to get into a rhythm for the first turn, and
trying to ignore the 300 metres of couloir ghosting down to the loch. Total commitment; diagonal double pole plant for stability and launch into the fall line, upper
body quiet, skis turning in mid-air, pulse racing…. I'd underdone the turn; an
instinctive twist of the skis across the line of travel and they bite – great, the form
was there, and I could relax and enjoy it. The slope was steep, perhaps over 50
degrees, but the quality compensated, so it was one turn at a time down the edge
to the narrows – it was tight – then a hop over a lump of ice and I could cruise,
relishing the situation and linking fast turns to the brightness on the far side of the
corrie.

Next was a long climb up the fine southern slopes of Bidean a 'Ghlas Thuill to
the next objective, the attractive-sounding Hayfork Gully. This was to be done from
the top, on sight, so I was hoping for a great trouble-free ski, and so it proved as the

descent looked – and was – brilliant, curving down creamy and virginal through massive sandstone walls. Far too good to miss and skiing at its very best.

A superb area for linking great descents is, of course, the Cairngorms. Many I enjoyed so much they were often repeated. A regular afternoon trip away from the office (I was Chief Instructor by then) saw me away down Diagonal Gully on Stag Rocks, across Loch Avon to traverse Ben Mheadhoin, back up to the shoulder on the north ridge of Cairngorm then down the headwall of Coire Laogh Mor.

The Lairig Ghru and Braeriach plateau offer some intriguing possibilities. I went there from a variety of different access points, but one trip was particularly memorable. I'd been there a week earlier with a helicopter, filming couloir-skiing with Hamish McInnes, so I knew the cover was great. At this time it was well into April and there was quality spring snow down to 600 metres. The weather was serenely perfect. Using the first lifts in Coire Cas, it was up to

Martin Burrows-Smith

Richard Mansfield skiing the Third Prong

Cairngorm summit, then a schuss down and around the head of Coire Raibeirt and Stob Coire an t-Sneachda into upper Coire Domhain. The early morning snow was iron-hard and very fast! A careful descent down the side of Hell's Lum Crag was followed by a big traverse underneath it, keeping as high as possible, working all the way round to the Garbh Uisge on the far side.

The late winter scenery here is simply stunning, with terrific crags, frozen falls, exploding water and Loch Avon ghosting away into the wilderness. Here I could look back at the great gash of the Lum itself, with hanging icefalls on its left and what is now a Dave McLeod E10 on the right. I'd skied the Lum two years previously at my third attempt. I'd been chatting with Allen Fyffe after a day's work and he'd casually mentioned that the Lum was full. He said nothing more but the look in his eye was perfectly clear – 'You won't be able to resist that, will you?'

So at the Garbh Uisge it was on with the skins for the first time and a steady pull, steep at first then pleasant enough, up to the summit of Ben Macdui. By now the sun was working its magic on the snow and for the rest of the day it remained perfect, firm but with just a little melted mush on the surface. There's a choice of descents into the Lairig and on this occasion it was the Allt a' Coire Mor which gave a wonderful ski; big, wide, fast turns at the top then tighter and steeper on the flanks of the Allt itself to cross the Lairig Burn and traverse across to the other side.

Martin Burrows-Smith

Martin skinning up the Feidh Buidh, with the Lum of Hell's Lum Crag behind

The snows of Angel's Peak looked irresistible, so it was on with the crampons for the climb up the North East Ridge. A little ice to play with on Lochan Uaine's exit burn, then up the ridge itself, eyeing up the best line down the face on the left. The summit was a dramatic spot for a light lunch and then it was an atmospheric ski back down to the dark lochan and the Garbh Chôire bothy.

From here it was yet another big skin up to Braeriach following the edge of Coire Bhrochain. I'd snow-holed here once in a cornice at the top of one of the gullies. It was a three-day, two-night winter ML Assessment course with two candidates I knew well – a memorable trip. There's a choice of gullies here, and this day it was the east; straight and narrow, snow still nicely turned, down into the great bowl of Bhrochain, retaining height on the left for a big traverse round to the top of the Lairig.

The usual exit from here is a long, tedious trudge along the pass and over the Chalamain Gap. But I knew better and I had enough energy to spare for the final climb of the day up the March Burn and on to the summit of Cairn Lochan, down its couloir on to the Great Slab and back to the car park. Not a bad day …

Today, from a comfortable base in Switzerland, I can on any day be climbing or skiing in any of three countries in a huge variety of areas and altitudes. In summer and autumn, when the body allows, I boulder and clip bolts. In winter, my local hill is a 1,500-metre skin, which I hope keeps me in nick. I have at least a dozen different ways off it. All I have to do is cross the road from my home and start skinning and four hours later I'll be back with a beer on the balcony.

But – and it's a biggish but – it's all too easy. I'm unlikely to move back to Scotland, but there are often far too many other folk out touring here in the Alps. It is becoming increasingly difficult to find peace, quiet and virgin snow. After any fresh dump there seem to be tracks everywhere, however remote.

So no surprises then; I find myself keeping a weather-eye on the conditions back in the Highlands and, on occasion, wishing I was somewhere else. Is that link from Sgurr Fiona into Lord's Gully complete? Will the Posts ever go? Can anyone get in at the top of Cresta? Is anyone else out there? So why Scotland? Well, when it's bad it really is horrid, but when it's good it's simply the best.

IN MY BACKYARD

Rob Collister

Even in the midst of yet another summer when low-pressure systems seemed to queue up in the Atlantic like jumbo-jets at Heathrow, there were isolated days of such perfection that it was easy to forgive and forget the rest of the time. Cycling the shady lanes of the lower Conwy Valley on a fine June morning, when the air felt pleasantly cool on bare legs and the hedgerows were full of honeysuckle and strident wrens, I was reminded why I have chosen to live most of my adult life in Snowdonia. The car was off the road for its MOT and this

A perfect day in which to enjoy being in the mountains. With the carefree style of an impromptu jaunt, combined with the careful consideration and concentration of soloing a mountain climb in the Carneddau of North Wales, Rob Collister describes a day when the British mountains are second to none.

was clearly a day to be in the mountains. Making a virtue of necessity, I was making my way through Rowen and Llanbedr y Cenin up into Cwm Eigiau. From Llanbedr, the Ordnance Survey indicates in bold green dots that the track is a Byway Open to All Traffic, but it is clearly not much used. Bracken, cow parsley and nettles clogged my wheels and forced me off the bike for a short distance until a sunless tunnel formed by hazel coppice subdued the vegetation and made for easier, if muddier, going. The path, brightly edged now with foxglove, campion, herb robert and vibrant blue veronica, narrowed and dropped steeply down to the Afon Dulyn.

The boulder-strewn riverbed was overhung by oak and ash and felt almost tropical in the green luxuriance with which bark and rock alike were smothered by lichen, moss and fern. I carried the bike across a neat, unobtrusive footbridge and up onto an unremittingly steep, twisting council road which called for bottom gear and maximum effort. Gradually the angle eased and, as the high tops of the Carneddau hove into view, the road emerged from birch woodland onto a moor of tussock grass and rushes and a few sheep.

With easier cycling, and gates to open and shut, there was much to see and hear that would have been missed in a car. Simple things like the crimson breast and lovely rufous-brown back of a linnet perched on a gorse bush; the descending cadence of a meadow pipit's flight song as it parachuted down to earth; the strange fishing reel call of a grasshopper warbler, were all familiar enough but at that moment they were a source of wonder and delight. As I pedalled on towards the mountains I was grinning to myself.

An atmospheric view, looking across from the top of the Amphitheatre at the summit cliffs of Craig yr Ysfa

<blockquote>Rob Collister</blockquote>

At the road's end where cars were parked, it was a simple matter to lift the bike over the locked gate and continue along a wet track to the dam wall, never repaired after it ruptured with tragic consequences in 1925. Beyond the wall the track became rougher and rockier and it would have been a struggle to ride without front suspension, at least. Even with this, it was quite sufficiently challenging for me. Some hill-walkers seem to dislike mountain bikes on principle, yet in a situation like this they represent a valid example of what Fritz Schumacher called 'intermediate technology'. A modern bike is a highly sophisticated machine, yet it is non-polluting, an extremely efficient form of transport, and great fun to boot.

At Eigiau Cottage two members of the Rugby Mountaineering Club were re-slating the roof. A farmer, quad bike idling, had stopped for a chat. Suddenly, Cwm Eigiau felt almost busy, if not quite like the nineteenth century when the farms were occupied and the quarries active. The grassy track steepened and the riding was made difficult by several washouts. Finally, sweating and beginning to burn at the back of my neck, I reached the old slate quarry, abandoned since the 1890s, and hid my bike inside one of its roofless dressed-slate buildings.

Overhead reared the dark verticality of Craig yr Ysfa. A steep little path wound up through scree and bilberry to the broad, stony gully known as the Amphitheatre. I was detained awhile by the spectacle of a black beetle gamely manoeuvring a twig three times its own length, but soon I was at the foot of a rock ridge forming the left wall of the Amphitheatre, the start of a favourite rock climb. The guidebook describes it as Amphitheatre Buttress; 275 metres long, it was first climbed in 1905 by the Abraham brothers from Keswick and graded Very Difficult, which means that, in climbing terms, it is not very difficult. However, it is by no means a scramble and there are several places where the obvious line is not the easiest, so route-finding acumen is called for. Its popularity over the years is evident from the way holds have been rounded and smoothed by the passage of many feet, demanding extra care.

I was carrying only a bum-bag containing a windproof jacket and some sandwiches. With no rope, helmet, harness or rock shoes, the preparatory rituals were reduced to cleaning mud from the soles of my trainers. Solo climbing is obviously more hazardous than with a partner and a rope, but this route was well within my technical ability and soloing confers a freedom to focus totally on the rock and to be absorbed by the place without the distraction of belays, climbing calls and all the paraphernalia that normally goes with climbing. Feeling a little stiff and awkward at first, I soon started to relax on solid, slabby rock, reassuringly in balance. Gaining height I began to revel in the precise placing of hands and feet and the flow of continuous careful movement. The crux, 90 metres up, was a steep little rib, its holds polished, the drop down into the Amphitheatre horrifying. More than ever, it was a time to suspend the imagination and focus intently on the short section of rock immediately ahead. A hand twisted inside a crack provided a perfect jam for a strenuous pull-up and a jug-handle hold just where most needed made the moves above feel exciting but secure.

I paused for a moment to savour the situation. Ledges on the far side of the Amphitheatre were a distinctive blue-green flecked with yellow; the fleshy leaves of roseroot and the yellow orbs of globeflower hinting at a different, less acid geology. Overhead, the sky was still a flawless blue. A peregrine ducked silently behind the skyline and did not reappear. A series of short walls and little paths in the heather led to a pinnacle, or gendarme, just over 3 metres high. On the far side of this feature the ridge narrowed to the proverbial knife-edge. George and Ashley Abraham were professional photographers who made a habit of taking a huge plate camera and tripod with them whenever they went climbing. A photograph in their book *Climbing in North Wales* (1911) shows a climber sitting uncomfortably astride this ridge, edging forward with difficulty. One hundred years later, it seemed simpler to swing across the slightly overhanging left wall on enormous handholds.

Above, the ridge steepened again to a final bastion. Interesting climbing all at once became too hard for comfort and I was forced to beat a retreat and find an easier way. Finally, a line of holds led leftward across a gully wall and then abruptly the ground was horizontal, the climb over. In front, on the far side of Nant y Benglog, the Ogwen Valley, were the hazy grey shapes of the Glyderau and the

Rob Collister

Looking back at Craig yr Ysfa

familiar dark cone of Tryfan. Far below, specks of colour and faint shouting indicated another party embarking on the climb, but the top of Craig yr Ysfa was deserted. Eating my lunch overlooking the Amphitheatre, it seemed quite likely that the Abrahams and their friends would have sat in the same spot all those years ago. I wondered whether their provisions were as substantial as their camera.

The summit of Carnedd Llewelyn beckoned and it was much too fine a day to ignore the summons. After the care-filled concentration of the climb, the walk up was a blissfully untaxing stroll. Others were picnicking at the cairn, so with a nod and a smile I crossed the summit plateau, a confusing, disorienting place in mist or storm, and descended a boulder field towards Foel Grach. Just past the little outcrop known as Tristan's Cairn I cut right to reach a branch of the Afon Eigiau, passing chunks of metal debris from a crashed aircraft and the bloated, buzzing carcass of an unfortunate sheep that had ventured too far onto a patch of bright green floating sphagnum. In no time I was back at the bike and clattering down to the dam. Another wet, potholed track led to Coedty Reservoir above Dolgarrog through damp woods of willow and alder, filled with the repetitive call of the chiffchaff and the limpid song of its almost identical cousin, the willow warbler. My way home took me past the Dutch Pancake House near Rowen which, to anyone tired, hungry and exceedingly thirsty, is thoroughly to be recommended.

Back home, browsing through a journal of the John Muir Trust over yet another cup of tea, I came across a reference to 'the spiritual qualities for which humans value wild land: freedom, tranquillity and solitude'. It struck me that I had experienced all three for much of that day in Cwm Eigiau.

MAIN WALL

Mal Creasey

Working as a guide based in North Wales in the rainy seasons of autumn and spring (often the quieter times of the year away from the Scottish winter and seasons in the Alps) does add a good deal of variety to the work. Operating at this time of the year will, however, require (by default) the ability and wherewithal to deal with some pretty wet rock at times and, believe me, British guides must be some of the most rained-upon climbers in the world! However, there is always a silver lining as, in between the raindrops, there have been some very memorable days when the sun has shone and the rock has been warm and dry. That is when North Wales is at its best – although at times it has been difficult to see where the next good day was coming from!

The trick, of course, is to time your visit with one of the all-too-brief interludes of dry weather, avoiding the weekends if possible, in May, June or September, well away from the main holiday periods. Empty crags, beautiful clear skies and some of the best rock-climbing in the world. When there's wall-to-wall sunshine it's warm enough to have to seek out the shadier north-facing crags out of the sun. In anything less than perfect conditions these higher crags can be dark, inhospitable, dank and uninviting, but when conditions are good these can offer some of the best climbing in the world. Clogwyn d'ur Arddu, or 'Cloggy' as it is affectionately known, on the flanks of Snowdon, can certainly stake a claim as simply the best crag in the UK (unless you know differently) and without doubt has more than its fair share of iconic routes. The best climbers of the day have enjoyed the classic routes such as Longlands, Pigotts, White Slab, Great Wall and many others.

Through the course of a climber's life, a classic mountain route in their home area is likely to be climbed more than once. Over the years and after many ascents of one route in particular, Mal Creasey has come to appreciate not only how climbing protection and tactics have evolved through this time, but also how his approach to climbing and guiding have developed.

Looking back on one's youth, with all its lack of knowledge and experience, from a viewpoint of operating as a guide today, it's perhaps easy to feel sentimental about going back to those early days; but it does help you appreciate what it's like being a learner again.

Main Wall top pitch circa 1970s

One of my personal favourites, however, is Cyrn Las, high on the south side of Llanberis Pass. During the summer months the sun will strike this north-facing crag only briefly in the morning, yet if the sun is strong and there is a drying breeze, it just needs a few days to dry the seepage lines and create perfect conditions for any of the routes that weave their way up the steep grey ramparts. There are some hard, uncompromising lines on Cyrn Las and The Skull epitomizes an era in the 1960s when the leading climbers of the day were really pushing the boundaries of what was possible because of huge advances in equipment and technique. With the new equipment came the belief that harder and harder lines or features in the rock could be attempted and if one challenger was repulsed, a new one would emerge until either the line succumbed or was left alone for future generations. Although nylon ropes and specialized footwear had been around for a few years, it was the huge advances in protection for the leaders that really allowed them to push the boat out and explore what had been impossible just a few years earlier.

On the other hand, Main Wall is one of the easier routes on the crag yet arguably the best route of its grade in the country. Some may not agree but, in reality, there are few other contenders. (Although I have no doubt that any self-respecting Scot would sing the praises of Ardverikie Wall instead!) At a good old-fashioned Hard Severe, Main Wall was a massive undertaking in 1935 when it received its first ascent. Hobnailed boots, 30 metres of hemp rope and possibly a few short slings to either place over a spike or tie around a chock-stone – that would have been about it.

After an initial awkward move and a little scrambling, the route weaves around, taking a series of ramps – first right to an awkward chimney, up this, then left and back right again following the line of least resistance. Retreat after the first couple of pitches would be difficult, even today. Heaven knows how the early pioneers could even have contemplated a safe return to terra firma as a 15-metre classic abseil would have left them dangling on the end of the proverbial umbilical cord, well short of safety. The first ascent must have been a step into the unknown, partic-ularly on the fourth pitch as a bold move takes the leader around a corner and out of sight from the rest of the party and, although the technicalities ease, there is still a long, narrow slab where the exposure certainly becomes more apparent. Here, at least, the sun may well be shining as the aspect has changed to face the east. The mood of the route changes too as it becomes much more direct and, with longer ropes and better protection, one big, long pitch will normally suffice from this point.

I first led Main Wall as a young and probably very naïve climbing instructor and in those days it was considered appropriate to wear boots and carry a sack on easier mountain routes. And talking of boots, mine on that particular day were what could only be described as 'bendy' – anyone who was climbing back then will know exactly what I mean by the terminology of 'bendy' boots (or to be more precise, Hawkins Walkins boots). At the time Hawkins were a manufacturer of good old-fashioned hiking boots and a legacy of bygone days; a rounded toe with eyelets and a few hooks for the lacing, and a Vibram sole. Quite modern for the day really, with a good rocker to ease the walking action and rigid metal stiffeners, which would, under normal circumstances, add some rigidity to the sole. However, in my case these didn't do anything apart from prise the boot apart as the screws that were supposed to hold everything together via the midsole had long since parted company from the boots, so each instep resembled big smiley faces once any weight was put on the toes! In any case, it didn't make much difference as both stiffeners had broken in half and didn't really add anything apart from a little extra weight to each boot. So, as you can imagine, it was a real baptism of fire for a budding young instructor and the two clients! We didn't have harnesses and for protection I carried two or three slings and about half-a-dozen chocks, including at least one 'moac' and of course the sack (a Whillans with a leather base), which I remember vividly as it jammed in the bloody chimney! 'Moacs' were the first-ever manufactured nuts and used to fit everything, or so we were led to believe! Before these appeared we mostly used drilled-out engineering nuts in which we wrapped carpet tape over the threads in an effort to stop them wearing the slings out! Suffice to say that we won out on the day – I learnt a lot and have since been back to the route (and crag) almost countless times.

The last time I did Main Wall it was one of those beautiful days of early summer. There was no one in the cwm and the few people who were on the hill had been left far behind in the valley, either bouldering or on the roadside crags. As we arrived in the cwm there was the usual discussion as to where we were going to leave the sack. My preferred option has always been to take one sack with a bit of grub, a brew and maybe a light waterproof if conditions are not guaranteed for the day, and also some comfy shoes for the walk back down. Thankfully the Hawkins Walkins were no more and these days there are any number of lightweight boots available which are perfectly adequate for climbing to a reasonable standard and remain comfortable on steep grass and loose rock on the descent. The other option whilst climbing in rock shoes is to tie a lightweight pair of approach shoes on the harness, stash a Mars Bar in the pocket and maybe a light windproof around the waist, because if you take nothing you can always guarantee a cool breeze higher up.

If you do take one sack, the other can be stashed, to be picked up on the way down. There is a problem, however, in that the start of the route is a good 150 metres of scrambling above the point where the descent route intersects the approach, so it really is worthwhile putting a little thought into choosing the right spot. Although it sounds silly, make a note of where you left it. I've heard of a number of teams over the years floundering around in the darkness after getting stuck behind a slow team on a bank holiday simply because they didn't make a decent note of where they had left the sack!

Heaven help any party that neglects to take any spare kit at all, unless the weather is perfect, and it is guaranteed there are no slow, incompetent parties using siege tactics in front of them. It's very embarrassing being bloody cold when that comfy little belay jacket is 150 metres vertically below!

These days, modern light footwear, lightweight insulating jackets and small rucksacks are a million miles from Hawkins Walkins and leather-based sacks specifically designed for getting jammed in awkward chimneys. Forty-odd years later it's a different ball game – it is still the same magical route, with the same decisions to be made over how to plan the climb, but today these seem somehow easier. That particular ascent just a few years ago was brilliant and I even got some good pictures for the client.

Not all days working as a guide in North Wales can be spent on one of your favourite rock climbs; however this one is the icing on the cake! I have no doubt that one day Main Wall will be climbed as a winter route as, in very wet conditions, it does carry a good deal of drainage. I'm all for exploration and progress, but in this case just a few crampon scratches would detract enormously from one of the true classic rock climbs in North Wales. If you haven't done this route, do it sometime and enjoy!

GUIDING POINT FIVE GULLY

Mike Pescod

It's not easy to make a film of a climb that puts across what it feels like to climb the route. In the film *The Pinnacle* there is steady spindrift pouring down on Dave MacLeod and Andy Turner as they climb Point Five Gully. All of this spindrift was created by me kicking out ledges at the belays ahead of them and makes the film depict what is commonly experienced on the climb. Actually it was a completely calm day, so there was

Following in the footsteps of Scottish ice-climbing history, on the great ice cliffs of Ben Nevis, local connoisseur Mike Pescod describes a day to remember amongst the many he has experienced on the mountain's most famous winter climb.

no snow being blown around at all and no spindrift coming down on me climbing the gully ahead of everyone else. I think I got the best deal that day. It was my job to climb the route first so Donald the rigger could follow and fix a rope for Diff, the cameraman. Dave and Andy followed behind, taking the hit of any debris that fell down the gully. With three people climbing ahead of them they were always going to get some debris falling and Diff needed some big, comfortable ledges to film from!

This climb was part of a week-long project celebrating the achievements of Jimmy Marshall and Robin Smith fifty years earlier. In 1960 Jimmy and Robin made first ascents of six ground-breaking climbs including Orion Direct, plus the first free and single day ascent of Point Five Gully, all in a week. They took a day off as a rest day in which they walked the length of the Grey Corries and hitch-hiked back to Fort William. They got arrested after stealing a set of dominos from the pub, were released and walked back up to the CIC hut ready for the next new route the day after.

Andy and Dave set themselves the challenge of climbing all the routes again and walking the Grey Corries, being filmed by Paul Diffley of Hot Aches Productions. *The Pinnacle*, the resulting film, is a brilliant portrayal of Jimmy's and Robin's achievement, with footage of the modern-day climbers and interviews with Jimmy. During their own efforts, Dave and Andy were continually reminded of the scale of what had been achieved during that winter of 1960. Climbing all the routes with modern equipment and techniques was hard enough, but Jimmy and Robin did it all by cutting handholds and steps in the snow with one ice axe each and fairly meaningless protection. There was also little chance of retreat from the climbs for them – the only way off was to reach the top. Imagine standing at the foot of the Orion Face before it was ever climbed knowing that, as you start up the climb, the

Mike Pescod

Observatory Gully on Ben Nevis, bounded on the left by the north-east Buttress and by Tower Ridge on the right. Point Five Gully is central to the view

only way off the face is to reach the top. The commitment displayed by Jimmy and Robin was outstanding.

What the film does not show is the effort required to rig the climbs to get the cameramen into the best positions. Ropes were fixed early in the morning, or the night before. One or two of the routes could be accessed from above but most just had to be climbed before Dave and Andy got there. There were long days with lots of lugging ropes around the mountain, but also with plenty of great climbing.

The project was fascinating and it was a great privilege to play a small part in it. We were blessed with outstanding climbing conditions and excellent weather. One of the climbs, Minus Three Gully, has only been in condition once in the last decade. Thankfully this was the perfect time for it to make an appearance. As well as a lot of planning and preparation, you need a bit of luck sometimes.

The first time I climbed Point Five Gully was in my first winter of living in Fort William. Having climbed two ice-climbs previously I thought I was ready for anything. Angel Falls, a grade II ice cascade in the Cairngorms, was my first-ever taste of ice. Even with bendy boots, walking crampons and two walking ice axes I was instantly hooked. The potential for some serious fun was obvious to me and it seemed a very natural thing to do. Clearly I was quite young without such a well-developed sense of fear as I have now. Ice-climbing is still serious fun for me now I've been doing it for nearly twenty years, but I'm not convinced that it's a completely natural thing to do. Evolution did not lead to us going ice-climbing!

After that first time on ice I went out and bought some technical ice axes and rigid crampons. It wasn't until I was in Russia that I got to use them, on a trip to the Caucasus to learn to ski. Being -25 °C all winter the streams and waterfalls in the valley were frozen cascades that looked as though they would offer some enter-tainment on a day off from the skiing. They did, I survived, and I needed no further convincing that I was an expert ice-climber and ready for anything.

So, at the tail end of the winter of 1995, after biding my time for the perfect day and climbing conditions, I went up to Point Five Gully for a look. I remember there was a creep slot at the base, not unlike a bergschrund. There had been brilliant

Two sets of climbers on Point Five Gully, V 5, the top team being established on the Chimney Pitch

Looking down into the Chimney Pitch (pitch 2) from the foot of the Rogue Pitch

snow cover that year and late in the season the snow pack creeps downhill gently, opening up a gap between it and the stationary snow in the gully. This provided the crux of the whole climb and I was glad I had waited for the snow to be perfectly crisp and solid to pull on. The rest of the climb went very smoothly, even waiting for a roped team as they led up the Rogue Pitch. I had a slightly awkward conversation with the belayer, discussing the weather and the condition of the climb, trying not to mention the fact that I was soloing right past them.

I was already determined to be a mountain guide, but climbing this route certainly reinforced the idea. I thought if I could have the chance to do climbs like this as a job and make the experience possible for others, then this was what I wanted to do. It took a few years to build up the prerequisites and work through the training and assessment scheme, but eventually I reached the position of being able to guide people on Point Five Gully and many other Ben Nevis classics quite regularly. Since then I've experienced quite a range of conditions in the gully, from perfect to impossible!

Quite often my clients have time restrictions imposed on them by bus or flight timetables. With one such deadline of catching a bus at 1 p.m., guiding Point Five Gully took just two and a half hours. It was the culmination of six days of climbing, enduring some prolonged thaw conditions before the weather and quality of the ice finally improved. Vanishing Gully was memorable for the water cascading down it and the rate at which it *was* vanishing, melting away in front of us. We were very grateful to get inside the cave for a respite before the main test of waterproof gloves and nerve on the steep, soft ice. Slav Route was another slightly drippy climb on the crux, but at least the weather was dry and it was a fine and long day out.

So, with one day of climbing left it was nice to know it would freeze properly and be dry and calm, for the morning anyway. The challenge was making it back down in time for the bus. We got to the CIC hut at 6 a.m. and started the first pitch of Point Five Gully just before 7 a.m. We walked up the approach snow slope roped-up so I could carry on straight up the first pitch. The Chimney Pitch and Rogue Pitch were done in standard pitches, but the second half of the route was climbed moving together, with anchors every now and then in one long pitch. We topped out at 9.20 a.m. and got down with time enough for a beer before catching the bus. Getting in a good climb against the odds always adds to the satisfaction.

Sometimes you can move quickly, but other times you need to climb very slowly and carefully. Knowing what to expect on a climb is all part of guiding, but looks can be deceptive. One time when Point Five Gully looked to be in great shape it turned out that the snow was still snow and had not yet transformed to ice. It required having four points of contact with the 'ice' in order not to slide back down with picks and front points cutting through the ice. Standing still was okay most of the time – it only became awkward when it was time to move either an ice axe or a foot, reducing the points of contact to three, below what was required to remain in one place. Extra purchase was possible in the Chimney Pitch with a foot out on a rock ledge or a hip wedged into the side. The Rogue Pitch was slightly unnerving though, as ice screws were easily placed but of no value at all in holding a fall. Jimmy Marshall might well have described the quality of snow as perfect – it was soft enough to make big steps quite easily and make them strong enough to hold body-weight. For someone who has never seriously cut steps up a climb and is entirely

Always an airy finish

dependent on front points and picks for purchase it takes a while to get used to the idea. Having no other option is a good motivator though, so I kicked steps up the Rogue Pitch and managed to remain in balance with some wide bridging so I did not have to pull on my ice axes. In retrospect, I was in good company had things not worked out well. I was climbing with two mountain rescue team members on a training course, getting to know the routes on Ben Nevis a bit better. They were quite impressed with the climb.

It's not just the snow you're climbing on that can be difficult; it can be the snow coming down from above that causes problems. Climbing Point Five Gully can become impossible owing to the spindrift pouring down it and this is just the same for a guide as it is for anyone else. On one occasion when it happened to me it was clearly windy as we walked-in and spindrift was always going to be a problem. Looking at the gully from below gave us more confidence though. We could see some spindrift coming down the bottom every now and then, but with long clear spells in between. This is how it worked out for the first pitch and the *névé* was brilliant. It wasn't long before we were standing below the chimney pitch where the funnel effect of the gully is most evident. An 80-metre section of the cornice funnels down into the metre-wide chimney. What is a thin dribble of icy dust sliding down over the exit slopes is magnified into a mini-avalanche of biting icy shards, big enough to engulf grown men, swallowing them head-first.

So I shut my eyes and started up the chimney. Every now and then I was able to open my eyes to see where I was. Most ice axe placements were made by feel. I couldn't see them under the spindrift even when I did open my eyes. Thankfully the snow did not build up on my arms as it sometimes does; the chimney is too steep for that. Standing and belaying under the Rogue Pitch was quite nerve-racking though, as we waited for the next wave of snow to land on us. So we called it a day and abseiled back down. The thought of pulling over the Rogue Pitch just as a wave of snow came over the top was too much after the experience of climbing the Chimney Pitch blind. Sometimes guiding is about knowing when to turn back.

Guiding is also about knowing when it's safe enough to get onto a climb in the first place. It's a very rare thing to have Point Five Gully all to yourself on a Saturday in February, but this is how it was for me once and we had great climbing conditions and weather. Recently, there had been quite a big fall of snow and the avalanche hazard was high. Most people were avoiding the north face of Ben Nevis completely, and with good reason. But the wind turned northerly and strengthened, and I guessed that Point Five Gully would have been scoured clean of soft snow. So we headed up Observatory Gully, picking our way round areas of soft snow. There was certainly plenty of wind slab on the approach slopes underneath the gully and these are easily steep enough to engender an avalanche. The last slope to the gully itself required careful judgement and choice of line. By hugging the foot of Observatory Buttress we were able to stay clear of the open slopes and avoid the worst of the avalanche hazard. When I'm making decisions like these I try to remind myself that most people who get hurt in avalanches already have an in-depth knowledge of avalanche hazard! I try very hard to make independent decisions, unbiased by my desire to achieve what I set out to do. Heuristic traps are very easy to fall into.

Having reached the gully it became clear that my guess was right. There was no soft snow left in it at all and we climbed on hard ice and névé all the way up. The following day there were four teams climbing Point Five Gully after word got out that it was safe enough to approach the climb. We watched them from Hadrian's Wall Direct which again we had to ourselves on another sunny day. Climbing the route is only half the job. Deciding what to climb is as much a part of it and it's a great feeling when you make the right calls.

But of all the times I've been in Point Five Gully, the climb with Diff the cameraman filming Andy and Dave for *The Pinnacle* was the best by far. The snow ice was exactly what Ben Nevis is famous for; solid enough for great climbing but soft enough for ice axes to penetrate easily. The rock was dry, as was the ice; there was no wind and no spindrift. The sun was shining and the air was crystal clear. The view went from the Cairngorms to the Cuillin on Skye, with seemingly endless snowy hills in between.

After the filming on Point Five Gully, Donald and I climbed into The Basin on Orion Direct to rig ropes for the following day. Coming down in the evening light we chatted with a French mountain guide about climbing, guiding and just how special it is to have the opportunity to climb on days like these in such a beautiful place. He went off to solo Orion Direct to reach the summit as the sun was setting. After a full day of guiding this was his time to make the most of this perfect day.

It was a day to savour, not to rush. A day to remind me why I endure the wet days, the thaws when I have to climb in rubber gloves, double waterproofs and waterproof socks in my waterproof boots and still come home soaked to the skin; the days when I battle the wind to get to a climb and crawl off the summit plateau; the days when Ben Nevis seems to want to spit you off in a foul temper.

This was the day when the history and tradition of Scottish climbing, the beauty and grandeur of Ben Nevis, the unique brilliance of the climbing and the shared experience of working with my friends all came together. When people ask me why I became a mountain guide, this is the day I remember.

A CUILLIN TRAVERSE IN NOVEMBER

Martin Moran

A truly magnificent route, a traverse of the Cuillin Ridge on the Isle of Skye is a major undertaking of Alpine proportions. Martin Moran and Jim Marshall had climbed together for years but how would the route go at this more testing time of the year?

Unpredictability is the eternal frustration but also the occasional delight of Scotland's climate. Autumn is traditionally imagined as the season of cold rain and high winds, yet in November 2011 the north-west Highlands luxuriated under clear skies, a balmy Mediterranean breeze and a full moon. The resident climber must be adaptable and opportunistic. Winter kit was mothballed in favour of chalk and T-shirts for bare-handed struggles on deserted Torridonian crags. Each evening the sun set in spectacular ribands of gold over the Cuillin. Though November's days are short the possibility of making a traverse of Skye's great ridge pricked my conscience and begged some action.

In Jim Marshall I had the man for the task. We maintained a flexible guiding arrangement. He had been waiting since June to weigh anchor and drive north the moment I signalled two days all-clear on Skye. He is a veteran of Eiger, Matterhorn and Norwegian ice campaigns. Compulsive climbing and manic rock drumming are his release valves from a repetitive day job as skipper of the Gourock-Dunoon ferry across the Clyde. A torn Achilles' tendon had scuppered the climbing for a year and he wanted to prove his return to fitness.

Midweek's weather prediction was perfect, with only slow deterioration towards the weekend. I made the call to Jim and our fate was sealed. Vital dental repairs detained me on Tuesday and Jim was already on the road from Glasgow when slight doubt over Thursday's trend materialized into a distinctly 'iffy' forecast. By then we were committed and Jim walked in chock-full of bluster looking like one of Parahandy's crew with his chinstrap beard. He had persuaded his relief skipper to step in till 7 a.m. on Friday. With Jim there are no half-measures. I tried to forget Thursday's predicted rain-bursts and we strode out from the frosted shadows of Glen Brittle on the dot of 6 a.m. on Wednesday morning.

A one-day traverse was not an option at this time of year. McLaren and Shadbolt took twelve hours end-to-end on the first-ever traverse in 1911; Es Tressider ran it in three hours seventeen minutes in 2007. Even I had laid my step on this path

with a traverse a shade over three and a half hours in 1990. Don't be fooled! A one-day traverse needs perfect conditions, prior knowledge and intense commitment: count on eighteen hours. In any case there is much to commend a two-day engagement, despite the need to carry overnight kit, and it is still a tougher assignment than the Matterhorn. Over two days the aesthetic appreciation is enhanced, especially during the chill bivouac high above the misted glens, with its view of a Minginish sunset followed by a Scavaig dawn.

The classic traverse goes from south to north but the initial approach is tedious. We decided to go up Coire a'Ghrunnda instead of flogging up the screes to Gars Bheinn, which doesn't save any time but gets you up to all good things on the Ridge considerably quicker. Leaving our sacks under Sgurr nan Eag, we struggled in the glare of the newly risen sun on the southward march to Gars Bheinn. We were relieved to turn about at 10 a.m. to begin our traverse.

To begin we skipped nimbly across dry boulders, revelling in the grip and precision of lightweight rock shoes. We both wore approach shoes with stiffened toes to allow stability on the rock-climbing pitches. A kilo saved in the weight of footwear is worth 10 kilos in the sack – so the saying goes; but it left us vulnerable to wet and cold if the weather changed. Although complex route-finding is required to get to the outlying Munro Sgurr Dubh Mor and back to the main ridge crest, confident scramblers won't require a rope until the T-D Gap is reached.

A moody Cuillin Ridge at the end of autumn; here the view is of Bruach na Frithe, Am Basteir and Sgurr nan Gillian at the north end of the ridge

Jim Marshall stood atop Sgurr nan Eag, the most southerly Munro on the Cuillin traverse

Many an epic has unfolded in this evil chasm. Any wind is funnelled through the slot, while the rock is polished and chill to the touch, but today the Severe chimney exit was almost a pleasure, and Jim romped it. We were up Alasdair at 2 p.m. and mounted the (Very Difficult) King's Chimney on to Sgurr Mhic Choinnich as the first tendrils of approaching cloud licked the ridge. Jim was keen to incorporate all the highlights in the traverse so we moved together up An Stac buttress, then led through up the Inaccessible Pinnacle as a peaceful twilight settled over the landscape.

The comfort and security of a cave – nicknamed Hotel In Pinn – was just a few minutes away, but every step of extra progress can be vital to success on the traverse. We sacrificed cavernous luxury to press on to a rather more exposed bivouac somewhere after Sgurr na Banachdich, halfway point of the traverse. The last vestiges of light disappeared on the summit of Banachdich and banks of mist crept over the ridge from the east. The cut-off to the continuing link to Sgurr Thormaid and Sgurr a'Ghreadhaidh is tricky enough to find in daylight, but now my torch beam met a wall of white fog worthy of a set from *The Hound of the Baskervilles*. Visibility was barely 5 metres and for half an hour I blundered up and down likely descent lines, leaving Jim increasingly doubtful of my competence. Finally we got the line and scampered over Thormaid to a 'rest and be thankful' crow's nest under the coxcomb ridge, sheltered by a jutting prow of rock.

Martin Mora

Jim was easily fooled by my magnanimous offer to take the tatty nylon bivvy bag in return for the inside sleeping berth, while he got hooded Gore-Tex and exposure to any wind or rain that should blow in the night. We had less than two litres of water each, hardly enough to rehydrate after twelve hours of non-stop action, still less to fuel our second day. Having remembered seeing an abandoned stash of water bottles in the locality two years previously, I went on a hunt. A two-litre bottle of mineral water was duly excavated and we settled to an evening of hot sweetened tea and Super Noodles. Blissfully oblivious to whatever Thursday's weather held in store, I sunk into fathomless sleep.

A steady patter of water on my legs wakened me just after 4 a.m. A shower curtain was pouring off the rock overhang, and our feet were resting in a paddling pool. The forecast's promise of 'a little light overnight rain' was materializing as a deluge in true Cuillin tradition. We brewed and tried to doze until daylight at seven. Jim was getting the worst of the drips. He gradually edged closer inward until his whiskers almost brushed my face, and orchestrated a dawn wind concerto. Only then was it apparent that we had to move. Squeezing into damp socks and shoes, we emerged into a fug of supersaturated cloud at 8.30 a.m., but at least the rain had stopped. The forecast had indeed posted 'dry for the daylight hours'. With hopes raised we set off, believing we could reach Sgurr nan Gillean and get off the Ridge before nightfall, even with the rock wet.

Looking down into the T-D Gap

Martin Moran

All comforts at the bivvy site

The wind fell light and the air stayed exceptionally mild. Soon my toes and fingers were tingling warm and my approach shoes were doing the business, padding on the greasy slabs. We didn't even pause for breath at Sgurr a'Mhadaidh, eager to embark on the vital central sections over Mhadaidh's tops and Bidein Druim nan Ramh. We stayed roped across a slithery mix of sloping floors and lichened walls. The clouds parted as a southerly wind sprang to life. Shafts of sun played on the moors to the north. Were we to get a complete clearance? A heavy blatter of rain as we came off the Mhadaidh tops squashed that hope! Suddenly my spirit sank as I pondered the long chain of difficulties still to come, the black wall of cloud to windward and our wet, bedraggled state. It would only take one minor accident – a trip, a sprain or a ruptured tendon – and we'd be fighting to survive! We could forget any hope of a helicopter rescue in this fog.

'Jim, I'm thinking about binning this. There's too much against us,' I cautioned. I turned to see dismay on his face.

'Well, it's your call,' he answered, but I knew his true thoughts, and after all it was I who had dragged him up here on a promise of ideal conditions. At such moments of doubt even a professional guide has to admit that momentary portents can sway the day. The air stayed dry during a hesitant ten-minute climb towards Bidein and this was enough to rekindle some resolve. I pushed on and didn't think back. Scary down-climbs, misted abseils and teetering arêtes led us to the An Caisteal gap and the big climb on to Bruach na Frithe. Here, the wind rose to gale force and a blast of stinging raindrops was thrust across the ridge crest. We staggered to the summit and down to the Bealach na Lice.

Time was still on our side – just! We had three hours to get to Gillean and back before dark. The tempest precluded any attempt on Naismith's Route. Instead we ran down Lota Corrie into the wind and headed up Collie's ramps and gullies back towards the Bhasteir Tooth. Waterfalls gushed down every cranny. My spectacles became so steamed that I had to take them off and navigated by blurred vision and an increasingly blurred memory. I began to feel a sense of disembodiment; my actions no longer seemed driven by my thoughts. Was hypothermia setting in? For the moment I was still bodily warm, and Jim followed with surety of foot. We bagged the Tooth, and endured a sustained pelting as we traversed the slabby ridge of Am Basteir. The chimney on Gillean's West Ridge was mercifully sheltered and we picked our way to reach the summit in oppressive gloom at 3.40 p.m.

The Ridge was done but the car was 7 kilometres away in Glen Brittle. In the last vestiges of daylight we descended the ridge, abseiled the chimney and traversed the screes under Am Basteir. We had left all non-essential kit at the Bealach na Lice, and picked it up *en route* back to Glen Brittle. Jim had left his car at the forest car park. The rain still sheeted down as we squelched down the Fionn Choire. My feet were sodden and lumpen with cold. I dreamt only of getting home to a hot bath, log fire and big meal. Maybe I'd watch the news on TV with a can of beer. At the Bealach a'Mhaim we turned head-first into a storm-force sou'wester.

On nearing safety, just as my spirits began to rise in anticipation, a plaintive voice called out from behind: 'Martin, I've left my car keys in your van. I'm really sorry and I know I'm stupid!' We were instantly condemned to walk an extra 7 kilometres into the wind to get to my van at the beach. I delivered a verbal blast that overwhelmed the prevailing gale, terminated with the reflection that, far from needing the patience of a saint, a mountain guide needs the patience of Job and more. Jim was mute. Glen Brittle was black and deserted and vehicular assistance deemed unlikely.

With resignation to our fix, my mood gradually mellowed. What price another hour and a half in life's greater scheme? Halfway down the glen I admitted to Jim that I had once done the same with the keys on a 30-kilometre family walk. With the air thus cleared we finished the trek with happy banter and I ferried Jim back to his car at 8 p.m. Far from pitying my own travails it was Jim who deserved my sympathy; his onward prospect was grim. He faced a five-hour drive home, and had to get up at 5 a.m. for a twelve-hour shift on the boat. We shook hands and I advised him to procure a fish supper at the earliest opportunity. Come tomorrow I could envisage news reports of a Clyde ferry going round in circles, the skipper fast asleep and slumped at the helm. This Cuillin Traverse had personified the adage 'If you've got what it takes, it will take all you've got'; but, in truth, it is rarely any other way on Britain's greatest ridge.

FLANDERS

Chris Parkin

Outside of Scotland, the winter climbing potential of the cliffs of Snowdonia and the Lake District is remarkable, if only there were the snow and cold conditions on a more regular basis. Being on the scene at the right time is essential, and here, on the Ysgolion Duon – the Black Ladders – of the Carneddau of Snowdonia, local climber Chris Parkin was making the most of every opportunity.

We moved through the mixed terrain of the lower slopes; ribbons of ice, frozen vegetation and hollow, powdery snow. We were anxious to taste the offerings of the untapped winter possibilities and moved quickly past other teams, some roped, others like us racing solo. The sudden attraction of these great cliffs had been initiated by the magical change brought on by the seasonal weather transforming a usually quiet cwm into a magnificent winter playground. The other parties were heading for the classic winter route of this arena, Western, a deep crevice with a history of many a fight, and many a failure.

To the other climbers we appeared as contenders in the same race, but our objective was in a different vein; we had decided to abandon the claustrophobic confines of the traditional gully in favour of an exposed arête which towers over their intended line. In my mind, my imagination was playing tricks, everyone became a threat; they were all heading for 'our' line. While most stayed on the ice flow which dripped from Western, I stepped out left onto the steep vegetation and rock, pushing on at a reckless rate, determined to get to the base of the first steep section of Western before anyone else. As I reached the belay peg on the left wall I was pleased to see evidence of yesterday's retreats, a new-looking sling through its eye. This pleasure was not that others had failed, but that we were probably the first to this point today.

Flanders is the name given to the summer route up the left arête of Western Gully, first climbed by Crew, Lowe, Alcock and Brown in the summer of 1969; it is described as an excellent mountaineering route, 220 metres, and HVS (Hard Very Severe) from the start of the major difficulties. To us it was a winter challenge with many uncertainties. I had friends who had failed on this route in summer; if it was anything like the routes on Lliwedd, we had no chance at HVS! To me a winter ascent had been an idea for several winters, but I had always kept the idea to myself, waiting for conditions. Yet since a comment by Nunn in a certain tick book (*Cold*

The snowed-up cliffs of the Black Ladders, nestled beneath Carnedd Dafydd

Climbs), the idea was open to all, and now the precipitous steps of Ysgolion Duon (the Black Ladders) displayed their best conditions for years.

As Dave and I moved a little to the left of the classic line, the arriving team were pleased to see that their way was clear. This pleasure was not shared by us; the clear evidence of human passage up the first pitch of our intended line took the glow from our faces, leaving us in a state of semi-shock. Who? How? When? Had we been a day too late, or had our contemporaries adopted nocturnal habits, and were presently doing battle with the upper reaches? If so, could we possibly catch them up? Not to overtake them and steal their glory, but to commend them on this, the prize of North Wales (to us at least). We had to pull ourselves out of our disillusioned state; if the route was worth the effort for a first ascent, it must be worth repeating.

I set off right-ward across a cracked slab, following their scrapes and scratches, to reach the difficult groove.

Climbers approaching the base of Western Gully; Flanders takes a line to its left

The author starting up the lower pitches of Western Gully from which one can access the main Flanders line

Steve Long

It was virtually bare of ice, protection and holds; only the thinnest hooking on small iced edges allowed an exit onto the easier ground leading to the belay. A small spike shrouded in abseil slings provided the main belay attachment, a reminder of previous retreats. As Dave followed on the ropes below, I strained to survey the ground ahead: two grooves, both steep, the right-hand one overhanging. It was difficult to see which our unknown friends had taken; I'd just have to wait for Dave to probe his way when he arrived.

Our spirits had been lifted a little by now, but Dave was tentative about this next section and after several forays he was expressing doubts; my encouragements failed

Lee Roberts on pitch 5
of Flanders

and he returned to the stance to exchange places. He was pretty sure that no one had climbed either groove – well, not recently at least. What could I think? It did look hard, and if our mysterious friends had succeeded on the last pitch and failed on this, it must be so. Oh shit! What was I to do?

I decided to go all-out for the right-hand option. Having passed Dave's high point I was situated at the bottom of the intimidatingly steep groove. The crack in the back was chocked with frozen mud that provided reasonable axe placements, and the rugosity of the walls gave some purchase for the spiked footwear. After placing a small stopper and my micro ring-peg, I turned on to 'full steam ahead'. Grunting and groaning I gained enough height to eye a 15-centimetre edge over my right shoulder. Without consideration of the consequences I threw my foot on to it, palmed off the left wall and lunged my right axe at the vegetation, which I hoped it would find at the top of the groove. Yes, good turf, and a small spike runner into the bargain. Thank God for that! I smiled down at Dave and calmed my racing heart before climbing steep vegetation to a comfy ledge below a line of overhangs. That was going to be the end of my lead for now! My feelings at this point were unexplainable as I eyed the ledge for any sign of previous passage: none! I was now sure that we were on virgin ground.

After following two very difficult pitches, Dave's doubts were replaced by such determination that he hardly stopped at the belay to rack up. As he broke through the overhangs on the left, that was the last I was to see of him for over 60 metres. He dispensed with the summer pitch 3 in no time at all, even though it was probably a good grade V. Where a 6-metre traverse right leads to the continuation of the summer line, Dave chose to stay on the more natural winter line, and just kept going straight up. A series of steep walls allowed him to enter an open corner, holding a slender column of snow-ice. This dwindled in width to less than

Tim Neill

Chris Parkin seconding pitch 5 of Cannon Rib, VII 7, a route found to the right of Flanders

30 centimetres as he gained height, requiring very careful footwork. When the ribbon of ice stopped, so did he, and placed a half-inserted friend and two tied-off blade pegs; and this he called a belay! Perched on his crampons, he balanced a stance, not daring to load the 'belay' with his weight. Then he shouted 'Come on up', to me, his mobile second, already 15 metres above my secure stance, gripped out of my box, not knowing what the possessed bastard was up to.

'What brilliant climbing, Dave!' I thought to myself. 'Why didn't you split it? Is that really a belay?'

With the utmost care I passed him in search of security – to cock it up now would be rather grave for both of us. After 8 metres of the most nerve-racking climbing, I gained a capped ledge on the left. Wires, pegs, friends, anything was rammed into every conceivable fissure to obtain the much-required mental relief. Now we could talk, express ourselves in the knowledge that we were not going to die! Well, the good thing was that any time we may have wasted below had been made up for; time was still on our side – just gone 1 p.m. – and we were well up the cliff.

Exiting from the ledge involved pulling through a bulging band of shattered blocks to reach more amenable ground that led to the large pinnacle that stood clear of the upper arête. I viewed the cwm at its most splendid; crisp, clear, black and white, with a blue sky into the bargain! It's at times like these you can absorb the unique beauty of the British hills.

Dave arrived and quickly crossed the knife-edge to gain the upper arête. Here, he took a stance below a daunting off-width. As I moved to join him I was surprised at the exposure, and peered down into the upper reaches of Western Gully. We were above its final difficulty, the crux slab, and a team were just finishing this off before climbing the gentle snow fan which leads to the summit ridge. It was good to feel the human contact of fellow mountaineers, who I knew would be on a 'high' after their completion of a difficult climb. For us there were technical pitches to go. How hard? We could only guess. It wasn't difficult to judge that the next 10 metres, the off-width, was going to be very awkward.

Once more at the sharp end, I moved across to the base of the crack and arranged some protection. From this position I realized its width; at 25 centimetres – oh dear – this was not the best location to practise 'arm bar' techniques. With my right axe-wielding arm thrust into the crack, I managed to place a peg with the other hand. It was just to the left and a little above the base of the crack; this would have to be it until the top. With the prospect of no more gear there was no reason to hang about, so off I went. Standard techniques have no place here; only squirming seems to work. With one arm deep in the crack, twisting the axe and scraping for purchase, the other flailed at the blank left wall. I wondered whether it would be better if I faced the other way – a question never destined to get an answer. With my feet a little above the peg, the fine balance between grip and gravity was toppled and I slid downwards. Luckily my foot stopped on the protruding peg eye and another attempt began. Slightly higher; gravity took over again, but this time I was not so lucky. I stopped upside down 6 metres below the base of the chimney, facing out at the top slopes of Western. Hanging thus, I felt a sling fall from around my neck and watched it go snaking down. I hoped it didn't hit anyone.

The next attempt was more successful. Adopting the same stubborn style, yet this time swapping hand tools over, I landed on a large sloping ledge at the top of the crack. With great effort I crawled, sweat running down my neck and heart pounding, to a sizeable block to secure the ropes. With a similar struggle Dave landed himself on the ledge, gasping and unable to talk. Here we took a rest and consulted the summer route description. With not far to go and over an hour of daylight left, we felt we were on the home straight. Dave took a groove to the short corner which was to present the last of the difficulties. He was surprised by its steepness but pleased to find both walls encrusted in a thick rime ice. Up he went; the axes took well but the ice crumbled at his toes, not allowing him much success. He adopted a new method; by bridging across the corner with his feet placed sideways he was able to spread his weight to allow the crust to support him. Once 'the method is mastered the problem relents' and a singing pioneer sat braced in the rocks that marked the scramble to the top.

Buzzing with excitement we strolled along the tops to the descent that took us back into the cwm. As the light faded our efforts were rewarded with a clear, starry sky and a brilliant full moon. Laughing and joking, we regained the base of the cwm to view the soaring arête as never before, highlighted against the cliff by the lunar glow. Here, we took a short break and savoured our experience; the stress, the strain, the questions and finally some of the answers.

* * * * *

The above is an account of a good day out on the first winter ascent of Flanders, Ysgolion Duon, incorporating well over a thousand feet of technical winter climbing in one of the best cwms in Snowdonia, the approach slopes being grade II/III, the rest being good grade V and above. After the first two hard pitches it would be best (and safer) to belay at 25 metres, then on the overhang capped ledge. The mystery friends succeeded on the second ascent the next day and were greeted at the top by Dave, who was out for a walk. All in all a good effort by all!

The summer HVS route Flanders received its first winter ascent in 1994 by Chris Parkin and Dave O'Dowd. The North Wales winter climbing guidebook rates it as grade VII 7 and gives it four stars.

A GUIDE'S LIFE – MORE UPS THAN DOWNS!

Ron James

The eventful story of a young man becoming a climber and aspiring to become a mountain guide turns into a history of the development of climbing protection and mountain rescue techniques, and culminates in the development of the guiding profession itself.

In 1941 Hitler's blitz was at its peak and for our annual holiday my family wanted to get out of Birmingham and find peace (and butter, eggs and fresh greens!) in the country. A farmhouse near Llan Ffestiniog was the answer. The packed train arrived at Maentwrog Station late at night. I was eight years old and installed in a single room. I woke early and opened the curtains. Across the farmyard the ground fell steeply to the Vale of Ffestiniog. I looked up above a cloud layer and saw a sunlit shape. My dad told me it was a mountain (Moelwyn Bach). That morning a desire to climb mountains was born. Later that week, Moel y Gest at 263 metres became my first summit.

Future holidays were mainly in North Wales, with days spent walking on the hills or along the coast. My equipment was minimal: a cut-down school raincoat, hobnailed old shoes (I still have the bunion to prove it), a 1 inch OS map and an ex-army prismatic compass. In 1947 I did the Snowdon Horseshoe alone. My parents took the train to the summit and checked me through. On Lliwedd, the awesome feeling of height was disturbed by a gentleman who emerged from the face with a rope trailing behind him. Real climbers! The pleasure was spoilt by the ticking-off I received for being up there alone. 'Make your parents hire a guide for you, if you want to do dangerous things like this', I was told. One word stuck in my mind and later, when my favourite teacher set an essay topic: 'What I want to be when I grow up', I had no problem finding a rather different topic from the 'fighter pilots' and 'train drivers' in the class – a mountain guide! Unknown to the class, the teacher kept the essays.

A couple of years later I bought decent nailed boots from Timpson's shoe shop and hill-walked regularly.

In 1950 I went up to Birmingham University and joined the mountaineering club. There I started climbing seriously both on their weekend meets and in the long holidays. I met good climbers and pushed up my standard. One was Johnnie Lees with the RAF Valley Rescue Team, who invited me to climb with them. He was not then a guide but his belt and braces approach to safety has stood me in good stead ever since.

In my final term, a lecture from the distinguished mountaineer Jack Longland was fascinating and opened up new horizons. When asked for his definition of a good mountaineer, he replied 'One who climbs until he retires!' This was my target for the next sixty years!

I started work as a teacher and bought a van. This allowed me to climb a lot of rock, initially in Snowdonia and the Peaks but later in the Lakes, Scotland and the Alps. (No motorways then!) At that time, the basic philosophy was that the leader must not fall. Climbing shops were rare; in Birmingham there was just Blacks. In the late 1950s Arvon's shoe shop in Bethesda would nail boots for climbing and sold the odd rope and sling. Hemp ropes were non-stretch but luckily hawser-laid nylon ropes (very marketable in the Alps!) were becoming available. Protection was minimal and the BMC recommended just one full weight sling. Tying-on was with a bowline. Karabiners were crude, often ex-War Department, and at least one opened on a leader fall, causing a fatality. One good thing came out of the ex-service equipment and that was moulded Vibram boot

Ron James

Young Ron in 1948

soles. I was slow to change and, in the list of routes included in my later detailed guides' application, I had Tennis Shoe on Idwal Slabs in nails as a good early 1950s ascent. I realized I was climbing quite well when a Manchester climber refused to believe that I had, by then, led Ivy Sepulchre above Llanberis Pass, then graded Exceptionally Severe. That put my standard into perspective, so perhaps I could become a guide!

In 1953 a leaking cylinder head gasket on my Austin 10 van helped with a big breakthrough. Protecting a climb had moved on to the use of runners, such as slings and inserted natural chock-stones. These were carried in old socks tucked into the hemp waist belt that had replaced the bowline for tying-on. I realized that a cylinder head nut might be better than a stone – and more so if a loop of thin line was threaded through it. I started with three different nuts on each sling but I was criticized by some climbers who thought nuts were as bad as pitons! A year later I did Central Buttress on Scafell with Frank Davies. He was amazed at the nuts and told me that it was the first time he had seen nut protection. Years later he was selling thousands in his Ambleside shop!

Scottie Dwyer was the leading Welsh BMC guide and I regularly stayed in his barn near Capel Curig. We became friends and he encouraged me to aspire to getting qualified and let me assist on his bread and butter Mountaineering Association courses. I learnt a lot, although I was in trouble for giving the clients too much information! I realized his was a precarious existence. Later Scottie became one of my referees.

In autumn 1958 Trevor Jones discovered that Ogwen Cottage, an old guesthouse, was for sale. We decided to buy it and start Ogwen Cottage Mountain School. My contacts through the Birmingham schools and my teaching experience

Faces from the Welsh climbing scene: George 'Scotty' Dwyer, Kenneth Leach, unknown, Paul Work

made it a viable proposition. We recruited a third partner in Tony Mason, a Bangor land agent, with whom I had often climbed. Tony had good security and a friendly bank manager and we opened in 1959. Obviously one of us needed a qualification and I set to work preparing an application for a BMC Rock-climbing Guide Certificate. My list of rock-climbs in Wales and the rest of Britain was very comprehensive but I had only five Alpine seasons and parts of those were in the Dolomites. My ice-climbing outside Wales was limited, with only a winter ascent of Green Gully on Ben Nevis of any note. I was nervous on ice for three of my closest friends, all excellent winter mountaineers, had died on the final slopes of Zero Gully attempting the first winter ascent. I could have been with them that weekend but chose Llanberis Pass instead.

I applied and had a test that lasted one full day! Don Roscoe of Rock and Ice fame was the BMC assessor and Douglas Milner (the photographer) and his young son were my clients. Milestone Buttress was the venue and all went well. On 1 May 1960 I received my badge and certificate, both still very treasured possessions, and I received a congratulatory telegram from my parents who incidentally thought I was an idiot for giving up my good job for this uncertain existence. By post came a letter from my old teacher telling me that I was the only boy in my class who had achieved his life's ambition!

The basic work at Ogwen Cottage was with school groups, mainly on twelve-day mountaincraft courses. The instructors were my climbing friends and others just appeared. The climbing standard was high and many new routes were climbed in our free time. The Cottage was also a rescue post and sadly rescues were quite frequent, so Johnnie Lees gave us some training in rescue rope work. I also worked with Dr Ieuan Jones, head of Bangor Hospital casualty unit, to produce a comprehensive first-aid course for mountaineers. The rescues were distressing (I was involved in 365 in the ten years I was at Ogwen) but a study of the causes enabled me to create an approach to our activities that worked. I realized that 'safety is an awareness of danger' and this became our mantra and our teaching. In the same period, the only accident to pupils was a broken leg on a ski slope!

From this approach came the *TAPES* equation. It was based on an approach that did not select the final *Target* until various factors had been evaluated. The sum of *Ability* (leaders and clients, including awareness and experience), *Prevailing Conditions* (past, present and expected), *Equipment* (available to all) and *Strength* (physical, mental and numbers) honestly assessed indicated a *Target* that was safely attainable. We did this sum every day and amended the activity accordingly!

The other spin-off from mountain rescue was the development of self-rescue. Tony Mason, by then qualified as a BMC Mountain Guide, got a 35 mm film of the Innsbruck Team in practice. We spent hours experimenting with karabiner brakes, crevasse rescue, improvised rescue, alpine baskets and so on. I obtained a German edition of Wastl Mariner's book and refined our techniques. Later I demonstrated many of these techniques to the first two Mountaineering Instructors Assessment Courses at Plas y Brenin and Glenmore Lodge. These new methods are now considered standard. We just found them great fun!

I enjoyed the repetitive work with the youngsters but needed the extra joy and income from guiding. The daily rate for rock-climbing when I qualified was £2 10 s. (£2.50). I added £3 for three Very Severe climbs, £5 for selected harder routes and new routes. One client was very ambitious but very nervous. An early booking at VS found me on the Shadow Wall crux, with him on the exposed stance. His violent trembling coming up the rope, instead of the slack I needed, caused me to retreat. I got him to take me off belay and I then soloed the pitch. I had always treated guiding as soloing and he convinced me I was right. A year later he fancied White Slab on Cloggy but insisted on a back rope on the first pitch. He paid Johnnie Lees to come as third man. It drizzled as we started and he could not follow but Lees and I could do it so he ran round taking photos! The same client made me reconsider the £5 specials. Pete Crew had recently climbed Great Wall on Cloggy with some pre-placed protection. I fancied an unprepared second ascent; the client agreed. I belayed him to a low peg, directly below the route, in case of an upward pull. Using two long rescue ropes, all went well until about 9 metres above today's peg-protected intermediate stance. I was on the wrong foot with poor handholds. I warned him I was going to do a hop foot change. If I missed, I faced a long fall! Tugs on the rope and a scrabbling noise made me look down to see him frantically trying to undo his belay while shouting, 'Don't land on me!' Rage helped my retreat down and ended the profitable relationship. Even worse, Dave Yates on my staff made the clean ascent two days later!

Shrike, Clogwyn du'r Arddu

New routing with clients was the best of both worlds and Lavaredo Wall in Cwm Penamnen and the Amphitheatre Girdle on Craig yr Ysfa are good examples.

Being independent, we were free to provide courses for anyone. A memorable course was one for the SAS in 1960. The aim was to select, in three weeks, a mountain troop of six top grade leaders from sixty hand-picked men! They were under pressure and so were we! A long day was planned to include an unexpected bivouac. One of my staff decided to bivouac on Belle View Terrace on Tryfan. The men had slept in worse places but were not impressed when their instructor produced his extra food and bivouac bag. Once he was safely tucked in, they quickly slipped three rope loops round him and lowered him 6 metres down Scars Climb. They slept, he didn't! After the course finished, he quit Ogwen Cottage! By week three some could safely lead extreme climbs like Erosion Groove on Carreg Wastad. I was down to twelve possibles and was determined that the losers would be happy with my final selection. A race over the Welsh Fourteen 3,000-foot (910-metre) Peaks was proposed and the men agreed, provided we instructors raced as well. Luckily one of my staff finished first while I just lost third place to the soldier who dogged my tracks and outsprinted me on Foel Fras! The last night party was very memorable!

Ron James

Amphitheatre Girdle
traverse, Craig yr Ysfa

By 1964 Birmingham LEA were buying thirty-seven weeks of courses each year. Suddenly they decided they wanted their own centre, so sadly we had no alternative but to sell Ogwen Cottage to them, at their valuation! The sweeteners were that I got a Headship and Tony became Chief Instructor. Advantages were a proper electrical supply, good sanitation, a new building and teachers' holidays. The big disadvantage was that guiding and mountain rescue was not included.

K.C. Gordon, by then a guide, had been kept on. In order to organize guiding, we formed the North Wales Mountain Guides Association with me as Chairman and K.C. as Secretary. Also, Tony Mason and I set up the Ogwen Valley Mountain Rescue Organisation, essential to cover the area during the school holidays, when we were all away. At that time the Valley and Ogwen teams had been involved in several big rescues for young people under so-called 'instruction'. Johnnie Lees and I pressed the BMC to do something about this and the Mountain Leadership Certificate was initiated.

The change and increased income enabled me to give more time to my own Alpine climbing and two selected climbs books, *Im Extremen Fels* and *Im Schweren Fels* became my tick lists. The ticks were frequent, but crosses also appeared, no doubt influenced by the old climber's motto 'Better to explain to the lads in the valley why you retreated, than explain to St Peter why you didn't.'

Initially, while I was a BMC guide, Alpine guiding was sometimes difficult. In Chamonix, a local French guide not only made sure that I could not get any concessions on uplift or huts if I was with a client but also once tried to stop me even using a lift. Luckily, in my favourite area, the Dolomites, I had no problems and had good relations with the local guides. One memorable guiding experience combined both aspects. I was climbing in Chamonix with Dai Rowlands, a very strong Welsh guide, when I met one of my North Wales clients employing a local guide, Christian Mollier. Dai and I were on the east face of the Grand Capucin and they watched us from Le Trident. We must have impressed Christian for, when the weather broke, he was happy when the client invited us to join them in the Dolomites. I drove the hire car and selected and led the routes. Four days, three guides and one client! I led with no sack, Dai was the porter and Christian led the second rope. We made very fast ascents of Diagonal Crack in snow at the Sella Pass, the Steger in Catinaccio and the Yellow Edge on Tre Cima. My only mistake was to order *quaglia* for us all in a Cortina restaurant thinking it was a kind of chicken. It's not; it's quail and not very filling! However it was still a very enjoyable job!

At this time, at an international avalanche conference, I learnt about the meaning of the different colours of snow. I also recall an instruction from André Roch to a group going out to study avalanches: 'You know you are all avalanche experts, sadly the mountain doesn't!'

In the 1960s Johnnie Lees and I produced a list of the hundred best climbs in North Wales. Some were on crags about which little information was available. A guest at Ogwen was Walter Poucher, photographer and walking guidebook writer and he suggested that I do something similar for Welsh rock climbs. He introduced me to Constable Publishers and they liked the concept. When the Foot and Mouth outbreak in October 1967 forced a five-month closure of the Welsh Hills, I took unpaid leave and wintered in the Alps, studying Alpine rescue methods and working in an Austrian ski school. Whilst there, I wrote the first collected climbs guidebook *Rock Climbing in Wales*. It was published in 1970 and I still meet climbers who were inspired by it to start. This success prompted other writing work, and my knowledge and love of the Dolomites led the Alpine Club to commission *Dolomites Selected Climbs* (1988) and *Dolomites East and West* (2006). Another spin-off was the invitation in 1974 from the BMC and BBC to perform in a TV programme *Rockface*, an instructional series of ten programmes. I was heavily involved in the planning and scripting of much of the content. It was shown three times on British TV and in other countries and I also wrote the book accompanying the programmes.

After ten great years with thousands of pupils, hundreds of clients, numerous hard climbs and thirty-five Welsh first ascents, I left Ogwen Cottage to become Principal Lecturer of Outdoor Education in Liverpool.

The BMC guides moved on too. In 1972 I convened a meeting in Liverpool between the Welsh and Lakeland Guides and the BMC to take the first steps to break away from the BMC and to form our own national organization. The Association of British Mountain Guides was formed and over the next few years developed and gained, with difficulty, international (UIAGM) recognition. The proviso that Alpine and ski-guiding components be added to our training posed no problem for me, as by then I had plenty of good Alpine experience and was British Association of Ski Instructors qualified.

All this was a great introduction to my fifty years of being a guide. I went freelance in 1985 and from 1996 until 1999 I served as BMG President. Finally, my two proudest moments as a guide came when, in December 2004, the Association made me an Honoured Guide, and in June 2009 when the Queen awarded me the MBE for services to mountaineering.

Today, at eighty, I can look back at Jack Longland's definition and realize I had become 'the good mountaineer who retired'.

On the crux of Grey Arête, Idwal

Ron James

Mal Creasey

On the summit of the Aiguille du Chardonnet, looking east towards Switzerland and the Grand Combin

Mal Creasey

Tea break on the Ottema Glacier during a traverse of the Haute Route

Mal Creasey

another hundred years from this golden age of Alpine mountaineering and things were very different.

Snell's Field; Dave Robinson in 1970

During the 1960s and 1970s a few British guides had worked occasionally in the Alps with private clients or students on outdoor education courses, but few were basing themselves out there for the whole season. Ron James certainly had some private clients around either Chamonix or the Dolomites and John Brailsford took his Bangor Normal College students out every summer, and by the late 1970s Plas y Brenin and Glenmore Lodge were also running courses, usually in either Chamonix or Ailfroide, but these would be for only limited periods. The first British guides to base themselves in the Alps for the whole season were the husband and wife partnership of Geoff and Brede Arkless and Terry Taylor. I, Martin Barnicott, Nigel Shepherd, Rob Collister, Phill Thomas, Richard McHardy and a few others followed very soon afterwards and we would regularly bump into each other, mainly on the classic routes (or occasionally in the bars) around Argentière.

Working as guides in those days was a steep learning curve for us all; it was only a few short years since many of us had been raggedy-arsed climbers habitually using the infamous Biolay or Snell's field camp sites as they were free.

We did occasionally pay at Snell's Field for the privilege of crapping in the woods, or dicing with death in some contraption that had been built over the icy-cold murky waters of the river Arve which flowed past the campsite. How that particular thunderbox didn't collapse and dump some poor unfortunate soul in the river, never to be seen again, is a mystery to me – perhaps it did! A few folk even made occasional use of the *douche municipal* in Chamonix – the highlight of the week for some!

Mal Creasey

Brede Arkless guiding
on the Écandies Arête

Anyway, just a few years later we had become respectable – or at least semi-respectable; we were still dossing in the woods but in real tents and not something concocted out of a kiddie's play tent and some plastic sheeting! And we had moved up the road to Argentière, which felt much friendlier, which is not surprising as the Chamonairds had been putting up with the Brits dossing in the woods since the 1950s!

During those early seasons I worked with Geoff and Brede Arkless, who would pack most of their kids, usually about six or seven, into the back of an old ambulance and head for the Channel, then drive overnight to Chamonix to arrive at some point next day, hopefully with the kids having slept through the overnight journey.

Not a chance there! I only travelled out with them once; after that I took my own car! They would set up camp in the woods behind the town with a big frame tent as base and at least two other tents for some of the kids. So it's not surprising really that the locals were becoming aware of our existence. I wonder what they thought of the nightly pilgrimage to the village water pump to fill the camp water containers and I'm certainly not sure what the local guides made of all this – although we were soon to find out!

Aiguille d' Argentière (3,901 metres) via the South West Flank (Milieu Glacier)

Initially we were regarded with suspicion as we would regularly meet the local guides at the hut, or on the route. Some would openly question us as to how we English could possibly be guides and operate effectively on glaciers without having any in the UK where we could at least have learnt the basics! On one such occasion I had opted to do the normal route of the Aiguille d'Argentière, which one guidebook referred to as 'an elegant and scenic glacier expedition taking a direct line to the summit'. It was, however, certainly a baptism of fire for me. There had been a period of poor weather, and booking in the *Refuge d'Argentière* as a British guide with poor French certainly raised the suspicions of the *gardiens* and no doubt caused some gossip amongst the local guides. We were probably the first British guides to have booked into the refuge with clients and word had got around! Also, we were pretty

Mal Creasey

green about start times and the various protocols to be followed concerning what times we should get up, and why we should sleep in the dormitories allocated – such details were all new to us!

The next morning we got up and managed to get out on to the route without causing too much personal embarrassment. It had snowed again overnight and the route was untracked, with about 15 centimetres of fresh snow, but otherwise safe and the weather set fair for the day. So off I went, as a naïve young British guide with so much enthusiasm – I just couldn't understand why everyone was hanging back! The way was free, you could clearly see the route (albeit under fresh snow) and the sky was cloudless, with the weather looking settled for the day. So why was everyone so hesitant?

A couple of hours later it was beginning to dawn on me. Naturally, I thought at least someone was going to offer to take the lead from me. Numerous times I politely stood to one side with a magnanimous gesture of waving someone through with the best '*Après vous Messieurs*' I could muster, only to be greeted with an equally magnanimous, but far more Gallic, gesture with the hands declining the offer – oh, and of course their beautifully accented '*Non merci, Monsieur*', along with lots of other words I didn't understand, which I'm sure were very polite, but totally wasted on me! So I had no option but to plod on, and as we got higher the snow got deeper. On crossing the bergschrund it was way over ankle depth and by the time we were approaching the summit it was knee deep! Again and again my '*Après vous messieurs*'

The author sits on the summit of the Aiguille du Moine, with Mont Blanc and the Chamonix Aiguilles behind him

was politely declined with yet another Gallic shrug of the shoulders and a *'Non merci, Monsieur'*. It was certainly hard work doing all the trail breaking and those French lads (the guides) must have been laughing their socks off. In fact I bet there are some aged French guides who still talk about the incident! Almost everyone from the hut was following me as no other routes were in condition, yet I couldn't persuade even one person to help break trail. In those days there were few rock routes just behind the hut and in any event you just didn't go to the Alpine huts then to do rock routes – we must have been blind to the opportunities that existed back then. Still, at least I got to the summit first – but boy, was I knackered!

Aiguille du Chardonnet (3,824 metres) via the East Ridge (Forbes Arête)

On another occasion just a couple of weeks later I got the opportunity to do one of the classics of the Chamonix Valley – the Forbes Arête on the Aiguille du Chardonnet. This is one of the classic routes of its grade anywhere in the Alps and although only graded AD, it does have a big 'feel'; it is not to be underestimated, particularly if conditions are not perfect. My client for the day was of a similar age to me; I had climbed with him in the UK previously and he was a fit and capable climber. We did the Petite Aiguille Verte as a quick warm-up route and then, with a good forecast, as he had only a couple of spare days, we went straight up to the *Albert Premier Refuge* that afternoon.

My first mistake was walking from Le Tour, as in those days the *téléphérique* closed for a couple of hours over lunch but, being young and enthusiastic (or just plain daft), we couldn't be arsed waiting around as we had just missed the last bin before lunch. It was Kev, my client, who suggested that we might as well walk from the valley rather than sit around for a couple of hours waiting for the cabins to start up again and I readily agreed, not realizing what the knock-on effect might be the next day. It was a long walk, especially as it was a blisteringly hot day. Although, having been out in the Alps for several weeks, I was feeling pretty fit, I was aware that Kev had only been out for a few days. The normal approach these days contours around the hillside from the top station before a couple of steep zigzags, then follows some more gently rising ground and the final steep pull up the moraine to the refuge. However, walking in from the valley the route initially follows the cable car then bears right at the first station and follows a long, steep, upward pull before joining the path, which contours around from the top station. By the time we reached the moraine we were hot, dusty and knackered in spite of the doze in the afternoon sun earlier on –which was in itself a bit of a silly thing to do, as we had both nodded off and had sunburnt shoulders!

There was no chance of taking in the view and relaxing in the sun outside the hut, as it must have taken the best part of six hours (including the snooze) to get there. By the time we had the dorm allocated and sorted the sacks it was time for some grub and, before we knew where we were, it was bedtime, especially as it was a 2 a.m. wake-up call. There was not time to have a quick look at where the route went in the morning, which is always a recipe for disaster, although I had completed the route previously. But you can't be too careful, particularly on 2 a.m. starts.

After a fitful sleep we were up and away with just one other team out, but they disappeared into the night before we emerged from the hut. There was no chance

Mal Creasey

of latching on to the couple of locals to find the way through the rocks up to the glacier. I had recognized the leader the night before as one of the local guides who had let me break trail a couple of weeks earlier, although he pretended not to recognize me and looked away every time I caught his eye. However, as it happened, we found our way and reached the edge of the glacier without any mishaps. Crampons and rope on, with a fine moon just rising to illuminate the route with the promise of a perfect day, and things couldn't have looked better, apart from our sacks just beginning to make themselves noticeable on our sunburnt shoulders! In the semi-conscious state of early morning the pain didn't register but as we warmed up and started to sweat things did begin to feel a little sore. The snow was frozen and our crampon points scrunched every time we moved, but we could see where we were heading. Up past the rocky island of the Signal Adams Reilly, etched starkly against the moonlit glacier, and in that cold, frosty pre-dawn we could almost imagine Victorian explorers huddled up, with their cloaks gathered around them. We were moving well and could put up with a little discomfort from the sunburn and we were even catching up with the couple in front of us – not that we were in any way competitive, but the trail-breaking episode still rankled a little and I was not going to let this guy have any reason to think that we Brits were only good at wading around in deep snow.

Initially the route heads up the left-hand side of the Glacier du Tour before crossing the glacier high up, then heads back down and round in a semi-circle,

Setting out on the Glacier du Tour

Mal Creasey

With clients on the
Forbes Arête

which avoids the worst crevasses, to the start of the route proper. Dawn found us approaching this with a carpet of diamonds at our feet as the early morning sun danced off individual crystals of frost that coated the glacier. We were now just ahead of the other two and I thought I'd be damned if I was going to let the guide overtake me. Kev was going well despite little acclimatization or rest. If I'd thought things through a little I would have realized that it would hit him later in the day – and it did! However, at that time he was still going like a train, so it was up the steepening ground and then a traverse right (well it was in those days) before whipping up the ice boss showing all the hard-won skills of someone who had cut their teeth on the Ben! None of this namby-pamby new-fangled French style of side-stepping and crossing feet whilst moving diagonally backwards! Back then it was good old front pointing, smacking the axe in and running the front points of the crampons up in a flurry of flying ice chips! Nothing could stop us now as rocky gendarme followed icy crest, with a few delicate moves on front points then back to icy crests – tightrope walking – this is what Alpine mountaineering was all about, with lots of exposure either side.

All too soon it was over as I scrambled up an icy chimney to the summit and a chance to really admire the views. Our Gallic friends arrived a few minutes after us and, believe it or not, we did get a cursory glance and a nod of acceptance – it must have been our performance on the ice boss that impressed the guide when we romped ahead. To be one of the first British guides this local had ever seen in action was a matter of pride. Since he was one of the guides who had seen me off on the Argentière, maybe now the story he would relate to his mates in the valley might just be a little more respectful! However, the day was not yet done – as ever, getting to the top is optional – getting back down in one piece is not an option; it is a necessity.

Needless to say we were a trifle slower going down – descending quickly has never been a strongpoint of the British in the Alps (although the Scots would argue that point vehemently as it is something they, with their predominantly bigger hills, have had to do since time began). Whilst Kev took a break on the summit he became aware of a violent headache and suddenly started throwing up as the lack of acclimatization and the events of the previous twenty-four hours suddenly started taking their toll. Time to go, and our French colleagues overtook us within two minutes of leaving the summit and ten minutes later were out of sight, only to reappear a little later as mere specks on the glacier below the Col Adams Reilly. Meanwhile Kev was moving ever-more slowly as I kept him on a tight rope, either belaying him or lowering all the way to the Col – it took an age! Below the Col we could at least move together towards the main glacier as Kev recovered a little with decreasing altitude, but he was shattered. The *rimayé* on to the Tour Glacier loomed, which the guidebook in those days stated, and I quote, 'often required an abseil or a heroic leap'! Well, I didn't fancy a heroic leap for Kev as he was all in, so I lowered him and decided the only option for me was the heroic leap! It was a hell of a distance and I didn't feel particularly heroic but it had to be done! And what of our Gallic comrades by this time – disappeared out of sight – probably back in the hut drinking a *panaché* or gently meandering back to the top station and contemplating a gentle ride

On the Forbes Arête

back to the valley. Once established on the Tour Glacier, the distance to the hut appeared deceptively short – and it was, by comparison to the long and circuitous route recommended in the guidebook to avoid the worst of the crevasses. So, for once, not to be enticed into a short, but evidently exciting, route directly back to the hut, it was a long, hot haul in the cauldron of the glacier as the sun reached its zenith and beyond. Finally we made the hut at 2 p.m. – early afternoon, but we had started at 2 a.m. with little sleep and, for Kev, little preparation but lots of enthusiasm. Six hours up and six down – not bad, but the French lads got down in four hours – mmm – must do better …

A brilliant day though, which has stayed in the memory for over thirty years. As for Allain – *monsieur le local guide* – he became a firm friend and was instrumental in persuading his colleagues that we Brits were okay really. Since then we have swapped many a tale over the odd *panaché*.

A TRAVERSE OF THE CHAMONIX AIGUILLES – THE HARD WAY!

Rocio Siemens

Many Alpine ridge traverses naturally involve a fair amount of terrain in descent, but you would like to think that to reach the summit, most of the time would be spent climbing. So when the opportunity came of traversing the many pinnacles that dominate the southern skyline above Chamonix, Rocio Siemens and companions knew exactly how they would go about it.

I'll say straight from the start that it wasn't my idea – it was Tania's. For the last year or so, Tania had been harping on and on about this mega-traverse of the Chamonix Aiguilles, and how to do it in the most *aesthetically pleasing way*. As described in Lindsay Griffin's Mont Blanc guidebook, it could only be done one way: north to south, by starting with the lowest of the aiguilles and finishing at the Aiguille du Midi high point. This way offers the best climbing, rather than the best abseiling. It made sense to me; after all, I pride myself on being a competent rock-climber, and make nothing much of being a competent abseiler. This traverse follows the amazing skyline that catches your eye in the summer's evening sun when the Blaitière, the Ciseaux and the Fou stand out as pointy granite giants amongst the bulkier and snowier peaks around.

In the months preceding our mini-expedition, Tania had been dutifully compiling all available information, route descriptions and topos, which extended over several pages of back-to-back paragraphs and photos. The majority described the route south to north, so most of the time had been spent working out things back to front. To make the best of the traverse, Tania had added her own little twist to our mission: to start on the Mer de Glace face of the Grepon, which meant climbing 800 metres of beautiful granite slabs. This would guarantee a double triple-ticking: three AD routes and three *Difficile* routes, all stand-alone lines in their own right, over 4 kilometres of granite peaks and troughs. In the standard and the most commonly followed description, the south to north traverse is suggested to be a one- to two-day affair for a competent team. It was suggested that the reverse route would take two to three days.

I flew out on the last week of August and sat at Tania's place, negotiating the gear

Tania Noakes

The author on the
Aiguille du Grepon,
day 1

and food we'd need. The pile of gear grew with crampons and axes, ropes, sleeping bags, rock shoes, chalk bags and a stove. We weren't sure how much mixed climbing we'd encounter, so axes moved from one side of the living room to the other: would the second need two axes? Would the leader need two axes? Could we get away with one axe each? What about crampons? Should the second take aluminium ones to save weight? Having the same shoe size, we decided to share rock shoes and chalk bag, something I had never done before with any of my other climbing partners in the Alps. Then we came to deciding on the food. Tania was convinced we'd do it in three days; I put food in for four – I hate the feeling of an empty stomach. The forecast was good for three days, with a storm forecast at some point after this …

My husband Owen was at a bit of a loose end and, with his new toy, the GoPro video camera, asked if he could join us as film crew. Both Tania and I thought climbing as a three would be more fun, so he was welcome to join us.

Our starting point was the Envers hut, and after an early breakfast we made our way to the Mer de Glace face of the Grepon and climbed the 800 metres enjoying the rock, the views and the company. Six or seven hours later, a few abseils down the other side took us to the Col des Nantillons, where we stopped for a while as the cloud cover thickened and thinned to reveal the Spencer Couloir. With clearing skies, we pushed on for a bit further and spent our first night at the foot of the north summit of the Aiguille de Blaitière.

Packing away our gear the following morning in the orangey light, I felt rather queasy and proceeded to vomit up all my breakfast. This was my body reminding me that not acclimatizing has a price. Luckily for us, Owen's GoPro had gone dead the previous day, cutting his filming mission short, so he was roped in to help with the

Tania Noakes

Tania Noakes
approaching the top of
the Mer de Glace Face
on the Grepon with the
Aiguille de Roc behind

team ascent. Both Tania and Owen took it in turns to lead us through the rest of the Blaitière summits. Tania did a phenomenal job of route-finding her way past the Ciseaux, reams of guide-book descriptions stowed away as complete fantasy and make-believe. We were now on our own, following our noses through what looked like uncharted ground, with plenty of fresh-looking rockfall. I took over in the afternoon, moving past the Aiguille du Fou and the Col du Fou and down to the Col de Blaitière.

A bit further along from there, we descended from the Col du Caïman, towards the Envers side. We lost our way for a bit, going far too low and having to climb back up again. It was getting towards the end of the day, and where we had hoped the route-finding would start easing off, it did anything but. We were among a sea of slabs and walls which all seemed as much possible ways ahead as they did dead-ends. In the dimming daylight we made our way to the foot of what looked like a steep groove that we'd be able to climb. I cooked our last shared meal, clipping the hot container to a sling for Tania to pull up to her ledge. After melting enough snow for drinking the following day, we settled in for the night on our two-tiered bivvying place and tried to get some sleep.

Another day, another sunrise; another opportunity to be reminded that I wasn't yet acclimatized. I felt hollow from the exertion of rejecting my breakfast once again. The steep groove turned out to be very loose indeed, and Tania did a great job leading it, but just as she was exiting the groove, she triggered a massive rockfall which narrowly missed Owen and me. The smoke generated by the broken rocks, and the smell of fresh granite, reminded us that in this world which is over 72 per cent silica in composition, our organic carbon-based bodies are no match in tough-ness. Being a warm, fleshy lump in the cold vastness of this granite empire, I could suddenly appreciate how, if not continually exposed to its rudeness, infrequent incursions during summer holidays would make any human feel well out of their comfort zone.

We were now in what we thought was *wasterra incognita*, arriving at this shoulder with no obvious line towards the summit of the Dent du Caïman. I led us up some walls and open grooves, all of which seemed quite improbable. When I topped-out and saw an abseil station, I was ecstatic! A few abseils down very loose-looking

ground took us to the Brèche Croco-
dile-Caïman, where we celebrated,
expecting the bulk of the difficulties to
be over. However, the ascent of the
Dent du Crocodile was tougher and
more complex than expected. This
ground was very involved and required
some meaty mixed climbing. Tania
tackled a brutal off-width and Owen
made swift progress up icy gullies. We
were grateful we had decided on two
axes for the leader and heavy-duty
crampons for everyone.

Progress was slow and we made it to
the col below the Aiguille du Plan as the
sun was setting. Tania made a strategic
phone call to our friend Miles in the
valley, asking him about the thunder-
storm that had been forecast a few days
ago. He said there was nothing forecast
for that evening. From here we could
see the lights of Chamonix and, realizing we had about four to five hours left
to do of reversing the Midi-Plan
traverse, with tired legs and empty
stomachs we opted to spend our last
night out under the stars. We spent a
good hour making a rocky ledge as flat
as possible and shared my last bag of
couscous and a spotted dick between
the three of us. The cloud thickened as we settled into our sleeping bags.

Rocio and Owen at the bivvy, looking more relaxed than the story might suggest!

Soon afterwards the weather deteriorated severely, with a full-blown thunder-
storm several times striking the summit of the Aiguille du Plan, which couldn't have
been more than 100 metres from us. We spent the night counting the seconds
between the visible lightning and the roar that followed, until lightning and thunder
were one ripping action making the granite shudder and our hearts flutter. When
you have layers of buffs, hats and hoods covering your head, it's hard for your hair
to stand on end!

It snowed and snowed and snowed. I kept waking up laden down and having to
dislodge snow from the bivvy bag I was sharing with Owen. I was also very cold –
so cold I thought I was going to die of cold. I remember thinking it wasn't actually
such an unpleasant way to go, since it was pain free.

The morning did finally arrive and we slowly got out of our bivvy bags, all damp
and sticky. We shared two chocolate bars between the three of us. There was thick
cloud all around us and some 10 centimetres of fresh snow, which made for very
difficult progress. We were now on the reverse of the Midi-Plan traverse, which I
had done with a friend some six or seven years earlier. In the poor visibility, we lost

Tania Noakes

Rocio leading on the
Dent du Caïman, day 3

our way, once again heading too far down. Our mood and sugar levels were very low. I knew that we all had to dig deep here, both to stay with it and keep forcing through until something positive came our way, and also to force ourselves to not lose it with each other and keep working as a team.

We reversed our steps and gained some height. As we were skirting the bottom of the crag, an unusual shape caught my eye through the cloud. Having the best eyesight of the three, I had spotted what looked to be a rope with frozen rime on it, the sort that only stands out against a dark granite wall after a wintry storm. I led the team to it and was relieved to realize that this was the step we needed to find to get us on to the ridge proper. And of course, as soon as we found it, the cloud mysteriously vanished and the sun came out and we were again in glorious sunny alpine morning sunshine, which quickly melted away the fresh snow and dissolved the knots in our stomachs and throats.

We were now well on our way to getting back to the Midi top station, with the chance of reaching it before midday. I was leading us down past the first rocky section, where it steepened up before the drop on to the glacier proper. I spotted a good place to belay and bring Tania and Owen together for an abseil. In my mind I had already fed the sling through the thread that was *in situ* as I made a quick double step over some black ice. Expecting the slip, I anticipated my bounce off with my left hand on the flat granite block pushing me forward in one swift, dynamic move to safety. But I was slow to extend my left hand and I slipped with a bit more speed than anticipated, so what struck the rock was not my flexible and shock-absorbing hand, but my hard left elbow. The impact shot up my humerus with such force that it jammed through a sweet spot in my left shoulder joint. That caused the head of the bone to jut out between the tendons and ligaments that would normally hold it in place. The pain was instant and paralyzing. I could not breathe; I could not make sense. Tears streamed down my cheeks and I shouted Owen's name again and again. I checked in with myself, trying to control the pain somehow. I was crouched as I had fallen, a heap of shrieks and babbles. I realized I couldn't stand up, such was the pain. I focused on my breathing and tried to think.

Calm down, think. Think!
What have I been shown on
all those years of first-aid
training about sorting out
shoulder dislocations?
Think! What? What was
it? OK, lean forward,
slowly … the pain is less …
keep leaning forward …
let the arm hang down in
front. … Clonk!

Tania Noakes

With a loud sucking noise the head of the humerus slotted itself back to its rightful place and the relief was instant. Owen arrived a few seconds later. In between my lessening sobs, he produced several ibuprofen tablets which I swallowed dutifully.

What followed was a slow procession, tired, thirsty and hungry as we all were, with me trailing behind in pain, with a weak and tender left arm which would not take much weight. What should have taken us about two hours from where we were to the Midi top

Rocio climbing above
the Aiguille du Plan
north face

station, took us about three. We still had some interesting ground to negotiate, including more scrambling and an abseil. Under any other circumstances, we would have negotiated the final steep exposed arête (near Pt 3626) before the shoulder within twenty minutes of the station without much thought. As it was, we all straddled it, *à cheval*, as the French call it, placing ice screws and crawling up, dragging our bums, with me bringing up the rear. The thought of the sweet, fatty fumes of a Poco Loco burger fuelled us on.

Our relief at making it to the Midi top station was palpable. Making Tania's epic Chamonix Aiguilles traverse a dream come true had been a real challenge. Sometimes it felt that we had bitten off more than we could chew and, as always, the brain is very good at forgetting how much commitment, effort, uncertainty and suffering you endured during your last Alpine adventure. And that's why I keep coming back.

The grand gendarme is a significant proposition in the early morning light

was worse. Leads down and keeping moving upwards, we finally got there and it was all starting to come together.

We had heard that the approach to the climb was long and the ridge, once reached, was quite technical. We seemed to breeze up the buttress behind the hut the next morning but it was a long way up the snow slopes which followed, in the dark. I thought the subsequent rocky section was quite serious with other teams ahead of us who could contribute to rockfall. Not far from the ridge there was a delicate slab and a flake which Mark thought we should/could have avoided. Too late … I was away and round a tricky corner at the top of a snowy ramp and then it eased off a touch. There was a lot of very loose rock hereabouts and I was glad I couldn't see much in the growing but still poor light.

Once on the ridge proper, it was much safer. With quite a lot of snow now the angle had eased; we climbed in crampons for the rest of the climb, up and down. But as Mark pointed out, I was in my element now; easy but sometimes steep rock – in crampons it's great!

I attacked the grand gendarme more or less head on, maybe IV+ for 10 metres, as per the guidebook, but it wasn't too bad. I was really flying. It felt so good being on a really big climb after a number of years of doing the plods.

Before we knew it we were behind some other climbers. I chose a direct approach to avoid them, which went fine, and I was now looking at less steep ground all the way to the top. All good things usually finish too quickly. Soon we hit the plod to the summit. The finish came as a narrow crest but it didn't feel too exposed and it was all over. Well, just the whole way down to come.

The Dent Blanche south ridge in distinctly wintry condition

I have to admit, it all went very smoothly. Mark was backing me up superbly and we found just the right chain to abseil diagonally down the steep couloir alongside the grand gendarme. A loose block at the chain worried me so I waited a fair while until another guide (without a helmet) had moved off a belay on a lower line.

When he'd moved from directly below me, I swung across on the abseil ropes and discovered the dammed rock was part of the mountain! Our abseil was much easier and safer. A few moves up easy rock and we were back on the ridge and away down straightforward rock. The point at which we had hit the snow earlier was more logical when seen in the light of day, and we now avoided the icy gangway and the loose flake I'd been concerned about that morning by taking the direct route.

I've perhaps used the words 'easy' and 'easier' too often to be believed. In general, it was all very serious but we were hitting the obstacles head-on and dealing with every question thrown at us. We clambered down the final ridge on to the snow and were soon at the hut: six hours up and five hours down. It was still a very tough day; tough enough to wait until the next morning before we departed from the hut. The long walk down to Ferpecle was very tiring, but Mark was in his Five Sisters mode and I resumed my usual place on his heels. The walk seemed to pass very slowly. The Silver Surfer (my Citroën) was a welcome sight. Next stop, meeting a strange man who ran a hotel in Randa.

The Weisshorn: 22–23 July

The strange man who ran the Alpenblick Hotel in Randa also seemed to be a one-man disco showman; his large van on the private hotel car park was decorated with his disco wares and adverts for gigs. He was indeed a strange character, fumbling about with his computer and papers, while Mrs DiscoMan steamrollered over anyone in her reach, the perfect businesswoman.

We had rolled into Randa around 4 p.m. intent on getting a much-needed shower after our long day on the Dent Blanche. The room was comfortable, and while Mark nipped up to Zermatt on the train to replace his lost gloves, I showered and then relaxed, taking short naps which were interrupted by fleeting memories of the great climb we had just pulled off.

I couldn't really rest, as deep in my head were the thoughts of things to come. The Weisshorn – even harder than the Dent Blanche? We'd be finding out soon enough.

The locals piled into the restaurant and sampled the good barbeque that evening. I scored by being a bit cheeky and asking for more salad. Two platefuls each solved our hunger all right. It was quite early when we hit the duvets; a quick check on the telly showed only CNN worth watching, and like the proverbial *Magic Roundabout*, the stories went around and around, until we'd seen enough.

Next morning, we didn't have to get going too early. We had driven backwards and forwards the previous afternoon, until finally fixing the way to the start of another long four- to five-hour hut walk. We did make it a little more quickly this time (four and a half hours) but it was altogether steadier and a little steeper than the Dent Blanche hut walk. However, it wasn't all plain sailing: the starting hours were steep and relentless, but yet again, we clicked into a mode I'd missed out on for a few years and soon we were gulping the cool water at the building called Jatz, at around 2,300 metres and a couple of hours from Randa. The guidebook described the continuation of the trek as 'more gradual'; I would have said 'just as steep'. Still, I don't write the books.

The final quarter was quite demanding but we eventually tumbled into the perfect Swiss scene; a lovely small but neat hut (places for thirty), with a couple of pretty Swiss girls working; the guardian's daughters.

The beer was bottled, which was a shame. Still, it was pretty cold so still very good.

The bunks were tight for space, so it was a good job we weren't staying too long. An American solo climber received a sharp retort from me for rustling his paper bags while we tried to rest in the afternoon. I initially thought little of this chap; why was he there on his own? Didn't he know it's a massive beast of a route? Would he even come back alive? Later in the day, I'm sure my humble pie tasted good to him. He turned out to be a very good and extremely fit climber indeed.

After a subdued breakfast we left with a throng of twenty or so climbers and headed for the waterfall, a key entry point to the long snow slope leading to the rocks. But instead of following this entry, the lights in the dark from the leading locals went much higher on to the area from where people had been descending the previous day. We followed the tracks of crampon points and occasional lights up ahead and, sure enough, found ourselves on the long snow slope we wanted. On and up we forged, quite quickly, as we seemed to be being pushed by that American. We

The Weisshorn as seen from the Zinalrothorn

climbed up in the dark and finally reached the dogleg through loose rocky ground before the ridge proper.

Mark was going well again and I, too, felt good. But when a rock the size of a football whistled past me in the growing light, I quickly remembered where we were.

Above on the snow slope called the Wandfluelücke, we realized we were still keeping to guidebook time, and we settled down to following the leading groups. We came along a rocky ridge, down into a dip, and then back on to the ridge to below our second grand gendarme. I recall the traverse across the left-hand side of this imposing tower better from our return journey, but obviously we were on route as the steepness (going directly up) would have put even me off in the half-light. We traversed into a snow couloir and climbed this, and did then some zigzagging up mixed ground which led us back on to the ridge above. We were now in the notch the book mentioned, behind the grand gendarme. A quick look at the book and, yes, we were on time, and actually enjoying the climbing. It wouldn't last!

The next bit, however, *was* my cup of tea. With Mark comfortably keeping up, I reached a smooth, steep tower. It looked quite a size, but the helmetless guide in front went straight up it in his boots without too much effort. I wasn't going to waste any time either and promptly dispatched the 40-metre grade III pitch in my crampons. There were plenty of small square holds and a few bolt runners making it fairly straightforward. At this point Mark said that this was why he liked climbing with me on big routes. I wasn't messing around today. There were good belay anchors, so I brought Mark up. There was still some steep stuff above me but it wasn't too bad in these good, dry conditions. After a tricky leftward traverse with some bolt runners I found myself under a sizeable overhang. I reckoned there must be a way up here as there was a fat rope sling hanging over it. My first attempt got me too puffed so, after a quick rest, I saw the trick was a sloper foothold under the roof. Next attempt, no problem.

Now it got easier and we were moving together again, but looming up was the part I was not looking forward to; the final 250 metres on the snow to the summit. I had now visibly slowed. The way was easy, but at over 4,300 metres what was making it harder still was the length between each footstep. These Swiss have long legs: I virtually had to climb into each next step. I could have done with following some shorter climbers, but it was not to be. I was now out of my comfort zone with this desperately hard work. Mark shouted encouragement from behind and somehow, oh so slowly, we gained height. So I struggled on, the demons in my brain yelling at me to forget the summit and go back. But it was so close. After what seemed an eternity (10 minutes, Mark, told me later) we were there.

I could now start to look around and savour the place. We'd actually done the Weisshorn in guidebook time. I was so pleased and Mark was as well.

Important refuelling with chocolate and water/hut tea followed, then we finally had to admit, it was time to go.

As with every big peak I climb, I'm another person on the descent. We raced down, taking every tricky section in our stride, although we did have quite a rest while I waited for the helmetless guide to clear from his lower traverse. We simply abseiled diagonally down and in a few final upward, easy moves, we were back on the ridge and past the hardest obstacles.

The ridge did go on and on (and on) and it was two pretty tired climbers who were eventually caught by another Swiss team descending a bit faster than us. Now, however, we were heading for the loose and dangerous lower part, so I persuaded these guys to stick with us; I really didn't want them below us with this pile of rubbish to go past. The older guy was sensible and agreed with keeping close, and together our two pairs gradually got down on to better ground and on to the snow slope. We had also caught up with some other guys in front and they, too, were asked to stay close. They did for a while but once on the snow, they shot off.

Mark found the 'jack-booting' with the heels a bit tedious. I loved it and urged him on for a change. In doing so, we both lost a bit of concentration and we went past our dogleg turn back to the hut track by a short distance. It was decision time: go back up, or go down and then across and up. The latter route was chosen and I now had my second wind. The ascent wasn't far after going around the buttress, and joy of joys, we hit the good track to the refuge.

We had already decided that Mark's fifth and final day with me would be for doing nothing! But to achieve this we had to get down from the hut to Randa and the car, and I had to be prepared to drive the two and a half hours back over the Col du Forclaz and Col du Montet and then back to my place. Nothing would stop me, and around half-past eight, or maybe a little later, we swilled the Office Bar beer down like animals.

It had been one heck of a day, and one brilliant week.

I hope for more climbing with Mark in the future. It's one thing guiding average clients but a different ball-game when you have someone behind you who's good. Thanks, Mark, for a brilliant week.

ADAMELLO: SKI MOUNTAINEERING ADVENTURES WITH A HISTORICAL TWIST

Cain Olson

Bringing back-country skiing and mountaineering together results in many great adventures across the European Alps, climbing fine peaks and finding the route of a great ski descent back down again. From his base of the Adamello mountain range in the Central Italian Alps, Cain Olson knows of one such expedition that covers the whole range.

When I first moved to the Val Camonica twelve years ago, I did not realize how beautiful this lesser-known region was, or how much history was steeped into its mountains. While skiing, mountaineering or rock-climbing in the Adamello mountain range, one's mind goes back to the historical events that took place in this region: the 10,000-year-old Neolithic rock engravings, the strategic importance of this frontier land between Italy and Austria during the First World War, the resistance during the Second World War and the more recent pilgrimage of Pope John II to the glacier in 1984.

It is a huge block, large enough to supply materials for half-a-dozen fine mountains. But it is in fact only one mountain. For a length and breadth of many miles the ground never falls below 9,500 feet. The vast central snow-field feeds glaciers pouring to every point of the compass. The highest peaks, such as the Carè Alto and Adamello, are merely slight elevations of the rim of this uplifted plain. Seen from within they are mere hummocks; from without they are very noble mountains falling in great precipices towards the wild glacier-close glens which run up to their feet. Imagine an enormous white cloth unevenly laid upon a table, and its shining skirts hanging over here and there between the dark massive supports.

This is how D.W. Freshfield described the central Adamello massif when he first set sight on it on 25 August 1864. The famous British mountaineer was standing on the summit of Presanella and had just carried out the first ascent of this mountain. A century and a half later this white cloth has shrunk dramatically owing to global

Cain Olson

warming: from an area of 30 square kilometres at the end of the nineteenth century, to 25 square kilometres during the 1920s, 17 square kilometres in 1997 and to a mere 13 square kilometres at the most recent measurement in summer 2009.

Monte Adamello is 3,539 metres, Carè Alto 3,462 metres and Cima Presanella 3,558 metres. We had been talking about it for some time: to climb and ski these three highest peaks in the Adamello-Presanella mountain range over three days, using the winter room in the Rifugio Caduti dell'Adamello at 3,040 metres as our base for the two nights.

My two clients and companions were Paolo and Luca, both strong and confident skiers. Paolo, a strategic management expert, discovered the mountains in 2007. Until then the only sport in his life had been tennis, just under pro level in the Italian Championships. When he bought a holiday house in the ski resort of Ponte di Legno and saw hundreds of people each weekend beginning or ending the ski tours in the resort, he started wondering what was beyond the pistes. Luca, an insurance broker, spent his summers and winters in the resort of Pinzolo in Trentino, where he learnt to ski and nearly became a pro in snowboarding. Also for him, love of the mountains came when he bought a holiday house in Alto Adige, the German-speaking part of Italy that borders with Austria. Since then, we have climbed and skied on many peaks together across the Alps.

The mountain huts across the Adamello range open in mid-March for the ski mountaineering season, but close the first week in May. Conditions for skiing are often great until the end of May, so why the huts don't stay open until then, I don't know. Probably because it has always been like this, and in Italy traditions are very difficult to change!

Mandrone Lodge with the Brenta Dolomites in the background

Climbing the Adamello
east ridge

The hardest task was deciding on the right itinerary; we wanted to find a route whereby we could limit the amount of times we had to ski the same sections twice. We also wanted to be off the beaten track; a three-day tour that did not follow the normal routes. It was not a tour described in a guidebook, possibly because it involved some steep terrain and lots of altitude difference – approximately 5,000 metres up and down. Also, we did not want to use the Adamello ski resort lifts which help access the glacier on the south side of the mountain range.

Day One

At 4 a.m. on 15 May, my local taxi man, Sandro, drove us from Cedegolo, on the main road in Val Camonica, to Malga Fabrezza, at 1,450 metres the starting point of our trip.

'*Grazie* Sandro,' I said: 'See you the day after tomorrow in Vermiglio. I will call you as soon as we get a phone signal on our way down from Cima Presanella.'

'Okay *ragazzi, in bocca al lupo!*' ('Okay boys, in the wolf's mouth!' – which is actually a good-luck expression, even though it does not sound like it!)

The stars were shining, the weather forecast was good for the next few days and, with our head-torches turned on, skis on our feet, we headed off along the trail that led up into the valley. It was still dark but we could start to see the sky getting brighter in the east, the direction in which we were to head. After a couple of hours, we reached the Rifugio Pridenzini, a mountain lodge that is open only during the summer. Here, we stopped to drink some hot tea from our thermos flasks.

One hour further on from the refuge, the terrain became steeper and I decided to keep a distance of some 7–8 metres between us. There had been a considerable amount of new snow recently and we did not want to break the snow pack with our

Cain Olson

The author

On the summit of
Monte Adamello

weight, which might have caused an avalanche. I had to work a lot, setting a new track in the fresh snow, and when we reached Passo Salarno at 3,168 metres, Paolo and Luca thanked me and promised me a beer when we reached the lodge in the evening.

'*Il rifugio è chiuso*' ('The lodge is closed'), I reminded them and they started laughing, telling me that I would just have to wait until we got down to the valley. The view from this point was amazing: in front of us, the largest glacier in the Italian Alps. Imagine a smaller version of the famous Bernese Oberland: there, at the Koncordia-platz, the ice is 800 metres thick. Just in front of where we stood, the centre of the Adamello Glacier, Pian di Neve (Snow Plain), is 200 metres thick. This is roughly the proportion in size between these two Alpine glaciers – 4:1.

We rested next to the Giannantoni Bivouac, a little yellow tin hut that can accommodate up to six people in case of bad weather, then continued to push forward towards our first summit, this time roped-up as we were on a much-crevassed section of the glacier. After an hour of steady ascending terrain, we arrived at the base of the East Ridge, with about 100 metres of mixed climbing to the summit.

While Luca and Paolo strapped their skis to their packs and put on crampons, I shortened the rope so that I would have more control over my companions. We climbed with good teamwork, using the front points of our crampons on the little cracks and ledges on the granite. I climbed 5–10-metre sections at a time, then put the rope round a rocky spike and shouted to Paolo and Luca that they could start climbing towards me. As they advanced, I made sure that the rope was always tight so that if they slipped, it would hold them.

'*E uno!*' ('That's one!'), said Luca. We were on the summit of Monte Adamello, and what a view! To the north we could see the Ortles-Cevedale range, to the east the Dolomites, to the south Milano and the plains where the River Po runs and, to the west, all the way from Piz Bernina to Mont Blanc. It was midday and we had been on the go for seven hours; perfect timing according to my schedule. The weather was perfect and the temperature very warm considering that we were at 3,539 metres above sea level. Time for photos, some hot tea, a piece of Parmigiano and some brown bread, then skins off, tighten boots and we were ready for a great downhill section. First we skied down the south face of the summit, a 35-degree slope with nice compact spring snow. The lads loved it!

From the base of the summit and back on the glacier again, I decided not to rope-up seeing we had to cross a much safer area, with no crevasses, that would lead us all the way to the next uphill section. Some 7 kilometres of steady cruising skiing – just relax, let your skis ride and enjoy it! Within no time we reached the bottom of the day's last climb: about 500 metres of easy terrain up to the Rifugio. The original hut was inaugurated in 1920, based on the remains of an army barracks built by the Alpini (Italian Mountain Regiment) in 1916. This long mountain ridge was the Italian First Line during the First World War and is now the border between the Italian regions of Lombardia and Trentino. In 2000 the lodge slowly started to slide down the mountain: it had been built at the same level as the glacier eighty years earlier and now the glacier was 100 metres below the lodge, not giving it the support that it needed. So in 2005, the lodge was rebuilt in exactly the same position, with modern engineering and state of the art construction technology. It has the best winter room in the Alps; twelve comfortable bunks with clean blankets and a great view on the surrounding glaciers. Here, Paolo cooked risotto for us on his gas stove, and Luca melted mounds of snow to make lots of hot tea for the evening and for the next day.

Day Two

'*Buongiorno!*' said Paolo the following morning, with a big smile on his face. We had all slept well in our super luxury winter room with a view! Today was the day of Carè Alto, first climbed by two British mountaineers, H.F. Montgomery and S.T. Taylor, on 8 August 1865. Our plan was to climb the steep north face of the mountain and ski down by the same route. Ten years earlier, the access to the summit had been quite easy, given that the north face was completely covered by the glacier, with a gently ascending slope that was not steeper than 30 degrees. As a result of the more recent hot summers (often with seven or eight weeks of the freezing level being above 4,000 metres, there was now a distinct separation between the flat glacier at the base of the mountain and the steep 45–50 degree north face.

After breakfast, we packed light as we could leave stoves, extra food and night gear in the shelter. At 7 a.m. we were on our skis, descending from Passo Lobbia Alta, where the refuge was situated, down to the middle of the Lobbia Glacier.

'*Le pelli!*' ['The skins!'] Luca shouted.

'What? Don't tell me you left them in the winter room?'

'Yes, I hung them up to dry last night and forgot to put them in my pack this morning.' No worries, I always carry a spare pair of skins in my backpack, and I gave

A First World War cannon on Cresta Croce

them to Luca.

'*Un'altra birra, ragazzi!*' ('That's another beer, boys!')

We set off east towards Passo di Cavento, where another little emergency bivouac is placed. Once over the col, we headed south and our peak was right in front of us.

We reached the base of the steep slope in good time, gliding with our lightweight packs along the flat Lares Glacier. Just below the bergschrund we strapped skis and poles to our packs, put on our crampons and got our ice axes out. I roped-up my companions and we started climbing straight up the 150-metre slope, digging nice steps into the firm snow. The best way to learn about the conditions of a slope that you intend to ski down is to ascend it; in this way you can see and touch the snow conditions. Once on the ridge, I created a little flat area on which to leave our skis and poles by stamping down the snow. We then continued still roped-up, along the exposed rocky ridge with some tricky climbing moves up to the summit.

'*E due!*' ('That's two!'), said Luca.

Blue sky, ideal temperature, no crowds.

'*Fantastico!*' from Paolo.

We could see Lake Garda just below us to the south-east, and the Cima Presanella, next day's peak, to the north. Along the East Ridge we could see remains of military barracks and cableways of the Kaiserjager, the Austrian mountain regiment. We were standing on the Austro-Hungarian First World War front line …

We headed back along the rocky ridge to our waiting skis. Crampons off, skis on, rope back in my pack and ready to rock! Paolo and Luca were confident because they had already been on the slope. I descended about 40 metres and confirmed to the boys that the conditions were great. With Paolo leading, then Luca, both skiing like champions, not too concerned about the steepness of the slope, we skied back towards Passo di Cavento as far as we could. Then, where the glacier starts ascending up to the col, we stopped to rest, eat, drink and put our skins back on. It was still early in the day and, with spirits high, we decided not to go directly back to Rifugio Lobbia; instead we made a little detour to visit the Italian wartime 150-mm cannon, still based on the Cresta Croce ridge at 3,300 metres. An extra 300 metres uphill and a great descent on the opposite side that led us back to the refuge.

Day Three

This was the big day: to climb Cima Presanella by its west ridge and descend the steep 500-metre north face, with sections of 55–60 degrees. This slope was first skied on 8 July 1972 by Heini Holzer.

We had breakfast at 3 a.m. and were outside ready to go within the hour. I wanted to start early for three reasons: we have a long day, there's a long avalanche-prone south-facing traverse and finally, for the north face descent we would need good cold snow conditions. We said '*arrivederci*' to the Lobbia Alta hut and headed south, downhill for a great 800-metre descent in the dark. A half moon and clear sky, together with the light from our head-torches, made the visibility pretty good as we cruised down the Mandrone Glacier towards the Mandrone Lodge. We skied as far as we could, traversing along the south face of Cima Busazza.

As we put our skins on, we started to see the sun rise in the east behind the Brenta Dolomites. I told Paolo and Luca to keep their ski crampons handy because we would probably need them. In fact, after a short while, Paolo started to slip a little so I told them both to put the crampons on their skis to allow safer progression and save lots of energy. We traversed steadily up and then zigzagged the last short section to just under Passo Cercen. There, we found a cornice blocking our way and I had to take my skis off and work my way laboriously through the snow with my shovel. '*Okay, venite!*' ('Okay, come!') I told the boys that it was their turn to climb through the hole that I had dug. '*Bellissimo, fantastico!*' were the comments as they clambered one at a time on to the flat Presanella Glacier at 3,000 metres.

We stopped to rest and compliment ourselves regarding the good time we had made, seeing as it was only 8 o'clock. We then headed up the quite steep west face of Presanella towards Sella Freshfield at 3,378 metres. The snow there was not as icy as the previous traverse on the south-facing slope, so Paolo and Luca didn't need their crampons. When we reached the col one hour later, we were all happy that the last 200-metre uphill section was just in front of us. We descended slightly on the other side of the ridge, keeping our skins on for the ascending traverse. The last section was pretty rocky, so we strapped our skis to our packs and walked up to the enormous cross on the summit. '*E tre!*' ('And three') we all said together, embracing and complimenting each other – the third peak was in the bag! However, we had to maintain our concentration because the following descent was probably the tour's most demanding section.

It was 10 a.m., the time I had scheduled to be there. We prepared skis and boots for downhill mode while I took the rope out of my pack. We started to ski towards the north face; the first part was not steep, but all of a sudden the slope seemed to disappear.

Cain Olson

Skiing spring snow on
the Adamello Glacier

'*Ma siamo sicuri?*' ('But are we sure?'), said Paolo, a nervous look on his face.

'*Stai tranquillo* Paolo' ('Relax Paolo') – just think about skiing and having fun.

I was pleased with the snow conditions, but still decided to start the descent roped-up. I created an anchor by jamming my skis into the snow and let Luca descend first, with the security of the rope behind him connected to his harness. I told him which direction to follow and to create a ski anchor when he had skied for about 40 metres. It was Paolo's turn next, and he did really well with this additional help. Paolo retrieved the rope and I skied down to join them. We used this technique for four or five pitches on our way down, until we got past the steepest section and Paolo and Luca were confident that they could ski without the security of the rope.

It was still pretty steep – not the sort of place where you would want to fall – but, encouraged by the good performance further up and the perfect snow conditions, we all had great fun taking turns to show off our technique. When we reached the flatter part of the glacier we had to ski round several seracs, choosing the best route while I looked out for crevasses ahead of us.

Shortly afterwards, we reached Rifugio Denza at 2,300 metres and were finally off the glacier; I could relax a little, even though we still had 1,000 metres of descent to do and a long way to ski down. My companions were tired but had gone into party mode! While we rested in the sun outside the closed lodge, Luca danced and sang on one of the tables while Paolo was on his mobile phone all ready spreading the news … the adrenaline was still running. This was a comforting sign for me: spirits would continue to be high all the way down the final descent to the road, where we would meet Sandro with his welcome taxi.

SUPER SUDGRAT: A ROCK-CLIMBING EXTRAVAGANZA

Mark Walker

Now it's all very well marvelling at rainbows framing some perfect Alpine vista, but as we drove up the Lower Chelenalptal from Andermatt to wander into the Salbitschijen, I had to conclude that despite the beauty of the lush, mossy greens and stark glacial whites, it was, in fact, pissing it down! Our team was comprised of two guides, me and some American superhero, and two very handy and lovely 'regulars'. Now, for the guides this was a maiden voyage, not only on the route but also working with each other. Respectful 'sounding out' of each other on the walk-in was required. The choice of waterproof trousers: on or off? From the outset this was to be crucial in the process of deciding whether one

Maybe this is what guiding is all about – climbing amazing rock routes in a mountain location and on good rock makes for an incredible experience. The Salbitschijen in central Switzerland is a granite climbing paradise and the mountain's south ridge is a classic outing. It was here that Mark Walker's enthusiasm for climbing must almost certainly have been passed on to his client.

was, indeed, a Jedi or not. As our guys, Anne and James, both donned waterproof trousers and got on with it, we collectively declared it 'not to be really raining' and wandered up the hill. As our waterproof tops funnelled torrents of water directly into our Anglo-American underpants we collectively decided each of us was 'all right'; this was going to be an ace trip and Anne and James had got it right.

I like rock-climbing – well, quite a lot actually. A good thing too, because the goal was the Sudgrat. Millions of VS pitches in a row, classic and diverse, demanding all-round competence. Anne was my partner in this glorious adventure. We'd climbed loads before together and ticked off many a Welsh classic. You need a good partner for 'Alpine Justice', not just to climb with speed and efficiency but also to hand out sweets when it's all going 'a bit funny'.

It's quite a steep climb up to the Salbit Hut and a few delaying strategies are needed to grab a bit of respite. The Anglo-American banter continued as we neared an isolated garden resembling 'Gnome Land'. Now Father Christmas occupies Gnome Land and Santa runs some weird cableway to transport bags up and down the hill. Nice, we thought, and something to make use of on the way out.

Gnome Land is a sea of juniper and bilberry on the walk-in. An old ecology mentor of mine, years ago, once said 'Always walk ahead of your students so you can tread on the species you don't recognize.' I cannot, of course, condone such behaviour and thankfully this was one of those days when I recognized the lot! It was 'Calluna' this and 'Juncus' that. As we approached the hut the American contingent was discussing the ins and outs of modern punk and rock: I'm afraid I couldn't contribute. Meanwhile there was a nice little switch in the weather from 'pissing it down' to 'mainly pissing it down'. A significant improvement and the guardian of the hut looked relieved.

Röstis were purchased and, as I sat perched on the edge of a rather wobbly bench, I could not help but marvel at the smooth, slick operation in this immaculate and stunningly located mountain hut. I consider myself quite a connoisseur of mountain huts and it takes a lot to impress me. Wobbling around the side of the hut to catch my first proper view of the peak, I clocked the guardian picking fresh salad from his own personal patch. That patch, akin to Stalag Luft 3, obviously saw a bit of chamois action, but the salad looked amazing and I was pretty excited about dinner. The clouds cleared and the rain ceased. Harness and boots were donned and we sneaked out to have a little warm-up on the local granite. Looking up, there were wall-to-wall sheets of it; pretty inspiring and all emerging from rolling alpine meadows. Now, the Salbit has no shortage of *uber* classics and climbers are certainly drawn from one route to another in a desperate attempt to somehow embrace them all. The 'kid in a sweet shop' analogy doesn't really go far enough to describe the excitement I felt. Anne was a fraction apprehensive as the mighty Sudgrat bared all in the shifting mist. It is important to have 'plenty in hand' for a route like this and she had it! Just a few Tremadogs in a row – piece of cake!

Wandering back to the hut, slightly late thanks to a comedy American hiding our shoes, we found the guardian dishing out the fruits of his labour from his garden. A happy, excited atmosphere filled the hut and while the American superhero continued to get mileage out of the 'great shoe joke', I leant back with a glass of vino and planned our attack with Anne. An early start was needed, just arriving at the technical rock-climbing at daybreak. This would allow us the luxury of a whole day's light on the route. Light and fast seemed to be the way; 'trainer shoe Alpinism' – I liked the idea of it. The walk-off over the back didn't supposedly demand crampons or ice axe. My sack was smaller than my kid's lunch bag (although I have to admit my daughter likes a large lunch!). As the sun finally fell from the sky, the Dammastock chain turned scarlet and Pierre the Frenchman declared that someone had stolen his toothbrush; it was clearly time to hit the sack.

You don't often get nice bread in mountain huts – that's just a fact. There's no point getting upset about it or, indeed, forming unrealistic hopes. It is hard to know whether I was more excited about the super-fresh, home-baked masterpiece before me, or the forthcoming adventure. Either way, it was going to be a great day, and as Anne and I shouldered our sacks and Pierre emotionally embraced his long-lost toothbrush, we left the hut in the nippy morning air.

Not knowing the area particularly well, I had previously recce'd the approach the night before. I like doing this, mainly to avoid the embarrassment of getting lost in the Alpine equivalent of 'Telly Tubby Land'. Granite buttresses soared above us, we were moving well. We had a few teams above us, jostling for position on the

scramble approach. I wasn't bothered. There was plenty of time to enjoy the route and the Chamonix-style 'Wacky Races' had no place here. A peaceful ambiance seems to be the hallmark of this place. Relax and enjoy the climbing … relax and enjoy. Anne was doing well and as we floated up the initial gully the sun kissed the route – simply stunning!

Sunrise over the start of the Salbitschijen Sudgrat

I had a super-light rack – just a few cams and wires and six quick-draws or so. There is quite a bit of fixed kit on the route and multiple fixed rappel points to return to the safety of Telly Tubby Land. This, in my opinion, did not detract from the quality of the route and it makes the first ascent in 1935 even more impressive. The lads, armed only with hemp rope and homemade pitons, achieved quite a mountaineering feat.

The first pitch was a good start and landed us squarely on the ridge proper, with fantastic views of the Westgrat. That looked just as good as our route and already a plan to return that way was forming in my head. Although a more involved objective, the Westgrat has reputably equally fabulous climbing, awe-inspiring positions and, in the main, solid rock. Guiding that would be quite an honour, I mused.

We caught up with the teams ahead of us, including the American superhero. A couple of friends were, by chance, a few pitches ahead. A cheery 'hello' floated down the ridge and they were gone. The few teams ahead of us were climbing well and there was a cracking feeling of unity, fuelling the banter. The Sudgrat is relatively consistent grade-wise and as long as everyone is moving well, it is pointless to overtake. We dropped naturally into our position and sat back to enjoy the ride.

Each pitch linked smoothly into the next. The route was proving to be especially good but, most amazingly, each move seemed to link perfectly to the next. Some days when you are blindly fumbling around trying to find a little purchase for your fingertips on the chosen, 'it must be good', out-of-reach handhold, you can't help but believe the rock has something against you. I loathe that. You just can't read the rock, try as you might. Sure, you get up the beast but you feel dejected and seriously consider road-biking as a possible midlife pursuit. Good God, it can really be that bad! You might just be having a bad day, but sometimes I can't help but think the route is just being deliberately awkward. Every time you link a reasonably organized

Mark Walker

Exposure comes as standard on this route as you traverse numerous towers

sequence to some critical handhold, it fails you or, worse, fails you a bit! Tension builds on a par with frustration and you slowly but surely become knackered. The Sudgrat is quite the opposite. As you gracefully link move to move it continually rewards you with what you expect, within reason, fuelling a buoyant optimism in you. Fingers engage what they desire and send a message to 'central control' that all is good in the world. Engaging, thought-provoking, but eminently do-able climbing without 'sketching around'. As Anne and I 'fed our rats' we asked ourselves 'can it really continue like this?' Damn right it could, another eighteen pitches worth. Feast yourself, pilgrim, you're going to feel amazing!

And feast we did! I know some guides use posh trainers and leave rock boots in the valley but I must admit, as Anne and I racked up the mileage, poised on that wonderful arête, I felt pretty happy that I had my rock boots on. Not necessarily because it makes the climbing *easier*, but purely because it makes it more enjoyable. Precision footwork amplifies the quality of each and every move and you flow up the thing! Anne remarked over dinner later that she could not really recall the intricate details of each and every pitch. I wasn't surprised, as each one blended seamlessly into the next. Every belay was an exposed 'eagle's nest'. A place to re-rack, back-coil the ropes and reflect a while.

People get all excited about 'crux' pitches. Sure, there are some pitches harder than others but ultimately it all feels the same as you explore your route-finding options. On many Alpine routes I feel drawn to the line of least resistance. On this route you feel drawn to the best-looking climbing: very rarely does it let you down. Up and down pinnacles we continued until the summit of the Zwillingsturm. Having been so engrossed in the climbing, Anne and I relaxed in the midday sun, sharing a muesli bar and marvelling at the earth-shattering views beneath us. The

West, Ost and Sudgrat converge to the summit above us; the hut below spilt out 'post-lunch' trekkers on their continued journeys. Everyone everywhere was happy and content. We dropped down off the pinnacle and climbed the remaining awesome pitches to the Gipfelnadel.

What a summit!

If you cast your eyes over the topography of this area you might get the impression that your work is done at the top of the ridge. It seems at first glance of the guidebook that what follows is a funny little scramble to some random 4c pitch. By the time we had congratulated ourselves on what fine rock warriors we were, we had indeed completed the tiny scramble and emerged through a hole at the base of the fine pinnacle, the Gipfelnadel. This iconic monolith stands right at the summit of the peak, exactly where it should, and taunts the climber into one final pitch. It hasn't got an abundance of gear on it. The metal, summit logbook case was held to the wall with more gear! Not being too distracted by this, upward progress was made and happily we both made it to the top. Now the views included the Mittagstock and Winterstock to the south and the Galenstock to the south-west. The tiny summit was no place to linger however, and a quick rap off the north side soon had us down on terra firma. Lunch followed. What a trip to share with Anne!

The descent the other side is well signed, with cairns and red marks. Sure, you must keep your wits about you – it's not over until it's over. Trainers were adequate but I imagine, in early season, lingering snow patches could be troublesome. Descending to the hut for the night and a well-earned beer we clocked the guardian lovingly tending his salad patch. We'd soon be charming Santa into transporting our kit down the hill, but for now, our work was done. The American superhero dropped a couple more *panachés* on the tab and our two teams sat admiring the unique, granite architecture before us.

TO ARRIVE AT THE OPPORTUNE MOMENT

Hannah Burrows-Smith

With the development of lighter skis that have excellent performance and ski-mountaineering equipment that helps you adapt to a variety of environments, the appeal of steeper slopes has become more wide-reaching. The challenge is there to bring together many of the disciplines of the mountaineer and skier, to make an ascent and descent of a beautiful mountain in perhaps the most aesthetic way. Hannah Burrows-Smith is one of those trying to make the most of skiing in the Alps.

NNE Face les Courtes: 5 April 2009

I had arrived on the Argentière Glacier on the Saturday with no fixed plan; I'd not been on this glacier recently and it is quite an impressive place. It was good to have a look about. Here, you are surrounded by things to climb, and to ski; spires of granite, couloirs and glaciers on one side and vast, shaded north faces on the other. There had been a good week or so of stable weather and now it was the weekend so there were plenty of folk about. Much was in condition on the Droites' and Verte's north faces but I was keen to see what I could have a go at on skis.

I skinned up on the sunny side on the Glacier des Améthystes a short way and could see many dots booting up the Couloir en Y on the Aiguille d'Argentière. I watched them all, transfixed for a while at how it is possible to make out the actions of these human forms from such a distance. Eventually they all set off down the same couloir, skiing in teams of twos or threes; they seemed to be all in one group as they waited for each other after they'd skied it, all ten of them!

Meanwhile, on the other side of the valley, four tinier dots commenced their descent of the NNE Face on the Courtes. You could barely see them really, but their movement down the slope was accentuated by the spray of snow that came away from each turn. The first dot appeared to sweep down the face, taking on the fall-line with enthusiasm; the others that followed were a little more cautious …

The face they were skiing was just then going back into the shade after a short morning in the sun. So that would be it   I would have to wait around and prepare myself to have a go at this slope the next day …

I'd brought bivvy kit with me as the nearby mountain refuge was closed for reno-

vations and I was keen to avoid the mad rush of people heading in from the first *téléphérique* in the morning. I'd found a big, flat rock to sleep on below the Améthystes Glacier and was fairly well prepared, with a four-season sleeping bag, but not a lot else, just a rope and rucksack to lie on and some cold food. But I had a great view; watching ski-tourers returning home, the sun setting and then climbers getting ready for their ascents of north faces in the middle of the night.

Things were a bit slow in the morning; I had been just warm enough through the night! I skinned up to the base of the route and then started booting up the rest. Getting used to climbing the things you'd like to ski was relatively new for me, as opposed to approaching the descent by some other route, which is what you normally do in Scotland. I kept going for four hours; plod, plod, plod, breaking trail for much of the way as the footprints of the previous team had been wiped out by their ski turns. Should I keep going? Yes, what if, er … there was too much time to think about every eventuality. Then, after two and a half hours, I no longer had the place to myself; more dots were appearing at the base of the slope. Well then, I would have to keep going! The dots below benefited from the trail I'd been making and the stress evaporated when I realized that, at the pace I was moving, I should still get to the top before them.

Eventually I reached the top of the slope about fifteen minutes ahead of the next team. It was great to finally get there and have the space all around to myself for a short while, knowing what was about to happen next. My greatest fear of potential embarrassment at the time seemed to be worrying about *skiing* past the five other teams, rather than *falling* past them! Two teams had arrived by the time I was ready to ski.

Les Courtes: the NNE slope takes the obvious diagonal line of snow catching the sun in the middle of the picture

Hannah Burrows-Smith

About to set off down
the 800-metre descent

It was a bit steep at the top.... Got my first turn in as soon as I could, feeling the eyes of the observers watching me, and managed two more before the angle eased. I could hardly believe I'd got to be there … skiing for half an hour in this amazing place. The snow was great and the team the day before had only skied down the middle of the slope; the right-hand side was still without tracks …

What is it that makes a ski line appealing? A gully? A couloir? A line of white between rocks and improbable terrain that presents a daunting but daring challenge? A fine mountain that can be climbed, but then descended on skis with much more satisfaction and fluidity?

To experience enjoyable turns, to flow; to stand at the top of your intended descent, perhaps after countless days of planning, and of numerous hours during the ascent pondering the snow conditions; all have brought you to this point, where you can finally start skiing! And now, not only are you about to do your favourite thing (so it's a feeling of it being Christmas), but there's a sneaky inkling that it might just work …

When conditions are good, it is easy to become hooked. Flying down steep slopes with soft snow to land in, and be caught by, builds your confidence no end. Once captivated by this experience other lines of snow start to wink at you, but equally you have to learn how to make them happen, or at least learn how to wait for the right conditions, and be ready. Mountaineering often comes in as a handy reserve, knowing you can climb up or down to escape something that, after all, proves unconvincing to ski.

Things can look quite unlikely but then, with the right view, the right snow, they look possible. You think, beforehand, if I was actually there, standing there, how would it feel, would I be able to do a turn?

Looking down at the first slope of the Ferdenrothorn north-east face

Ferdenrothorn, North East Face – 17 April 2010

A beautiful 'S' of a couloir that winds its way down the middle of this rocky face and culminates in an abseil … Not a big mountain but a line that first winked at me from a film of when it was first being skied, and then on subsequent reconnaissance trips to this area above the Lötschental of the central Bernese Oberland.

I'd been here the week before but, on reaching the Gitzifurggu Pass, my intended ridge and route to the summit looked more complicated than I anticipated … perhaps it was a relief to opt out and save the descent for another day, but I needed to check out whether there was another way to the top of the descent, and to meet my clients later that day.

Off to Interlaken then, to meet the group and start a week-long ski-tour in the Bernese Oberland, the last day of which finished with us skiing down into the Lötschental from the Hollandia Hut, and the Ferdenrothorn was still there, waiting at the end of the valley. I still had to finish the tour round in Interlaken but a plan was forming to go and visit the mountain again and, with the Lauchernalp lifts in their final weekend of the season, it would be my last chance!

A nice meal in Kandersteg that evening was followed by finding a good place to park and sleep in the car, ready for the first lift the next morning. A pleasant start to the day involved heading up via the ski-lifts, then skiing down to the Lötschpass Hut amongst the grandeur and space of many exciting peaks, and the view of the Ferdenrothorn ahead. It was only on arrival at the skins-on point just beyond the hut that it slowly dawned on me that the three guys behind me, a boarder and two skiers, were also in possession of two long ropes … there could only be one place they'd be going – I couldn't believe it!! But far from communicating, saying hello and admitting where I was heading, I carried on up. All my gear was tucked away in my pack and I just kept going, hoping they wouldn't guess they had company … If they got there first, then fair enough, but I would just keep going as normal, and see what happens!

Once (again) at the Gitzifurggu Pass, this time there was no hesitation; a little research in an Interlaken shop had unearthed an alternative route for the solo mountaineer to venture. I scuttled down the other side of the col, skiing still in skins, to reach the easier snow approach on the north-west side. After some skinning and then booting up a couloir, I came to an abrupt stop on the ridge. There was a small buttress to the right which led to the summit, and some rocks and a snow crest to the left; the other team were still way behind (phew!); they had chosen to climb the ridge. I was aware that, while I had used human competition to reach this point, it would now be good to calm down to deal entirely with the mountain.

It was an exciting place to be; the top of the 'S'-shaped couloir started just to the right; I was 'there' – in the right place to start skiing! Yet I was a bit gripped; organizing myself at the top, working through each thing I needed to do to keep busy. In this small area I had to turn from a mountaineer into a skier; to eat, drink, calm down, be rational – to instill a sense that what I was about to do … I was choosing to do! From all this, my gut reaction was, without hesitation, to start with a short abseil off the rocks to begin the descent. The snow to the right was just too steep and soft, and I couldn't quite visualize myself skiing it. In his account of his first descent of this face, Rémy Lécluse described this bit as having 'ambience Base Jump' – not for me!

As I set off down the abseil the first of the other guys came into view on the ridge. I waved just to say, 'Yes, I am here too …' before I vanished out of their sight, knowing that my existence on the ski descent would have been a bit of a disappointment to them – but then I was gone into my new world and completely absorbed by every action; pulling the rope down and wrapping it around me with the least amount of movement. As I side-slipped down, a section of snow vanished down the cliff below; I gulped with relief that I'd chosen to abseil! Just below, the couloir curved off to the right; my way ahead. I took some photos: 'Hannah was here …'

If it seems a little crazy to be in such a place without prior knowledge of the slope, then I need to say that a big part of my reason for trying this face on the Ferdenrothorn was that, on the little film of Rémy skiing it, the slope itself didn't look too bad; not too steep in itself but just surrounded by cliffs on all sides, and particularly below. I felt that if I could do 'normal' turns, one after the other, I should be able to do this. It was only the top 20 metres that had fazed me, since it was that bit too steep … and the abseil at the bottom of the face – well, I've done plenty of them.

But what about the snow? Viewed clearly from below, the couloir itself was amazingly filled in. Watching, searching every corner of my intended descent, looking for
rocks or hints of ice … the couloir looked good. The true point of commitment
occurred on pulling the rope down.

Looking back at the
'abseil of avoidance'…

So the time had come to venture a turn … which was okay. More snow vanished
over the edge below me, as the couloir now curved back round to the left. The
slopes and snow were fine – actually very skiable. Nice turns. Just a little tension
about the situation; for some reason I was often out of breath, and had to keep stop-
ping to focus on this basic function. The snow stayed light for the first half then got
a bit heavier lower down. The slope was still in the shade. I took no more photos
on the face, but the image I had looking down the long, straight central section is
unforgettable. It looked like an abrupt end to the couloir, with nothing but a big
drop beyond. In fact it was, but from all my studying of the face previously I knew
there was a way across rightward at the bottom – and it was there.

It was weird to have to ski towards this edge. Keep turning, keep turning, keep
turning; a mantra to just keep moving, or at least keep thinking about it. The way
across to the right was fine, probably 10 or 15 metres above the edge – I don't know,

The Ferdenrothorn NE face as seen from the hut; the skied line takes the wiggle of snow slightly right of centre

I didn't look too closely! Then just a simple traverse round the corner to meet some heavier snow in the sun. Side-slipping and one last turn back under the upper line, to meet the couloir's end and a search of an abseil anchor.... I was prepared to make my own belay but any *in situ* contributions would have been welcome … and there it was; a peg that was attached to two others, buried under the snow. A 30-metre abseil got me on to the final snow slope, the continuation curve of the couloir that had been briefly interrupted by rock. Down this and then the open slope – yippee! A massive relief; I skied out, I'd done it, I could go home, happy!

The guys at the top of the face had waited for me to finish before descending themselves, and from the hut with my cake and Coke I watched them surf and ski the face, with snow pouring down the cliffs. It was great!

THIRD TIME UNLUCKY

Richard (Dick) Peart

The Dru, as seen from the Chamonix Valley, is one of the most compelling peaks in the world for a mountaineer. The first time I saw it in 1965 I knew I had to climb it. However, it was over ten years before I actually set foot on the mountain, after two abortive attempts, when we had turned back before even starting the approach. John Sheard, another Chamonix habitué in the 1970s, and I would often swap stories over a pint in the Bar Nationale over our respective thwarted attempts on the north face. He had actually got on to the face a couple of times, once with

The iconic nature of mountains such as the Matterhorn and the Dru has a lot to answer for regarding the hold they have on the minds of those who are bound, by these external forces, to climb them. Following disappointment from previous attempts going awry, Dick Peart knew he would be back to the Dru, to that north face that would not be won over so easily.

another character of the times whose alias was Dan Boone. They were pressing on upwards in pouring rain, when they met a French team descending rapidly. Dan, when asked by one of the team why they were continuing, responded in broad Mancunian, 'Us's got our caggies on'. Another chapter added to the British/French mutual incomprehension!

My own initial failures were much less colourful. The first was with a Scottish friend, Bob Duncan, an American friend called Larry, and his wife who is French. The *météo* notice board near the Tourist Office in Chamonix had been promising impending bad weather for three or four days, yet each day had turned out perfect. Larry had suggested that we should reach the base of the face in the afternoon, climb the first third, and bivvy on a ledge. Then, next day, we would complete the climb and descend to Chamonix. We decided to go in the hope that the forecast would continue to be incorrect for another two days. However, whilst waiting to board the *téléphérique* for the Grands Montets, Larry's wife rang the meteorological office in Geneva, who warned of a massive depression stuck over Dijon, which would release hell in the mountains once it started moving. We went instead to the Aiguille de Pouce with Larry and his wife, choosing to do a route called the Voie des Dalles (Route of the Slabs), whilst Bob and I chose a parallel route called the Kohlmann-Mazeud after the first people to ascend it. Standing on a belay ledge while Bob was leading the penultimate pitch, I could see huge cumulus clouds bubbling up from Italy beyond the Aiguilles. By the time I was leading the last pitch,

Dave Hobbs approaching
the start of the route
from the glacier

the thunder, lightning and hail had started. Bundling the ropes into the sack we raced along the ridge, whilst lightning strikes were hitting it. When we caught up with Larry and his wife, Larry had been knocked off the ridge by a lightning strike and fallen over 10 metres down the other side; he was very lucky to be unscathed.

My next attempt was with a young American, John Vogel, who was studying medicine in Paris. My main memory of that attempt was going to the pharmacist to get a prescription, as I had not been well. John did the talking to the pharmacist, and soon went into a giggling fit. He explained to me that she wanted to prescribe me suppositories, and found the thought of me trying to insert one whilst bivvying on the north face of the Dru most amusing.

In fact we had a very comfortable first bivvy in the workman's accommodation at the top station of the *téléphérique*, after we'd watched the staff leave for the night. The next morning dawned with a very threatening sky and streams of cirrus approaching from the west. We decided to head back for the valley, but in fact the day turned out to be glorious, and the threatened bad weather didn't arrive for another thirty-six hours. This is one of the biggest problems for an Alpinist who is trying to judge the weather: local storms can occur in moments, while full-blown depressions can get stuck crossing the French landmass and only arrive after a day or two. On the other hand, on British mountains a drenching can be pretty much guaranteed six hours or so after the first cirrus appears (or mare's tails, to give them their colloquial name).

The third attempt was the successful one, with a friend from North East England, Dave Hobbs. However, the early attempts should have given me due warning of the vicissitudes of the Chamonix weather – particularly on the Dru. We decided on the same plan as my first attempt: leave early on the *téléphérique* and traverse from the top station to the base of the north face, ideally to a bivvy on the west face. All went according to plan, except that I managed to pull a tooth out on the first heavily iced-up pitch, by holding my axe in my mouth by its leash whilst placing a runner!

A flaw in the plan became apparent when I started climbing the grade IV+ crack, leading up to the Fissure Lambert. By now we were directly under the prominent ice field in the middle of the face called The Niche. Despite the fact that it is north-facing, the late afternoon sun was melting the ice field in The Niche above me, so by the time I reached the stance I was soaked. We decided to bivvy there so that I could get into dry clothes. We had a minor panic whilst preparing food when the hot base of the gas stove ignited my foam mat that it was touching, and on which I was sitting!

The morning dawned fine, and the climbing went smoothly up the crack system above our bivvy site, despite the fact that the cracks were iced up. Below us we could see two other parties who had sensibly bivvied on the terraces, thus avoiding passing under the melting Niche. Unknown to me one of the pairs was British – Mike Mortimer and his climbing partner. Progress was not as rapid as I would have preferred because I was leading all the pitches, my climbing partner Dave having announced at the top of the first pitch that he was not prepared to swing leads (a climbing term meaning to lead pitches alternately). To be fair, he had told me before we left the valley, but I had hoped that he would change his mind once we got to grips with the climbing. Alpine climbing often produces setbacks like that, with partners behaving differently in the big mountains, as compared to the small ones back home.

A comfortable bivvy ledge; Mike Mortimer's team were climbing the north face at the same time as the author

Whilst I was cramponing up the final slopes towards the Quartz Ledges, a rushing sound from above caused me to crouch defensively over my ice axe, fearing a rockfall. However, when nothing happened, I looked over my shoulder and to my surprise was staring straight at a grinning pilot in a glider about 100 metres away from the face.

A few more pitches, mainly on snow and ice, brought me to a curious hole in the rock called the Cannon Hole, through which I was able to crawl, to emerge on the south side of the mountain. I was now on the Quartz Ledges, basking in sunshine, a dramatic change from climbing up ice fields in the gloom of a north face.

Dave wanted a rest and a brew on the Quartz Ledges before starting the abseil descent. My inclination was to push on, as the sun was beginning to drop towards the western horizon. However, he insisted, and unfortunately we dozed off in the warm evening sun, and were woken by a clap of thunder. In my entire mountaineering career, I have never known a storm come in so fast, with so little warning.

Looking down at The Niche

The lightning started immediately; I realized that my axe and metal climbing gear were beside me, so I reached out to move them away. Before I touched anything I was airborne, lifted up and over Dave who was sitting beside me. He grabbed me and pushed me back down. For a brief period I had been a marionette, leaping under the control of the electricity which had passed through my body. Stunned, we sat as torrential rain started, and bolts of lightning continued to crash into the summit of the Dru not far above us, lighting up the whole of the Aiguilles like day. I realized that we were sitting in a slight cave, and I had been caught in a spark gap by the electricity flowing down the mountain. In front of us was a large block on the ledge, which reminded me of a drawing in Eric Langmuir's handbook for mountain leaders, of a climber sitting on a block, with electricity flowing under him. With this in mind, I quickly put the carry mats on the block, and there we sat in the torrential rain, with the lightning continuing its relentless barrage. After about an hour, the storm began to lose some of its intensity, and the rain became more bearable. It was around midnight, but we decided that we would start down if we could, rather than stay there to be fried by the next storm, which we were convinced would arrive shortly.

Just along the ledges, Dave found two rock pegs connected with rope, which we could use as an abseil anchor. Throwing the ropes into the darkness, Dave set off first with our one remaining functioning head-torch. As I slid down the ropes towards his stance at the end of the second abseil, he said 'Watch out, there are two guys on this ledge'.

'Where are they?' I said as I landed.

'You're standing on them now!' was the reply. He shone his torch in front of me and I saw two pairs of very frightened eyes, peering at me out of the slit of a double bivvy bag. They were a pair of Czechoslovakian climbers, who asked in broken English if they could descend with us. We invited them along for the ride, and the four of us continued through the darkness and rain – the decision nearly cost me my life! After two or three more abseils, dawn began to break, and I led the way into a snowy gully, stepping gingerly over a precariously perched boulder before I got my weight on the ropes. Near the end of the 50-metre ropes I found two pegs on the rock wall, and clipped in, straddled across the narrow gully. The two Czech climbers were in between Dave, who was bringing up the rear, and me. I had noticed that one of them was rather uncoordinated, probably through shock and tiredness, but didn't reckon on him dislodging the boulder which I had so carefully avoided. It came bounding down the snow-filled gully straight for me. As I watched it until the last moment, it suddenly bounced into the air just above my stance; I ducked and it flew over my head. From above I could hear the yells of both my partner and his, swearing in their respective languages. He arrived beside me full of apologies; it had been far too close for comfort.

Another couple of abseils took us down to the Charpoua Glacier, where a previous team had left two 9 mm ropes in place, presumably to race across the glacier to the shelter of the Charpoua Hut. None of us showed any interest whatsoever in recovering the ropes, despite the fact that I could see that my few-month-old ropes were now seriously trashed by the combination of the wet

The climbing continues steeply through the upper walls of the face, with Rob Jarvis climbing here

Kath Bromfield commencing the descent down the south-west side of the mountain, following the normal ascent route

conditions and the grit on the ledges. (Years later when Mike Mortimer and I were regular 'Tuesday Nighters' – a group of climbers who meet in the Peak District every week – he told me that the ropes belonged to a Japanese pair, who he and his mate had helped down the descent, as they were totally exhausted.) All we were interested in at the time was getting down to the valley without further incident, and certainly without extra weight on our backs. Our two new friends thanked us and headed off to the hut, while we headed direct for Montenvers and a train for Chamonix.

At the campsite were two friends who had arrived from England the day before, who were amazed to see us in relatively good order. Later, whilst showering, I discovered a black disc-shaped bruise on my arm, presumably the entry point of the lightning into my body! At the time I didn't consider where it would have emerged from, nor could I see anything, but on reflection it was probably from my rear as I had been sitting down! The following night I was woken in the tent by dreadful screaming: it was Dave reliving our epic in his dream. The next day his wife arrived from England, and he left with her, abandoning any further climbing plans. It had all been too much for him, and it turned out to be the end of his serious Alpine climbing. I carried on for many more reasons, and also made visits to more remote mountains, such as those of Tierra del Fuego.

About five years later, in 1982, I finished my guides training to become a fully qualified International Mountain Guide, but with an even greater respect for electrical storms which, along with avalanches in winter, I use all my mountaineering knowledge and experience to avoid.

THE NORTH FACE OF THE EIGER

Mark Seaton

We stepped off the train at Kleine Scheidegg into a mini tornado, dodging the postcards which were being blown out of their stands. My fingers were too cold to slot the coins into the telescope. Huge metal bins bounced around and rubbish was strewn all over the place, driving the Swiss railway workers berserk.

Our plan to climb the north face of the Eiger was not looking good. Charles and I retired to the station bar to discuss the options. Despite the uninspiring scene through the window, the weather forecast was favourable, especially because it was to be cold for at least the next four days. Global warming has

Imagine that the first day you had with your new guide was on the Mer de Glace for a refresher 'école de glace'. Then imagine eighteen years of Alpine holidays later, each with the same guide, to find yourself on that most famous of north faces. For Mark Seaton the guide/client partnership comes into its own as he recalls this ascent of the north face of the Eiger, done in 2007.

meant that cold is the new hot. Everyone now craves for cold, none more so than a guide and his client attempting Alpine north faces, because if it is not freezing then large bits tend to fall off. There was a glimmer of hope if the wind dropped, yet the evidence outside suggested this was unlikely.

There is a view that Alpine climbing is all about being in the right place at the right time, and that you make your own luck. The next morning, at 4 a.m., the weather was clear and millpond mirror calm. So no excuses; we had better try. We had already scoped the lower slopes on earlier attempts so we decided to steal some time and use the Eiger railway tunnel and move on to the face at the Stollenloch via a small door just below the start of the 'difficulties'. While trudging up the tunnel we discovered that the light at the end of the tunnel was, in fact, a rouge train trundling down from the Jungfraujoch. If it had not been so terrifying it would have been funny. We panicked, swore and then dived into a hollow in the tunnel wall as the train's wheels brushed our sleeves.

We could not decide whether this near-death experience was a good or bad omen. However, climbing the north face seemed infinitely preferable to going back down the tunnel and having another silent movie Buster Keaton moment.

We could see, as dawn broke, that our excuses for binning the climb were diminishing. The weather was good. Nevertheless, I was sceptical as I ploughed through

The Eiger north face, as seen from Kleine Scheidegg, here in winter conditions

knee-deep snow and rotten rock until we arrived, at 6.30 a.m., at the foot of the first of the iconic pitches on the Eiger: The Difficult Crack.

Any British rock-climber knows that the adjectival grade Difficult is in fact very easy. However, in Switzerland, on the north face of the Eiger, it means 'prepare to be challenged'. An hour later, a pathetic 30 metres higher, and feeling that I had already enjoyed a good day's climbing, I shouted for Charles to follow. As he struggled up the crack he sounded like a man who had been arrested by the secret police and made to talk.

The guidebook states that forty-five minutes should see you to the next iconic section: the Hinterstoisser Traverse. It took us three hours of very taxing climbing, laboriously clearing the snow off every hold. We arrived at the Swallow's Nest bivouac at 2 p.m. and pondered whether to stop and bivvy or continue. The next recognized bivouac is Death Bivouac. Five hours of daylight could not be sacrificed and Charles is always one for carrying on, and so we did. Around the corner we were confronted by a slab of weathered limestone formerly known (before global warming) as the First Ice Field.

We continued, finally reaching some better conditions, arriving quickly at the Ice Hose. I was happy to see a fixed rope, which I used to help climb the crack. I was less happy to see that it was bootlace-thick at the point where it was tied to the piton.

Next was meant to be the Second Ice Field. Instead, I was troubled by more polished limestone – only this time, it resembled quarried marble. To add to the challenge it was covered in loose powder snow and I found no protection for the entire 60-metre pitch. I wondered what was going on – this was meant to be the easy ground! If that was a stressful pitch, the following one was the stuff of nightmares because it went sideways. I climbed it with my heart in my mouth, placing as much gear as I could to protect Charles. He climbed it by penduluming in an arc, ripping out all my gear plus a couple of antique pitons until stopped by a conveniently positioned pillar. Although visibly wincing with pain, he managed to put a positive spin on the incident, noting that falling sideways was faster than climbing horizontally.

We were now finally established on the Second Ice Field and witnessing a stunning sunset. Suddenly reality checked in; I said 'Sunsets precede darkness.'

'That's what head-torches are for,' Charles reminded me.

A memorable sunset

It was a pity, seconds later, that Charles got his head-torch smashed to bits as Eiger rocks came firing out of the White Spider high above us, thumping into the ice field and ricocheting into Charles's helmet. He arrived at the belay and handed me bits of plastic and a couple of batteries. 'Could be worse,' he noted.

Indeed it could. 'We could be on the north face of the Eiger in the pitch dark with falling rocks', I thought – but did not say.

We jammed the head-torch back together and climbed on to the top of the Second Ice Field, where I decided that we could dig out a platform on which to spend the night. It was 10.30 p.m. following an eighteen-hour day. Time for a cup of tea, so out came the stove.

I had a good night's sleep thanks to tricks of the trade – knockout sleeping pills. I awoke about six o'clock and started making breakfast. The weather looked superb and we were away across the Second Ice Field by about 7.30 a.m. I pulled out my mobile phone and reconfirmed the key exit off the ice field with a call to my friend Hans Reudi, a fellow guide from Grindelwald. We moved on up over the Flatiron towards Death Bivouac. Despite its name, this is the most palatial ledge on the entire route. A pity it was only ten o'clock in the morning. We stopped to melt snow and eat some food.

The Third Ice Field awaited; a steep traverse led to the foot of the Ramp. Up the ramp and suddenly it was 5.30 p.m. I was feeling 'well climbed'. Above us was the Waterfall pitch. This afternoon it was an overhanging ice-climb that looked as if it might revert to being a waterfall any time soon. Logic said we should bivvy and climb it in the morning when it was frozen. Two things stopped this from happening. First, we could not find anywhere flat enough to rest and second, I suddenly decided

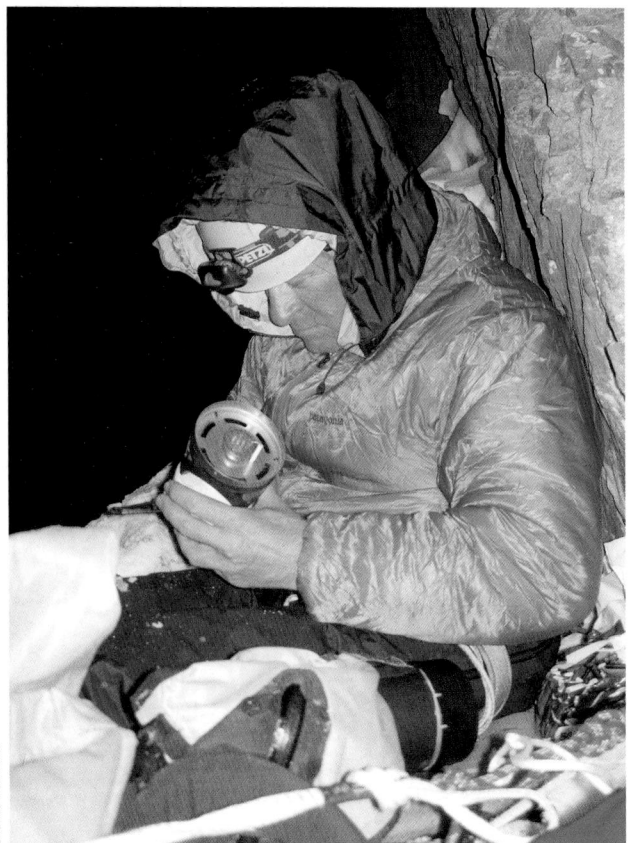

How does this work? Mark Seaton hopes the stove is going to start so that he can make 'dinner'

that I wanted to get up and over the Waterfall pitch now, because it is a climbing pitch to lose sleep over.

It might have been a melting ice-climb when I set off, but by the time I had finished floundering up the pitch most of the ice was at Charles's feet and he looked like a man who had suffered a bad accident with an enormous chandelier.

Charles followed with his eyes on stalks (he later claimed it was the hardest pitch he had ever had to follow). It was now dark as I climbed the Ice Bulge pitch: a steep chimney that was not big enough for climber and rucksack – rather like climbing inside an endless wet oil drum. I emerged on to an ice field and belayed. It was midnight. I could not find the next section in the dark so we hacked two seats in the ice and sat down for another cup of tea, after which I made us some dinner: couscous and my secret ingredient –

Charles Sherwood at the bivouac at the top of the Second Ice Field

half a litre of olive oil. There is nothing more calorific. We said nighty night at 2.30 a.m.

I shoved a cup of tea into Charles's hand at about 7 a.m. There was a sea of cloud below us, blue sky above us and it was windless. In addition, we could see exactly where to go. We packed up (carefully) and the Brittle Ledges immediately confronted me. I struggled to find any climbing rhythm and was not helped by a coating of verglas on all the useful holds.

Reaching the top of these ledges unlocks the key to the upper section of the face: the Traverse of the Gods.

We climbed horizontally while beginning to comprehend that we were in a very, very special place, yet at the same time trying to stay focused on not falling off. (It becomes more god-like towards its end.) We arrived at the foot of possibly the most famous mountain feature in the world, the White Spider

The view from the first bivouac looking down the Second Ice Field

The second bivouac above the chimney pitch was cut out of solid ice and we just sat there, exhausted

One of the iconic pitches in world mountaineering, the author on the Traverse of the Gods

Charles Sherwood

We now had perfect climbing conditions and we could move together quickly up the spider's leg to the penultimate obstacle, the Quartz Crack. I had heard horror stories about climbers getting lost in this section, yet everything fitted into place for us. It was now late afternoon and the sun caught the face, making it uncomfortably hot. We traversed left to the Corti Bivouac (not recommended as a bivouac because it would be like sitting on an upturned dustbin) and then slightly down by way of the aid of a fixed rope to the Exit Cracks. These were like some water feature in a house of horrors: a shallow gully made of shiny black shale with no protection and with water gushing down it. I paused to drink some of this 'free' water and tried to remind myself that this is one of the most amazing places few people get to see.

My confidence was immediately shaken as the first hold I grabbed became a rock in my hand. I struggled to maintain my balance and then swung out like a barn door slowly enough to view the void below. Fortunately I swung back and bridged my way up the gully until I found a trickle of ice into which I could tap my axe. There was just enough ice to steal some purchase and then I was cruising. The Exit Gully was below me; just the summit slopes now to deal with. However, it was going dark (again) and the slopes were not proving very amenable, with hard ice like sheet metal. Once again I was feeling 'well climbed' and the ice slope just went on and on, and it got darker and darker. The wind increased. I just wanted it to be over; I had had enough. At last I reached the ridge. I flopped over the other side to provide Charles with a belay and additionally I escaped the wind. Charles took what seemed like an eternity to arrive and when he did it was the first time in fifteen years he had admitted to being 'quite tired'. Fourteen hours since breakfast: it was 9.30 p.m. A dream had been fulfilled for both of us. We hugged. Further celebrations could wait until we were safely down in the valley. We carved out a ledge for the bivouac on the summit ridge and then I made some more tea.

Day 4, Mark Seaton on the summit of the Eiger

WORLD CLIMBING

HIGH ON THE SIERRAS

Tania Noakes

Whenever I am asked what my happiest climbing memories are, it always catches me somewhat off-guard. A calm pause normally follows, where I draw in breath and remember the Sierra Nevada Mountains in California.

Falling in love with the Sierras is easy. There is something about the warm golden granite, the subtle scent of pine in the air and the play of light on shadows that allows this mountain range to hold your heart forever. John Muir, the famous environmentalist of Scottish origin, would not disagree. He called this place a 'Range of Light' and spent countless hours exploring its wildest corners and scaling its most inaccessible summits. Some of the highest and lowest moments of my life are tightly woven around this hauntingly beautiful mountain range.

It makes me smile to know that I share my love affair with such a strong and passionate character as John Muir, a man who, in the 1870s, climbed to the top of a 30-metre high Douglas spruce

Everyone will have heard of Yosemite, with its spectacular granite cliffs and domes of rock; however, the whole of the Sierra Nevada mountain range is fantastic for adventurous and wilderness Alpine-style rock-climbing.

Tania Noakes describes a journey that starts with a traditional apprenticeship of aspiring to climb some of Yosemite's famous classic big wall routes and learns all about aid-climbing, but this evolves, visit by visit, into a memorable relationship with the spontaneous adventure of climbing in the greater area and a framework for a life in the mountains.

and clung there tenaciously so that he could experience first-hand the force and beauty of a fierce Sierra wind-storm. If you have not read any of John Muir's writing then allow me to encourage you to put this right. I cannot hope to capture the majesty and grandeur of the Sierra wilderness as well as he did, but I will endeavour to entice you to find out more.

I am fortunate to make my living working as a guide and spend most of my time in some very beautiful places. Not all of them are as wild and inhospitable to man as once they were and the same holds true for the Sierras. Their very charm inevitably ensures that they have to be managed to prevent them from becoming overly loved. My first experience of the Sierras was similar to that of 99 per cent of

Crossing the Merced River near Muir Trail Ranch, which is central to Yosemite Valley

other visitors. I went to Yosemite Valley, famous for its rock-climbing as well as the sheer grandeur and scale of the place. I was in my early twenties, reclaiming precious time from a busy job so that I could experience this climbing Mecca at first hand.

The American Indians who first lived there considered it a sacred place and it was easy for me to understand why. I was in awe as I stood in El Cap Meadow and watched twinkling lights appear high up on this 1,000-metre rock face – the head-torches of climbers settling in for the night. In the gathering dusk I tried to trace the lines of routes I'd read so much about, imagining what adventures my fellow climbers were having up there in their own, very personal vertical world. I wanted to be there too, but the granite face loomed over me, overpowering and intimidating. I didn't know where to start, and felt humbled and full of self-doubt, so I lost myself from these thoughts with as many free classics as possible in my two-week visit.

For a valley famous for aid-climbing and big-walling it isn't short of amazing granite trad routes. Central Pillar of Frenzy, Brail Book, Nutcracker, Lost Arrow Spire Tip, Royal Arches, Crest Jewel, Middle Cathedral, Higher and Lower Cathedral Spires … the names run easily off my tongue years later. Other memories persist too; like the way my body rebelled at first against the very physical nature of granite climbing. Three pitches into Central Pillar of Frenzy, my hands took on a mind of their own and clamped up into useless fists. I tried desperately to prise my fingers open with my teeth so that I could fit my hands into the crack and keep climbing. The specific and repetitive movements associated with crack-climbing had found out my British trad-climber's weakness. I'd never experienced anything like it before or since – serious hand cramp.

Tania Noakes

I left with sore hands, many happy memories and new friends; better at crack-climbing but still frustrated by off-widths and already planning my return. My memory of that first evening in El Cap Meadow burned inside me, lingering thoughts of unfinished business.

Two years later I returned, for longer and with more confidence and experience. I'd left my busy job and was making ends meet as a freelance instructor in the UK and on expeditions abroad. My climbing partner and boyfriend at the time suggested that we spend the first week of our trip in a place called Tuolumne Meadows, to allow time for the crowds and the heat to leave the Valley. I firmly disagreed. All my unfinished business lay in front of me and I was reluctant to let my objectives out of my sight so easily.

After some discussion I accepted the sense in his argument. I stared dejectedly into the darkness out of the window, convinced that I could see deep snow lying either side of the road. I soon found out that it was only the pale granite slabs shining in the moonlight and not the massive snowdrifts of my negative imagination. I was so Valley focused that I felt climbing on some scrappy granite domes would be a waste of time compared to the proud and soaring lines I felt familiar with. With a smile, I can reflect on how wrong I proved to be. If Yosemite is a climbing playground then Tuolumne is easily its tranquil and spiritual equal. We spent a week enjoying solitude and immaculate granite in cool, clear air which seemed to lighten any troubles and create a real sense of peace. Later that trip we would climb more challenging routes, but my memories of that week are some of my happiest. It would be the calm before the storm.

We climbed Cathedral Peak without another soul in sight, relishing our tiny

Having completed the Tyrolean traverse off Lost Arrow Spire Tip

The Domes of Tuolumne Meadows beyond Tenaya Lake

perfect summit. There, bathed in glorious sunshine, I caught a fleeting glimpse into the heart of the Sierras. To the distant east an unknown sweep of granite shot skyward; to the west the petrified rock wave of Mathes Crest seemed close enough to threaten the shores of our little mountain eyrie. In every direction, stretched out before us, were the serrated forms of other unknown peaks. I began to understand that there was so much more to the Sierras beyond the Valley.

We relaxed into a gentler pace and I found time and space to open my eyes. Regular Route on Fairview, West Crack on Daff Dome, the Eichorn pinnacle …. From high on almost every route we climbed, one particular peak drew our eyes. That clean-cut ridge silhouetted in the distance – it struck into the sky as sharply as it did into our imaginations. What line was that? To which summit did it lead? It would take another visit to the Sierras, a little older and wiser, before I found my answer.

Our week of quiet climbs in Tuolumne drew to a close. The American Alpine Club free coffee morning had long since packed up and each night seemed decidedly colder than the last. It was time to head to the lower elevations of the Valley. Inside I could feel the prickle of nervous anticipation. The flame of determination flickered and held … it was time to step up to my first big wall.

We had aspirations to climb El Cap, of course, but agreed to practise on a shorter, simpler route first. The route we chose, the west face of Leaning Tower, is never very hard, but the first pitches overhang relentlessly and the intimidation factor is undeniable. On the plus side, that makes for easy hauling – a factor insisted on by my partner after experiencing the horrors of dragging a large haul bag up Regular Route on Half Dome years earlier. With a mix of moderate aid pitches and some free climbing the route seemed a good choice for a first effort.

My memories of the climb itself are vague and indistinct. I remember much more about my second ascent four years later. On that occasion a close friend and I guided two relative novices up it. Remembering their wild screams (of excitement) as they cut free and swung out over the void still makes me smile, although I confess that my heart did skip a few beats until I knew the strange wailing from below was of joy, not pain.

What was clear from the start was that the methodical approach of aid-climbing, combined with the hard work, was something that suited me. Our success on the route helped me believe that something bigger might be possible. I helped ferry our haul bag back to the road with a light heart, scrambling down the last of the descent gully in darkness. Not much chance of a ride back to Camp 4 so late at night, so we set off along the road under a very black but starry sky. Strangely, I remember that walk back more vividly than the route itself. The Valley air still held on to a little warmth from the day and we were

Cathedral Peak,
Tuolumne Meadows

tired, but not overly so. In fact I could have walked on quite happily for many more hours. We had succeeded on something that I had thought would be hard, yet I'd discovered more in me than I had known before. I had found it challenging but fun and I had climbed it well.

That night, walking back to Camp 4 with my boyfriend, cocooned in a bubble of light and wrapped in our own thoughts, our paths diverged. My partner had been severely injured in a terrible fall in Alaska one year earlier. Physically he had fully recovered. In my determination to climb El Cap I never stopped to consider how much the exposure and commitment of such an undertaking can pick you apart from the inside. Whilst I reflected on my own transformation, my partner was experiencing a different one of his own. The next few days we relaxed and made plans, but something was not right. We talked about exploring the back-country on foot; quiet walks in the forest, swimming in the river and having some time for the two of us. I talked about climbing El Cap. It didn't take long for arguments to follow and it dawned on me that another big wall was out of the question. I remember feeling so disappointed and let down. Eventually, he agreed to try again, on a route he had done before; the north-west face of Half Dome.

Now Regular Route on Half Dome is a classic and popular route, but it also has

A student cuts free on the west face of Leaning Tower

one of the longest and most punishing approaches. We spent an exhausting day getting our gear to the base, finding the nearby spring, filtering water and getting ready for the climb. Our plan was to fix the first two pitches and cast off early the next morning. My partner took the first lead and almost immediately I knew that something wasn't right. I didn't want to admit what, inside, I already knew. Slowly, ever more slowly, he finished the pitch. Whatever thoughts were going through his head at that point I feel sure have stayed with him for a very long time. He wasn't ready to deal with the exposure and fear yet, and his heart just wasn't in it. I cleaned the pitch in silence and, I'm ashamed to say, in anger, and we headed down. I didn't understand and I wasn't forgiving. I carried the haul bag back to Camp 4 alone and frustrated, cursing all that hard work getting our gear to the base of the route, thinking only of lost climbing time and unfulfilled goals.

A close friend was also in the Valley at this time. One evening he asked if I would like to climb the Nose on El Cap with him before he had to leave in five days' time. I discussed with my partner whether it was a good idea and, to his enduring credit, he encouraged me every step of the way. Of course he knew, painfully so, how much it meant to me. At the time I thought that he was relieved to have any expectation removed from him. Now I look back and see something more – his selfless desire to help me achieve my dream.

I have mixed memories of that first route up El Cap. Its thirty-one pitches would take us four days to complete, with three nights on the wall. Of course it has been free-climbed in much less time, but this was a big adventure for us at that time. It remains the longest rock-climb that I have ever done. There is all that history, the amazing rock, so much exposure, the pleasure of working hard with a good friend for a common goal, the shared highs and lows. Our first night on the wall with such excitement and unexpected comfort; my friend catching the King Swing on his first attempt; completing the last pitch to Camp IV in darkness followed by a less-than-ideal half-seated bivvy. Aiding across the great roof and marvelling that any size of finger could find purchase on such a tiny crack; the glorious pancake flake and the gloriously perched Camp VI …

The route wasn't crowded but we were never alone. Humanity was evidenced by various sounds, from the muffled garbling of the Green Dragon tourist train and the hum from traffic below to the high-pitched screams from the French climber who dropped his rucksack at the top of the Stoveleg cracks. There was also silent evidence from the faster Spanish team who wrapped numerous religious artefacts around their night-time belays, from the piles of discarded water containers found upwards of Camp IV – and the off-putting smell of urine that arrived shortly before any decent-sized ledge.

Finally, I remember settling in for our last night at Camp VI and thinking about how I'd watched those twinkling head-torches from the meadow below two years earlier. I felt tired but content as we chatted and flicked empty pistachio shells off the ledge into the darkness below. After three days on the wall I'd reached a strange sort of calm. The first day I spent mostly scared and nervous about whether we could do it. The second passed so quickly because I focused entirely on the task in hand. The third day I began to relax and enjoy our situation, the exposure, the history and the route itself. That final day, the closer we got to the top, I only felt tired and strangely empty. I became less able to escape questions about my future which waited for me in the valley below.

On later reflection it became clear that this particular route held little about what I like most in climbing – those wild, inaccessible places, the sense of exploration and solitude, swift and sure travel through the mountains and freedom of movement. I felt something inside me begin to shift away from the Valley. I wandered down to El Cap Meadow again a few days later. Sitting for a while amongst the tall, dry grass I looked up at that wide expanse of granite which fills the sky from that point. In my mind I felt that the face had shrunk somehow once we had climbed it, and yet there in that meadow it didn't seem to have changed at all.

After my partner and I returned to the UK the cracks between us quickly widened into chasms. We were on separate paths, following different dreams. Unexpectedly, it hit home harder than I could have imagined. The fire for life that I had never questioned before seemed to have burnt itself out. I began to question whether the sacrifices I made in order to climb were worth the pain they caused and initially found that I had no answers. Sometime later the mist cleared and I was able to remember our amazing day on the summit of Cathedral Peak. It was there that I had glimpsed something which seemed to call me deeper into the Sierras. I started to research what else was out there beyond the Valley, beyond Tuolumne.

I learnt of a trail named after John Muir himself. It traverses almost the entire length of the range from Yosemite Valley in the north to Whitney Portal in the south: a distance of around 415 kilometres, traversing countless high alpine passes and weaving through the heart of one of America's great mountain wildernesses. A seed of inspiration was planted and I knew that I had to return the following year, so I organized and led an expedition for a group of students from Leeds University

Bivvying out with a
student group at
Bishop Pass

Officers Training Corps to complete part of the trail from Tuolumne Meadows to Bishop Pass, as part of my ongoing guiding work for the British Military. Over the last twelve years I have been organizing and leading mountaineering and skiing expeditions for the British Services all over the world.

My students and I shared that journey following one of the most troubled times of my life. Yet quiet reflection in some magical places helped me regain a sense of inner balance and perspective. My love of the mountains, which I had begun to question, surrounded me and supported me once again.

I began to take note of just how many beautiful summits we passed. Towering granite faces, Domes and Spires … a feast of climbing potential for any adventurous spirit. When we finished our journey I stayed on with several of my students who have now become good friends. We climbed several backcountry routes including an easy and fantastic rock ridge; the West Ridge of Mount Conness; a soaring granite blade recognizable from summits miles around. It became impossible to shift the smile from my face and I knew that I had to return.

The following year I organized another expedition for a larger group of students. One team would trek the entire length of the John Muir Trail from Whitney Portal to The Valley, whilst a smaller team of rock-climbers would sample some of the backcountry climbs I had seen whilst on the trail twelve months earlier. We started in Whitney Portal and gradually drifted north. The final ambitious stage of the plan was to rejoin the trekkers on the summit of Half Dome a month later. The range and quality of backcountry climbs in the Sierras is remarkable. There are excellent routes on beautiful summits at every grade. Even the popular ones are not crowded. For almost every route we climbed we had the entire *mountain* to ourselves, not just our route.

Inspired by the pages of *The Good, The Great, and The Awesome* (a guidebook that could only be found in the USA!) and a little local knowledge along the way, we sampled climbs on summits up and down the Sierras, from the high alpine routes on Whitney and Russell to the imposing sun-soaked Charlotte Dome; from the clean-cut lines on Bear Creek Spire to the somewhat loose monolith of Mount Goode; from Temple Crag with its fortress of soaring ridges, to the precipitous

pinnacles of the Minarets, from the blocky buttress of the Incredible Hulk, to the perfect hand-crack and mantle combo out of the vertical world on Mount Dana. It is truly a wild and inspiring mountain range.

Mount Russell in the High Sierra

Somewhere in amongst all this climbing I forgot to notice that my heart had healed. One evening we set up our camp below Mount Whitney with a plan to scale the historic east face. An American guide came over to let us know about two climbers missing in the backcountry and all I saw were a brilliant pair of blue eyes.

By the end of the expedition our climbing students were successfully tackling their own routes, independent of our instruction. They climbed Snake Dike on Half Dome whilst the other instructor and I climbed North West Regular Route in a day. We met up on the shoulder after our respective climbs, everyone buzzing with energy and excitement. I was intensely proud of what the team had achieved. The trekking team had climbed Half Dome via the cables and finished the John Muir Trail one day earlier.

At the end of the trip I stayed in the Valley for another week, climbing on my own. I returned to El Cap Meadow and shared an evening I will never forget. Lying back on the warm, dry grass to watch the stars frame the silently shining form of El Cap, I reflected on a summer of good company and golden granite. The warm air brushed through the leaves above my head with a gentle sigh, echoing a new contentment I felt in my heart. My love of the mountains and my love of life had never been stronger. Surrounded by an instinctive knowledge that somehow here was one of those profound decision points in life where there is no second chance, with a smile I looked back into those amazing blue eyes and decided to take the chance.

Nick Kekus

Climbing on the east face of Mount Whitney

Since then I have returned to the Sierras on numerous occasions. The region seems able to draw me back irresistibly and quite happily. Some of my adventures there have been whilst working and others, chasing personal dreams. The first moment I smell that familiar scent of pine and granite in the warm evening air I am almost overwhelmed by a wealth of memories; some of them make me smile while others bring me close to tears, but I would never want to part with a single one of them. It is difficult for me to imagine another mountain range which holds that same powerful magic, and it is the one that I am certain to return to again and again. If you ever find yourself questioning your love of the mountains, perhaps a little contemplation in the Sierras is just what you need.

Tania Noakes

The author tending the campfire, by Rosalie Lake

AUTUMN ON THE NARANJO

Ric Potter

We were both keen to try to find something 'meaty' as an objective – perhaps even something on a more Alpine scale, despite having only a few days available. A quick search for 'long rock climbs in Spain' brought us almost immediately to the Naranjo de Bulnes; a high tooth of steep limestone in the Picos de Europa, with a towering profile and a number of comparative accolades attached to it: 'the Matterhorn of Spain'; 'the Dru of Spain'; and 'the most spectacular peak in Spain'. We concluded that, with such an impressive write-up, it ought to fit our semi-Alpine requirements. In addition, and according to our research, its steep west face was proclaimed to be 'the longest continuous rock wall in Spain'. It seemed to us that an ascent of the Naranjo by any route would be a stunning prize, but we were particularly

The Picos de Europa may not technically be the Alps, but the scale of the climbing can be as committing as any Alpine rock route.

The autumn is usually a time to make up for lost opportunities over the summer, and with a few cold and dark months ahead, the idea of one last rock-climbing trip before the arrival of winter can be really appealing. With this in mind, Ric Potter and James Harrison decided that they could both do with a quick trip somewhere warm …

attracted by the orange-coloured sweeping west face that gives the peak its name and its notoriety, so an ascent of that would more than make up for any summer regrets.

Our plan was to climb in mid-October, which would be late in the season, but we hoped that an autumn high pressure would favour us, and temperatures wouldn't be too low for climbing. In reality, the decision was an easy one; it was the only time we could go. The Rabadá-Navarro route, on the west face, with 750 metres of climbing in twenty-two pitches, would definitely offer a 'meaty' challenge, but as it was the classic route of the face we hoped that the difficulties would be reasonable, allowing us a quick ascent in the shorter daylight hours. Based on this, and after seeking out photographs and topos, we decided to adopt a positive approach, and immediately booked flights to Santander, allowing five days for the round trip.

Autumn in the Picos is beautiful; with changing leaves and dappled sunlight, the forested valleys were quiet after the maelstrom of the summer tourist season, and we found ourselves alone in the campsite in Arenas. The weather was good, and we expected it to last for a few more days, so our confidence was high as we spent

Nick Kekus

The Naranjo de Balnes: the west face basking in autumnal sunshine at the end of the day

a day organizing our gear and buying food, and a disposable camera to replace the one forgotten item. The following morning we walked-in to the peak, carrying a tent and food for a few days, pleased with our luck with the weather and optimistic about our chances of success.

We were surprised to find the refuge beneath the Naranjo open, despite the fact that the summer season was over and there seemed to be a distinct lack of climbers or trekkers anywhere. We stopped to chat to the guardian and apologized for not bringing him more trade. Over a coffee he was able to update our weather information, informing us that it would only remain good for one more day before a change was due.

We hurriedly erected the tent and discussed our plans. Given the weather it seemed that we should make haste with the climb. We were doubtful that we could climb all twenty-two pitches in one day, especially as the daylight hours were short, requiring a chilly pre-dawn start. In addition, the early pitches were some of the harder ones. We decided to start straight away, with a plan to climb the first few pitches in the afternoon, before abseiling back down, leaving our climbing ropes in place. In the morning we would ascend our ropes in the dark and carry on climbing at first light, hopefully to reach the top before the change in the weather arrived. 'We had better take head-torches though', offered James, wisely.

The first few pitches were quite tricky and strenuous, and we decided on some 'alpine ethics' to make quick progress on a couple of the harder moves. We managed three pitches before the failing light encouraged us to descend to the warmth of the tent. After a quick meal we set the alarm for an early start, and settled down, happy to have dispensed with what we expected to be the hardest technical climbing on the route.

I have never enjoyed prusiking up single 9 mm ropes in the dark and this was no exception, but it was preferable to re-climbing the crux pitches in the bitter morning, and at first light we arrived at our evening high point, from where we launched back into the free climbing, up a series of bulging grooves. It was numbing with cold at first, and with no promise of sunshine for a few hours at least, so we started slowly, but gradually gained confidence with height and movement. The views were fantastic, across the jagged panorama of white limestone peaks to Spain's

Atlantic coast only 30 kilometres away. The sense of being on a big face was quickly upon us, as we followed the first part of the route straight up the wall into our new vertical world.

The Rabadá-Navarro takes the most amenable, yet traditionally protected line, up the west face of the Naranjo, and at about half-height the route makes a leftward traverse to avoid the blank walls which rise above. This traverse gives access to a second set of grooves on the left side of the face. As James led off on the first pitch of the traverse, immediately the sense of exposure multiplied as we left the security of the corners which characterize the lower part of the climb. Crossing the broad face in several pitches, the lines of bolts on harder, more direct routes arrive from below and continue above, offering inspiring objectives for a second visit, although preferably in warmer weather.

It was going well; we were making good progress and, above the traverse, with eleven or twelve pitches behind us, we had the feeling that we were on our way out. We began to climb directly again, and the easier climbing above promised to lead us swiftly via slabs and grooves to the summit. The only concern was the weather, which was looking increasingly cloudy and less encouraging by the minute.

On the Rabadá-Navarro route

Inevitably, as the day progressed, the cloud thickened, until finally it began to snow. After a brief discussion, we agreed that retreat would be equally as inconvenient as having to climb over the top in a snowstorm, so we decided on the latter course almost by default. With the slightly easier climbing, we had been making fast progress, but as the snow began to stick to the limestone slabs, and as our feet began to freeze in our rock shoes, our climbing slowed and time accelerated, as it always seems to do in these situations. Among the slabs were occasional overlaps, and awkward high rock-over moves, which became worryingly precarious with the thin layer of melting snow between rock and rubber, and with the widely spaced protection to concentrate the mind. After what seemed an age (and was therefore much longer) climbing what were easily the most terrifying pitches on the route, despite the lesser grade, we arrived at the summit as the daylight left it. We took a quick snap with the disposable camera, pulled on our head-torches and continued quickly, in order to try to locate the start of our descent on the shorter east face of the peak, before the darkness became impenetrable.

SNAKES AND LADDERS ON CERRO KISHTWAR

Andy Perkins

Every expedition has its ups and downs, and this trip by Andy Perkins and Brendan Murphy to Cerro Kishtwar in the autumn of 1991 was just an extreme case – periods of total despair when forward progress, let alone success, seemed virtually impossible, followed by wild elation when a small step took the team nearer to that elusive goal – to climb a big wall in a Himalayan setting.

It all started inauspiciously …

The Nightmare Scenario

I know you've imagined it in your worst dreams. The two of you there at the foreign airport at the start of your climbing holiday: you're waiting at the baggage reclaim for your two precious, irreplaceable rucksacks full of gear and only one appears. This was Brendan and me in Delhi; months of planning for our attempt on Cerro Kishtwar suddenly jeopardized by the disappearance of Bren's sack somewhere between London, Muscat and Delhi. I was torn between 'Thank God it's his sack that's missing, not mine' and the thought that, without it, our attempt was a non-starter despite 80 per cent of the kit having already been freighted in with the advance party. The missing 20 per cent included rucksack, pit, jackets, sunglasses, headtorch – all those things which are small but vital.

Instead of a couple of relaxing days of digestive acclimatization (aka curry eating) in Delhi before our flight to Leh, we spent four days running backwards and forwards across town in rickshaws, hopes rising and falling amidst the scream of scooters' two-stroke engines, and surrounded by exhaust fumes. The airline office and our agent produced no joy but, as always in India, someone somewhere has what you're looking for. We tracked down Mandip Singh of Ibex Expeditions in a quiet suburb and, in his air-conditioned office and Western furnished house, our hopes rose again. He could hire us the kit – and his own European gear at that; he would sell us a rucksack made by his own firm, and so on.

This pattern of up and down, hopes raised and dashed, grew to be a feature of our travels to and efforts on the mountain. One expects excitement, difficulties and reversals in Asia but this was an extreme version – a case of 'what can possibly happen next?'

The journey to base camp was correspondingly erratic in pace and nature – a flight away from the humid lunacy of Delhi delivered us to the computation heaven of Leh, with its open blue skies and brown boulder slopes studded with old monasteries. Weathered Ladakhi faces of sunburned leather were split by beaming smiles while children tugged at our clothes, not begging but just interested. I almost resented the pressure we were under to move on towards the mountain; I could have stayed in Leh for a week instead of taking a bus the next morning. That journey ended in Kargil where the only onward transport to the Zanskar Valley by truck-hitch took a day to find. A bone-rattling truck ride of thirty-six hours past the glories of Nun and Kun brought us to Padum. What should have been a good night's sleep turned into a surreal hell as a psychotic American with 'an anger problem' beat up his girlfriend, who then staggered round the hotel clad in only a sleeping bag insisting he be thrown out or arrested!

A jeep ride to the road-head the next day ended with a wheel falling off as we reached our destination. Mental well-being was then restored by witnessing a Buddhist fire *puja* by a visiting *Rinpoche* before the three-day walk over the Himalayan divide into Kishtwar.

The vanguard of the expedition had passed this way a week earlier and had done a sterling job getting all the porters and a horse(!) over the 5,300-metre Umasi La and finding a superb base camp site on the banks of the Haptal Glacier. We breezed in to find our tents already pitched and brews waiting under the base-camp tarpaulin. We swapped tales of our adventures and took a welcome rest day.

Cerro Kishtwar. The line of Andy and Brendan's route went directly up from the snow slope in the middle of the picture then took a line up and rightwards, taking in visible snow line features on the rock face to meet the shoulder beneath the summit. A direct line from here met a horizontal snow ledge en route ...

Here was the accustomed normality of expedition life: familiar kit unpacked from barrels; chapati omelettes for breakfast; even a friendly and helpful liaison officer – wonders will never cease! The sun beamed from a clearing sky on to the granite spires towering everywhere: Kishtwar Shivling, Dandagoporaran, Chomochior .... Partially hidden, only the top quarter of our objective, the north-west face of Cerro Kishtwar, showed itself, intimidating and yet enticing.

From an advanced base camp in a glacial bowl below the face, it looked just phenomenal. Mixed terrain rose from the bergschrund to a Patagonian-style sweep of granite draped with ludicrously steep tendrils of ice here and there. We gaped through binoculars and worried whether our seventeen days of food would last out; whether our 300 metres of rope would stretch between the ledges where we'd planned our camps; whether these would be big enough for our wall tent, whether the weather ... just stop worrying and GET ON WITH IT.

Looking down at the author jumaring up

The Ideal Sport Climbing Venue

We'd ferried all the gear up the mixed terrain and moved our capsule up to the base of the wall itself. Here, 300 metres above the bergschrund, we'd hacked a ledge out and hung the bivvy tent from the wall where it reared out of the mixed terrain in the form of ice-smeared slabs. Back in Britain, we'd pondered photographs, drawn diagrams and tentatively traced a line up this first section of slabs. There were no encouraging cracks or snow streaks on the photos to indicate how we were going to get up this first 300 feet (90 metres) of a 3,000-foot (900 metre) wall. We'd just applied the Longstaff dictum: 'Rub your nose in it before you are certain it won't go' (I doubt, however, whether Longstaff also said 'but pack the bolt kit in case it won't go'). Feeling distinctly apprehensive, I racked a massive range of big wall armaments – forty pins, friends, a triple set of wires ... Here was the point where we would find out just how presumptuous we were to assume we could climb this thing. Even using all the cunning gained from seasons of Scottish scratching, I'd only made 30 metres of progress in four hours: the tongue of ice I'd followed now shrank to just over 2 centimetres thick and 70 centimetres wide. I stood in an *étrier* clipped to my axe and pondered the blank 6 metres to the next good ice and the dubious pegs an equal distance below.

'It's no good – send me up the bolt kit.' All those outraged letters to the maga-zines about the value of adventure climbing and there I was placing 8 mm self-drillers in Himalayan granite. How easy it is to trample over your own morals in the pursuit of goals! I'd never placed one before and felt very guilty at first, as if the BMC Ethics Sub-Committee would jump round the corner and catch me at it. Half an hour later, with bleeding hands and totally wasted, I wished I'd brought a Bosch! Then, attempting to hook the existing rugosities, I took a fall in a scrattle of pegs, axes and hardware. Not content with placing a bolt, it seemed inevitable that I should have to dog it out! Brendan hung off the belay 30 metres below and barked in delight. From then on the gloves were off and progress was by bat-hooking, another new experience. (Do *you* know how deep to drill a bat-hook hole?) By close of play we'd made it to the next ice smear and, abbing to the tent, reflected on the day's climbing: 'The ideal sport climbing venue: afternoon sunshine, best quality granite, bolt protection and a café at the base of the crag!'

Over the next few days, we pushed out our 300 metres of fixed line, gradually instilling in ourselves the rigid discipline of the clip-on, clip-off mentality neces-sary in such a merciless, unforgiving environment. On the third day, I was in the middle of passing a belay point, when I suddenly found myself hanging one-handed from an ascender, having forgotten to re-clip into the new fixed line, and I was an instant away from a blurring, tumbling death. From then on concentration was absolute; procedures were religiously followed, and we acknowledged we had hold of items passed over. Even inside the tent, theoretically safe, a routine developed to maximize safety with minimum effort. Constant concentration just accelerated the attrition we'd already started to feel.

Brendan Murphy arriving at the snowy belay

Andy Perkins

The Hilton

Life at the Kishtwar Hilton

Beep-beep-beep-beep – 6.00 a.m: alarm off. Reach out of the pit. Jeez, it's cold: lighter in top pocket, light the tower stove, hand back in pit again. 6.20 a.m: unzip door, back outside for more snow for the pan, check the weather.

The weatherman says it's another good day: let's go climbing. 6.40 a.m: boiling water and we're ready for chocolate and another grope outside for snow and, careful, don't let any spindrift in. Sit up, trying not to tangle up in Brendan's safety leash from his chest harness to the tent tie-in points. Chocolate finished; time for muesli, then boil up again for a brew. Spin this out until the last possible moment to avoid the worst part of the day – God, it's awful getting dressed. 7.20 a.m. – reach into the pit for inner boots and socks (it smells like something died in there overnight). Down boots and dry socks off; yesterday's socks and inner boots on, Gore-Tex salopettes on, chest harness off, jacket on, chest harness back on again, outer boots on and we're ready for the big bad world. 7.40 a.m. – tent door open, clip on to fixed line, step out to immediate 500 metres of exposure to the glacier and temperature of -15 °C. Now another extremely unpleasant part of the day – the morning dump. Hang off the chest harness, fumble with a myriad of zips and flaps, try not to drop your bog paper, zip it all back up again, round to the other end of the tent on the safety line, it's harness on, hill food in left pocket, water bottle and ropes in rucksack. 8.00 a.m; right – I suppose we'd better go climbing, though maybe it's not quite sport climbing!

The climbing above the Kishtwar Hilton centred on the major feature of the route, 200 metres of corner formed where a massive buttress abutted the wall. Intermittent runnels of perfect ice gave some of the best Scottish gully climbing either of us had ever done. Where these ran out, progress by aiding was steady but, oh, so slow.

On one particular day, I spent five hours shivering on a stance while Brendan was totally absorbed in a sustained corner on blades, small wires and friends. On the following day the roles were reversed as the climbing continued at an unrelentingly difficult level. One section of the route required one foot becramponned while the

other boot smeared on rock. Then, at an apparent impasse where the corner became a hideous powder-choked off-width, a tension traverse out on to the overhanging right wall led to a perfect friend crack and access to the upper sections of the corner where angle and difficulty eased (comparatively). Every pitch was a microcosm of the route, progressing from total despair (this'll never go) to vague hope (I'll just give it a try) to elated incredulity. (I don't believe it! It's going!)

Reaching the top of the corner, we pulled the ropes up, had a hideous bivvy, and then managed to site the tent on a perfect ledge below the Texas Flake, the next impossible-looking feature of an impossible-looking route.

Friday the Thirteenth

It was a Friday and our thirteenth day on the route, but neither of us was superstitious – just very, very cold. The morning temperatures were the lowest we'd had yet and even getting geared up required underarm hand-warming every five minutes. Trying to lead out a pitch directly above the tent on steep rock and ice was excruciatingly cold on the fingers. Every move, I'd have to stop and warm them – but at least I was moving. Brendan hung uncomplaining on the belay and shook quietly.

I'd chosen to avoid the Texas Flake itself and started up a crack system in its front face. Climbing thin, ice-choked grooves and cracks presents such a dilemma. Do I leave the precious little ice there is and try to ice-climb (it's quick and I can keep my hands in my mitts, a good plan at -20 °C), or smash it off and torque/hook it (much more secure and I can get pro as well, but then I have to strip my mitts to

The Upside-Down Hotel handle gear and what if the crack's blind)? There's never a perfect solution to this dilemma but somehow progress materialized slowly and after two hours I'd scraped and hammered my way up 20 metres of some of the hardest mountaineering I'd ever done.

Higher up the pitch, the ice ran out and I was hooking and torquing to make progress on every move. Now this involves taking hands out of wrist slings and it's *very important* to remember to put them back in when the axe is retrieved from foot level. Inevitably there came a sequence where I dropped the axe to let it dangle on the wrist loop … and watched it spin away and down into the void. In those few seconds, there was sudden hope as it appeared to be heading straight for the ledge where our wall tent was pitched, then sheer horror as the axe plunged from 30 metres, straight through the roof of the tent. Thirteen days out, within striking distance of the summit and daily afternoon spindrift swirling around. I abseiled down to Brendan, full of contrition. He typically remarked that it was 'just one of those things', and we set to assessing the damage. In the end, we just turned the tent upside down and laid our Karrimats over the hole. It looked a bit of an odd shape and the poles didn't quite fit right, but what the hell – it worked and gave us a name for the doss: The Upside-Down Hotel.

Finishing the repairs, we returned to the fray with Brendan in the lead. My morale was at a record low, having wrecked the tent, and it also looked as though I'd led us into a blind alley where the crack system we were in widened into a hideously unprotectable off-width. However, Brendan was firing on all four cylinders and the next morning, after some wild pendule action, whooped in delight as a thin crack materialized to lead us to the top of the Texas Flake.

Andy Perkins

That afternoon, another desperate spindrift-lashed torquing pitch brought us to   Bold Brendan
within striking distance of the Scissors, two intersecting ramp systems from where
we hoped the terrain would ease. Would the mountain finally give us a break?

The End Game

It was make-or-break time (for the nth occasion of the route). Brendan had
traversed to the left-hand end of the Scissors and was peering round on to the
north-east face. I joined him and we contemplated powder-covered slabs and
broken rock, a total contrast from the clean, compact granite of the previous fifteen
days. I led a pitch leftward towards a vague gully line, floundering in the powder
which filled my wrist-dangling mitts and brought Brendan across. We stared up at
the gully which, after 100 metres, disappeared from sight at a cornice which we
guessed indicated the summit.

Just that distance between us and success – all that effort, to have come all that
way (that oft-used quote by Southerners going on to the Ben in evil weather and
conditions). I made the final few moves across to the gully, wading in powder,
screaming with the cold in my hands. Have you ever noticed how hideously cold
powder can be? More than that, the inner voice screamed 'NO!' as well – what was
it? We were 100 metres from success on a great route, state-of-the-art climbing. We
would be like Boardman and Tasker on Changabang (so we'd imagined in our
naïvety) but something about the situation was all wrong: we'd been climbing for
fifteen days and the attrition had been intense and unrelenting. There was no way
we could replace all the calories expended during such hard climbing and we were

feeling leaner and meaner every day. We'd had no sunshine for a week, and afternoon snow was gradually permeating our kit. My sleeping bag was frozen into useless clumps of down, so I wasn't getting much sleep. On one particularly memorable night (for Brendan), I'd taken two paracetamol and two Halcion (those sleepers that have now been withdrawn from sale). Apparently, I'd had Brendan very worried with violent Cheyne-Stokes breathing, switching my head-torch on and off, moaning in apparent pain from frost-nipped fingers and mumbling unintelligibly. When asked if I was okay, Brendan tells me I muttered 'My mind's gone!' Hmm.

In addition to all this excitement, the mental concentration we needed to remain safe had started to slip. I'd fallen 7 metres off a nominally safe belay through not being tied in properly. Brendan had nearly dropped a climbing rope. It was only a matter of time before one of us made a fatal error. Finally, we only had a couple of days' food left, which was allocated for the descent and, while our rations were meagre anyway, the prospect of eating nothing and drinking water did not fill either of us with enthusiasm.

It was a terrible decision to make, particularly being so close to success, but the chances of frostbitten fingers, the complexities of the descent and that final fatal error were getting uncomfortably high. It was with great reluctance and frustration that we finally decided to jack it in and, two days later, after a complicated descent that went like clockwork, we finally rapped over the bergschrund as night fell.

Walking out I was very depressed at having stopped so close to the summit, but soon afterwards I was able to rationalize it all and now I'm happy that it's one of the highlights of my mountaineering career. It's a direct yet natural line on a beautiful Tolkienesque peak. It demanded all the techniques of both climbing and survival that I'd built up over the years, and some new ones. Specially designed and selected items of equipment, from bivvy tents to harnesses and skyhooks, performed perfectly, enabling us to push ourselves close to our limit by a very narrow margin for a sustained period, then retreat in good order without injury – apart from the loss of a few more brain cells. The choice of capsule style was perfect, enabling us to cut loose on a Himalayan big wall, to teeter on the edge of the possible in an isolated world and become as aware and alive as I have ever been.

And that's success …

LION HEART

Rowland Edwards

The cold but dry sand forced its way between our toes as we quietly plodded our way through the village, passing by the black tents of the Bedouin. Their fires, in the centre of the tent floor, cast a golden glow which lit up their faces as they huddled round the light in the chilly morning air.

Dawn had not touched the sky yet, but life begins to stir early in the desert to avoid the intense heat of the afternoon. Bedouin dogs rushed out to warn us of their vigilance, causing the occupants of the tents to look out, and then acknowledge us with a blessing of the day.

We were soon through the village and out into the open desert. Slowly the horizon glowed with the rising of the sun as a new day was born. Suddenly, echoes bounced from wall to wall of the wadi as the Bedouin started the day's chant of prayers from the village mosque.

For Rowland Edwards, exploration of new rock routes and new rock-climbing areas has been his life – and still is! It's a passion he's shared with his son Mark on so many new climbs in Wales and south-west England, in Spain and further afield, but, as this story of a new climb on the desert rock towers of Jordan tells, it is still possible, despite these years of experience, to be caught out by a climb

By now the valley walls were gradually turning blood red as the sun started its journey across a clear, cloudless sky. The sheer beauty of this place stopped us in our tracks: if there had been no climbing here at all it would have been worth coming to Jordan just for moments like this.

Mark and I were on our way to explore a possible new line up one of the back walls of the Abu Aina Towers. These towers, situated in one of the deep *siqs* (canyons) of Wadi Rum, seemed to have very impressive grooves and cracks leading a way up to the very top of the wall. They looked tempting enough for us to get up well before dawn for this trek out into the desert.

This was my second visit to Jordan and Wadi Rum. I had been here the previous year with a number of European mountain guides, as guest of the Jordanian Government. The idea was to promote the area as a new destination for climbers. We had been told that there would be accommodation and transport available for guides who visited the area with clients. This second visit was really to test out if accommodation, etc. was in place before committing ourselves to bringing clients.

When Mark and I arrived in Wadi Rum we found the place devoid of climbers,

Desert walking

transport or officials. There were just the local Bedouin living in the valley. Talking to the Bedouin it soon became clear that they would provide transport, but at a very high cost. This was too expensive for just the two of us, so most of the exploring was done on foot, hence the early morning walk out to the Abu Aina Towers.

A little over an hour's walking found us at the entrance to the *siq* which led us up to the base of the tower. After a scramble up over boulders and loose rock we finally reached the base of the wall and the start of our new climb. By this time the sun had reached down into the bottom of the *siq* and what had been a cold morning's walk became pleasantly warm. When we had first arrived at Wadi Rum we had been troubled by very cold weather, cold winds, hail and even snow. This was something we really hadn't expected. The Bedouin had assured us that it would soon change and this warmth, we hoped, would herald that change.

The start of the climb was to solo a 20-metre slab at about 5a to the base of a deep chimney. The whole face leaned outwards, hiding the line we wanted to take; it disappeared with the verticality of the wall.

My first lead was up this chimney, which soon closed up. The rock quickly became awful crumbling sandstone which just disintegrated as soon as I touched it. Fortunately, a series of moves right landed me at the base of the first big groove and perfect rock, with what looked like good placements for gear. After 15 metres of this groove at 5c, as I ran out of rope, I reached a good foothold but with no chance of anything higher to belay on. I placed one bolt to belay from (by hand), and hoped that we would also be able to use this on our descent. The rope was taken in and soon Mark appeared, grinning all over his face at the sheer joy of climbing this pitch. This was just the start.

Lion Heart takes the left-facing groove/crack system in the centre of the tower. To the right of Mark, the 'large chimney' can be seen high up.

We exchanged the rack and he was off up the next pitch, a continuation of the groove system, bridging, jamming and lay-backing up this superb line, the rock still perfect. At the very top of this pitch some harder 6a moves up an open chimney led to a good ledge and belays.

From here on we had two options; a crack line going left or a more direct overhanging crack straight up. I elected to climb the direct line, which fortunately turned out to be the correct one, as the other one eventually ended up on rubbish rock and a blank section higher up. That's the way it goes on new routes. This choice turned out to be an excellent one; a gently overhanging 45-metre hand to fist jamming crack at 5b ending at a perfect belay ledge. The next pitch above didn't look at all promising; unprotected, it looked very difficult. The route ahead again was hidden by the overhanging wall above.

On pitch 2, the author climbing

Rowland climbing the impressive leaning corner

Rowland Edwards

Immediately above us was a short, steep wall which led on to a smooth, steep slab, ending at what looked like an impossible overhang. Mark climbed the steep wall and then on to the slab, managing to place two small RPs which would have been useless in any serious fall. At the top of the slab he disappeared leftward around the edge of the left arête. Suddenly there were whoops of joy and the rope started to run out steadily for its full length.

It was my turn to follow. The slab, which was about 6a, was really delicate, requiring a bold approach from the climber. On reaching the overhang I repeated the move left around the arête, and there it was – another perfect corner groove, with a perfect crack, soaring skyward for another 45 metres. This crack went a steady 5c with perfect protection; another superb pitch. From the belay, another corner and crack forced their way between the steep walls above, and again looked to be perfect rock. How lucky can one get?

This groove proved to be a bit harder than the one below, 6a, but equally enjoyable as there was no loose rock. As hand jam passed hand jam, and a bridging move led into delicate smears, I revelled in the sheer joy of this superb climb. All too quickly Mark called up that the rope was running out, so I took a belay.

I had now reached just below the chimney we had seen from the walk-in. From below, this chimney had seemed quite reasonable and looked as though it would lead us out to the top of the route. This wasn't to be. It was at least 5 metres wide, overhanging 7 metres, and a good 70 metres high. The only alternative was to try to climb the very impressive blank-looking wall on the left.

During the latter part of the climb the sky had darkened, covering the sun. It had also become cold again, just as it had on previous climbs. We just prayed it

Climbing in the upper reaches of the cliff

Dawn breaks

wouldn't bring snow. Darkness was only an hour away and we thought we had just enough time to reach the summit. We felt fairly confident we could find our way back down the route again in the dark.

Mark now started the next pitch with spots of rain splashing on to the rock around him. Just left of the belay was a slight groove leading on to the headwall. Mark climbed this, and then disappeared into a shallow depression to reappear later higher up, creeping his way upwards until he was once more out of sight. When seconding this pitch I could really appreciate the fine job he had done; the pitch was a poorly protected 6a. This pitch ended at the base of a series of grooves which seemed to head upwards in the direction of the summit. The rain, having held off for that pitch, now became a torrent. Before leaving this belay we placed another bolt, our last, as we had to return here to abseil off down the wall. We had limited ourselves to just two bolts and a couple of channel pegs which we had reserved just in case we needed them for abseils. It was now quite dark, but fortunately the remaining pitches proved to be quite easy, two long pitches of 4c and 5a.

By the time we reached the summit the rain had stopped, but we were in complete darkness. Sitting on the summit of the wall we could make out the head-lights of the Bedouins' vehicles (4x4s) far below, as they travelled back to the village camp of Wadi Rum. This day had been a holiday for them and they had spent their time racing through the desert far below us.

The night was freezing and, not really having the right kind of clothing for such temperatures, we soon started our way back down the route, soloing down the easier top pitches to the bolt we had left – and then the rain started again.

Saving weight, we had decided on bringing only one torch. Mark first attached himself to the belay then on to the abseil rope, preparing himself to abseil down after me. That way we could use the torch to check that everything was okay.

I then started the first abseil, swinging left and right as I descended, in search of any possible thread or crack I could use to belay from. Once attached to the rock, I arranged the next abseil, from either a crack or thread, then shouted up to Mark to start his descent. I pointed the head-torch up so he could use it as a guide: as Mark descended he would be guided by the small pool of light 40 metres below. Once he had reached the anchors he attached himself, then we pulled the ropes down, hoping like mad that they wouldn't jam. Once the ropes were down, Mark then started the next abseil with the use of the torch. In this way we continued down the wall, getting wetter and colder at each abseil. Waiting one's turn to do the abseil without the light was an eerie sensation, with only the dark outlines of the mountains and the steady hiss of the rain as it hit the rock around you. The ropes disappeared into the gloom; one hand constantly felt the rope going down to Mark who was abseiling below, making sure that there was still a weight on the rope. Far below, a small pool of light swung around, searching for the next abseil point.

The one abseil we really were not looking forward to was the one going over the overhang at the bottom of the wall; we just didn't know whether the ropes would reach and touch rock below. If they didn't, it would mean a 50-metre prusik back up to the belay. As luck would have it the ropes just reached, with not one metre to spare on the stretch. Our last abseil was down the easy slab and finally, after three to four hours of abseiling, we were at the base of the wall.

We started the scramble down into the siq. The rain had stopped but had left the boulders very greasy, making us stumble our way back down the siq, and our torch finally gave up the ghost.

We'd been travelling on pure guesswork, using the outlines of the mountains on each side to guide us in the right direction, when suddenly the whole siq was lit up with a blinding light. The Bedouin who, unbeknown to us, had been following our progress up the wall during the day, must have also been doing the same on our descent. They had driven their 4x4s up small mounds in the desert so that their headlights illuminated the whole of the siq we were in. Although, at times, this light blinded us, we did manage to pick our way back down to the desert floor, where we were met by an enthusiastic crowd of Bedouin. Dayfallah, one of the Bedouin we had befriended, came hurrying towards us, insisting on taking us back to his camp nearby.

As we entered the low black tent, Dayfallah's family were seated on the floor around the fire in the middle of the tent. Their faces turned towards us as we entered. Without exception, all had a friendly smile. We sat crossed-legged around the fire, sipping small glasses of sweet tea and eating small snacks. Everyone wanted to know how our 'new way' (our new route) had gone. These Bedouin were quite in tune to climbing and the challenges involved. Many of the locals had found 'new ways' up these rock walls to go hunting.

Our visit was over all too soon and Dayfallah insisted on transporting us back to our camp in Wadi Rum.

Lion Heart was to become one of the classic rock-climbs in Wadi Rum and has received many ascents confirming its grade and quality of climbing.

HAUNTED BY THE GHOST

Adrian Nelhams

Adrian Nelhams shares his experience of climbing one particular icefall during a successful trip to the world-class ice-climbing venue known as The Ghost in the Canadian Rockies of Alberta. His story highlights the plight that enters many a climber's thoughts – what if I truly get stuck on a climb and can't climb up or down? How do you work through the situation, in increasing fatigue and fear, to find a way out?

I stepped out of the cave and on to the steep pillar connecting the face. I looked down to my feet but my focus wandered and eyes shifted to the 200 metres of dizzy space below them. The smooth, steely blue ice just dropped away out of sight as if the whole route was overhanging. Canadian spruces crowded out the valley below. The exposure was wild, scary even; just the void absorbing all my thoughts. I imagined the ten useless crampon points that would all be hanging in space and stared at the two toughened orange steel front-points, 2 centimetres of metal that were actually penetrating the hard, steep ice.

My mind wandered – why bother with ten points, why not have two-point crampons? All this was going on in a second or two. My eyes shifted to the huge limestone amphitheatre that was wrapped around me: it was as if someone had thinly iced this central wall with a pallet knife as if they were icing a cake. I looked up above and the whole route appeared super-steep, almost overhanging.

'One step at a time', I said to myself. I refocused, straight arms pulling down, I looked down for my next foot placement and kicked in with a bent leg; my other foot came up and stepped out, giving me a wide platform. I pulled down with both arms and drove up with my legs; heels down, hips well forward, legs locked out. I looked up, locked off my left arm, lifted out my right tool from its secure position in the ice, reached up and replaced it in the ice above. Not too high – I didn't want to overstretch and come up on my heels. A swing from the elbow, letting the weight of the axe do all the work, then a flick of the wrist and the pick splintered a little ice as it struck the slim, hollow groove above. No crack, not too deep, no blade movement or wobble; it felt great. I heard a voice in my head: 'Never move up on a bad axe placement!' Yeah, yeah - that's easy to say on easier ground, but here? But it's a mantra I try to stick to, like the ice I was feeling my way up. I was happy with it though, so I needed to forget it and move on, to concentrate on the next foot placement. The sequence was almost robotic, although it flowed and felt fantastic over the steep featured ice – more like climbing on rock than it's over felt, where balance, body positioning and timing are everything.

I looked down again to see the ropes hanging in a great arc, free of the ice and disappearing around the corner. I looked at the ice above and focused on a thick depression which would take a solid ice screw. I stepped up again, feet wide apart, hips forward, right axe high and readied myself to place a screw. No need to clean the ice; I placed the left axe to one side and let go. Completely still, no sorting the feet, I felt I should be happy with them now that I'd committed to one axe. I reached down on my left side and unclipped a screw. The thick depression was chest-high and slightly left. I pressed the four sharp teeth of the screw hard against the ice and, just by leaning against it, made a full turn of the screw into the surface. The screw bit and I let go. Very carefully, I twisted my wrist to put another turn in the screw so that it would feel more solid. I lifted the express lever and drilled it in. It felt good, solid, no hollows or air pockets, no cracking of ice … the hanger stopped flush against the smooth ice surface. With the heel of my hand I knocked it even tighter in against the ice so that it hung down, let go and reached down to my harness again and unclipped a quick-draw, then clipped the hanger. I felt down between my legs for the left rope and lifted it up, clipping it into the bottom snap link of the draw, and relaxed.

Acrian Nelha ʼs

Stepping out from the comfort and safety of the ice cave on the Sorcerer, WI 5

Placing gear is about being totally organized and having a quick, clean system without upsetting any balance or overstretching.

I reached out and took hold of my left ice tool, lifted it out from the ice and replaced it higher, pulled down on both with straight arms, looked at my feet and the cycle continued …

Another 8 metres and another screw; I was enjoying the climbing. It was exhilarating, steep and technical in one of the world's most beautiful places. Huge, steep limestone walls and hanging valleys, once carved out by the Ghost Glacier. Steep bands of rock and turret-like rock outcrops almost fortify the flat summits from those that top out on the cliffs far below. Needle-like rock towers have also been carved out on steep ridges, creating the most amazing scenery.

This is the dry range east of the Bow Valley and over Devil's Gap. It may have

Adrian Nelhams

The Sorcerer, a steep ribbon of ice in impressive surroundings

very difficult access but generally has low avalanche risk. The access is made difficult from the drifting snow and icy river crossing, which only those in a 4x4 would bother attempting in winter. It's a wild place and, up here, bloody exciting!

Then wham! I got the worst pump of my life and, it came from seemingly nowhere. I went solid above my waist and my arms stopped working. I felt my grip of the tools loosening; my hands and fingers were totally pumped and solid. Then I was losing my grip of the tools; my hands were opening up and I couldn't do anything about it. I looked down at the ropes and they were just hanging there limp and lifeless, arcing away out of sight. I couldn't see the last ice screw. I looked at the void below and prepared for the worst. My heart was pumping so fast, sweat was pouring down my face and into my eyes. I was still losing grip. I tried constantly to get the weight back on to my feet but for some reason I couldn't. I felt as though I couldn't climb any more: why couldn't I get my weight back on my feet – everything felt undercut and overhanging. All my weight was hanging off my hands, over which I had no control, and which I could feel were still unclenching their grip on the handle of the ice tool.

I let go with one hand and tried to shake it out, hoping that I'd at least start to get some relief. But as soon as I let go with one hand the other felt as if it was giving out and I grabbed the tool again. I tried again, again and again, hoping that the slightest relief would start to loosen up the lactic acid that had gone solid in my hands and arms. I'd never had this before; my whole upper body above my waist was solid and I didn't know where this had come from.

I looked down again and the void started to engulf me; the exposure started to scare me and in my mind I could see myself falling and thinking 'This is going to hurt big time.' It's serious here, five pitches up, two hours of walking-in through thick pine forest and an hour of serious off-road driving to the roadhead. I looked at my hands unclenching; I focused on them and then my leather gloves. The gloves were short, with a short cuff which I could see clearly as my jacket sleeve had ridden up. As a final throw of the dice, I hooked the cuff of my glove over the heel spur on the very end of the ice tool.

Instantly I started to be able to wiggle my fingers a little and get some relief, the gloves and stitching were now taking my weight! I then grabbed the tool again and did the same with the other hand; amazingly I was getting something back, just a tiny amount but it was definitely something. I repeated the process forty, maybe fifty, times, which seemed to take an eternity. I wondered what Dean must be thinking with the rope not moving for so long.

I'd moved far enough back to try to place an ice screw. I reached down with my left hand, but my right started to give out again so I quickly grabbed the tool again with my left hand and shook the right out. I went through a long cycle again, shaking both hands out until I felt that I had enough power to get a screw. I reached down with my right, grabbed a screw, it didn't unclip cleanly. I fumbled and, as I finally unclipped it, my left hand started to give out. I put the screw in my mouth and quickly grabbed my tool with my right hand and shook the left hand out. I did the shakeout cycle again. I could hardly breathe with the screw stuffed in my mouth. I shoved the screw in with no time to think – the sharp teeth on the end of the screw embedded into the side wall of my mouth and it was complete agony, but I had to hang in there. I got enough back to retrieve the screw from my mouth and stop the pain; blood stained the teeth of the screw. I made a quick half turn of the screw into the ice, let it go and grabbed the tool again for some relief, hoping of all hopes that the screw would stick in and not fall out. However, I could see it starting to drop out slowly so, with the other hand, I made another quick half turn to secure the screw into the ice. I did this a couple more times until I was sure that it wouldn't drop out, lifted the hanger and started to drill it in. At this point the pump came back and I grabbed the shaft of the ice screw which was drilled in halfway. The change of hand grip gave me more relief and I changed the cycle from tool to screw until I could feel my body start to loosen up. I finished the screw off up to the hilt, clipped the hanger and then clipped the rope. The rope clipped easily as if they didn't even have me on belay. Christ, that would have been some serious airtime! I shook out, more relaxed now that the storm was over and everything was quiet. I placed one axe higher, stepped up and slowly continued to where the ground eased off, placed another screw and then continued to the belay.

I was totally wet with sweat, physically knackered and mentally spent; I rigged the belay, clipped on, sat back and just totally relaxed for a few minutes. I then picked up both ropes, pulled in the slack, clipped Dean into the belay plate and started belaying.

I looked down at the void below and felt physically sick, so I looked up to see the easier ground and flat-top summit; I fixed my eyes on this until I could hear the sound of axes hitting ice below me and a white helmet started to come into view.

I took in the rope, still trying to understand and work out what had happened, what went wrong. The steepness, exposure or technical nature of the ice weren't anything I wasn't used to, or hadn't comfortably climbed before. Only two days earlier I had led the pitch of my life, far harder, steeper and more technical, and I'd enjoyed every minute of it, savouring every axe placement. I hadn't climbed better, ever!

This felt as though I was a novice again, trying to pull up all my weight on my arms, arse sagging, not using my feet, not getting any weight off my arms, not getting my hips in … I couldn't understand it.

Dean followed up, unclipping the rope and pulling the screws. It looked great, steep and Dean seemed to be really enjoying the pitch. He got to the belay all smiles but was also pretty much pumped from the climbing. He said he felt tired after the two-week trip and, as it was the last day, maybe tiredness had just crept up on me. But I couldn't get my weight off my arms and on to my feet – schoolboy stuff.

Anyway, we rigged an Abolokov, threaded some old climbing rope through the

Acrian Nelhams

Steep and sustained
climbing on the Sorcerer

ice thread and tied it off. I took an end from each rope, threaded one end through the tied-off climbing rope, joined the two ends with an overhand knot, pulled it tight, tied a knot in the ends of both ropes for security and dropped them. The ropes just seemingly hung in space; the anchor felt good but even so we backed it up with another screw, Dean first, on with a prusik and belay plate and he was gone. I did the same, retrieved the backup screw and headed down.

Slowly I went back down the way I'd come up. I stopped at the place where I'd so nearly blown it, looked down again into the void below and took a deep breath – my heart was racing again. I looked across at the wall of ice, smooth and uninterrupted, but it was actually undercut and overhanging for 15 metres and I hadn't noticed. The ice had led me into a trap. I hadn't realized or felt it; I was enjoying the climbing too much. Sure, I was getting tired but I'd just kept powering up, not bothering to place a screw, thinking I'm happy on this ground, I'll place one soon. Face on and looking up it just seemed steep, but no, it was actually overhanging. That's why I couldn't get the weight off my feet and that's why I couldn't get my hips in and that's why my arse felt as if it was just sagging and my arms were taking it all. I'd climbed myself into a box. I shook my head. Earlier in the trip I would have just powered through it, or if I'd have been wearing leashes I probably wouldn't even have noticed. But after eight weeks of icefall climbing in the Alps leash-less and then this two-week trip out to the Canadian Rockies, I was tired but hadn't realized it. I hadn't given that any thought at all; I hadn't been looking after myself. Now this route and this wall on the last day was just one step too many.

I carried on abseiling. Dean had the next abseil already rigged, I unclipped my cow's tail from the rope we were pulling, clipped the belay and started pulling the ropes down. The knot came to the belay, the loose end whipped out over us and down the next pitch. I threaded the ropes into my belay plate, wound on the prusik and left the belay, abseiling down the next pitch.

It was dusk as we made our way back through the dense pine trees, following our snow trail which we'd plugged on the way in. Two hours later and headlamps on, the track, our 4×4, stashed the kit in the boot and made our way back in darkness along the track of frozen river crossings, boulders, windblown snow and ice. Back up the Big Hill, through and along the forestry track and then finally back to the main road. We both sighed with relief, the mental strain of the day subsiding and let loose, reliving the whole day again from start to finish.

Winter climbing in The Ghost is serious – full stop. It's a wild and adventurous journey into some committing valleys and climbs. It's a remote wilderness back there, of snowed-up summits, limestone rock towers, hanging valleys, dense pine forests, few trails and an array of wild animals like bears and cougars, which treat the area as their home. You only feel free from the place when you're back on hard tarmac and the road returning to the highway. Many people struggle just to get vehicles in and out in winter, let alone finding the climbs and climbing a route! You leave home in the dark and arrive back in the dark – that's The Ghost.

The chat in the car reliving the day was at fever pitch and the excitement lasted on into Canmore, the bar, and through the huge burger and fries they served – what an exciting, adventurous, serious, scary and wild day that was.

They say 'You should try to learn something new every day' – well I certainly found something out about myself that day in The Ghost!

I had never talked about it with Dean until recently. I'd run it over in my mind a thousand times but never told anyone. Recently, we were both sitting on a ledge in the Grose Valley, in the Blue Mountains, Australia. We'd just done a fantastic five-pitch rock route; sandstone, serious, exposed, scary, committing, adventurous, on a huge wall rearing out of the valley and Eucalyptus forest below. It's an amazing place, if you've never been there before. We both sat, having had a great climb, enjoying the views and precious time spent climbing together. It all came out, as I recalled that day in The Ghost; he had no idea. I was surprised how emotional I was just talking it through, reliving that 15 metres of steep, overhanging ice.

It's good to talk.

Adrian Nelhams

Hydrophobia, WI 6, plastered to the back of this amphitheatre in nearby Waiparous Creek

A MONTH IN PATAGONIA

Tim Neill

There can't be many places left in the world where Tim Neill hasn't climbed.... On a trip to Patagonia, factoring in the likelihood of appalling weather comes with the territory, but it didn't seem to dampen his and Matt Stygall's spirits and aspirations. Good teamwork, a determination to keep having a go, and modern technology all contribute to whether a climbing trip becomes a success.

One place I'd always wanted to climb was Patagonia – jagged, granite peaks and a bit of challenging weather. I loved the style of climbing in Chamonix, and I love the burly weather in the Scottish winter, so why not combine the two? Plus there is the attraction of decent red wine, big steaks and a good dose of adventure.

For years, living in North Wales, I'd got a sense of the connection between climbers here and the granite spires down south. A hefty list of North Wales-based climbers had made the pilgrimage and come away with wild tales and, sometimes, a summit.

An evening at the Cromlech boulders chatting with a friend, Adam Wainwright, had sown the seed for our own trip. He'd just returned having summited Fitzroy with Andy Cave. His words 'Even if you don't get to climb, you'll have a great time!' sealed the deal. The best way to commit to a climbing trip, they say, is to buy a plane ticket. So it was that a large cash injection got the ball rolling for a trip to Patagonia. My good friend Matt Stygall was also well up for it. He'd even been before. So, if he was keen to go again, it must be good.

So, in the aftermath of Christmas, a seamless journey from Llanberis to El Chaltén, in the Argentine Patagonia, saw us arriving on a beautiful evening with some otherworldly summits piercing the horizon. We pitched our tent, checked a forecast and thought we'd see what it was all about first thing in the morning.

A lot of walking seemed to be what it was all about. A big part of a day got us out of town, through a beautiful beech forest, up some scree, past a few lakes and on to the glacier that led up to Passo Superior. This col is home to the traditional snowhole site used as an advanced base for attempting any routes on the east side of the Fitzroy chain. In the big bank of snow there, we refurbished an old hole into a deluxe sleeper for two giants. A blue sky and amazing vista sent us to sleep.

An early alarm alerted the senses to a dull roar outside! The alpine tradition of resetting the alarm for the next hour just brought a louder roar. So, that's what

windy means down here. Kit was stashed, and a battle was fought until we reached the cover of the forest way below, and so the first lesson in remaining positive was delivered.

The peaks of St Exupery, Innominata, Poincenot and Fitzroy

This gave us a few days to find our feet in El Chaltén, the town used as a base for most of the climbing in this range. Very modern but still with a bit of wild west feel, it had plenty to keep us occupied during the inevitable periods of poor climbing weather. There were good bars, restaurants, gear supplies, internet access for weather updates and, more importantly to stop us festering too much, bouldering and rock-climbing, plus plenty of other climbers to chat to from around the world.

After only a few days in town the *météo* was looking promising for a reasonable one-day weather window soon. Lighter bags this time made the walk-in faster. The evening at Passo Superior was a jovial international affair with a great vibe for the day ahead. The dark hours of the morning saw us approaching the Whillans/Cochrane route on the east side of Poincenot. Good *névé* saw us moving fast at daybreak, and soon our hoped-for HVS chimneys were being scaled in a fashion more akin to Ben Nevis in winter. Crampons stayed on all the way up the iced-up rock to the breezy summit. A photo was taken to emulate the cover of Whillans' biography, then lots of abseiling back to the glacier and two happy, tired souls rolled into their snowhole, just as snowflakes blew in on the next winds.

The unheard-of happened after only a day or so back in town. Forty-eight hours of good weather and light winds were forecast for a few days' time. Leaving town in

Tim Neill

Matt tackling varied climbing conditions on the Franco-Argentine route on Fitzroy

squally weather saw us arrive mid-afternoon at the now-familiar snow bank. As the scudding clouds dissipated, the mountains looked snowy after the storm, and the usual doubts set our minds racing as we set in for the short sleep.

The approach to the east face of Fitzroy was perfect; bone-hard snow to walk on and the huge light of a full moon sped us to the bergschrund. Great snow led up to La Brecha, the col between Fitzroy and Poincenot, which was used to gain access to the technical climbing of routes like the California Route, or our objective, the Franco/Argentine. By daybreak we were already tackling the first technical rock on the route. This, the most-travelled climb on the peak, saw A1 cracks choked with ice that set the tone for the day. A few pitches later, a few moves with an *étrier* clipped to an ice axe got a new pulse record too.

The sun was doing its work melting a big snow patch high above us into a beautiful jamming corner that gave us both a good soaking, and a few others behind. As the sun wheeled around the mountain and the pillar came into the shadows, the rock went from wet to verglassed – and so did we. One by one, the other teams shouted up 'Good luck' and set their ropes for heading down. We weren't romping along like on Chamonix granite, as you might on a good summer's day – it was more like a big route in the Cairngorms in the winter combined with the occasional Yosemite big wall pitch, all with the associated slow and steady progress. But progress it was, and our pitch count had us well up the climb.

Tim Neill

The Fitzroy summit

We couldn't see any reason to bail except the prospect of a very cold night. Were we going to turn around because we were about to be very cold and uncomfortable? There was no wind or cloud to be seen, although there was plenty of ice and rime above. This, of course, didn't fit the topo which described mid-grade rock-climbing! We were used to that by now though – as long as the good cracks under the ice continued, so would we. A succession of memorable ice and mixed pitches, followed by some steep aiding, landed us abruptly on a big, open ice slope in the dark. A few pitches later saw us on a blunt ridge, and a ledge was hacked for the night. Bivvy sack over our heads, sitting on ropes with our legs in our packs, some soup and a bit of food helped us shiver through the relatively short night.

A great sense of exposure was our only reference point. The first rays of light illuminated an unbelievable vista out west over the icecap from one side of the bivvy. The other showed the summit only a quick climb above us. We packed our sacks and mustered cold bodies to make the snowy scramble to the summit – and there we were.

In this land of storm, barely a breath of wind, no clouds and an uninterrupted view north and south along the Andean spine of peaks. Out west, and just a bit below us, casting a sabre-toothed shadow were the mighty Torres, each looking fierce with their great rime ice summits. To the east were the great glaciers carved into lakes, fringed beyond by the never-ending pampas.

On the descent of the east face of Fitzroy

As usual on an alpine summit, thoughts of the descent soon urge you to turn your back and head down. The normal thing would be to abseil the way we'd come; we down-climbed to the big ice slope and started abseiling towards the edge. As we committed over the edge on to the pillar, the sight of many of the pitches we had inched our way up in such conditions the day before was inspiring stuff. At the time I think we were just concentrating on the next short stretch. Abseil after abseil got us down the wall into warmer temperatures. Only one rope snag had to be sorted. We met quite a few climbers on their way up, many impressed by the sight of our head-torches the night before. We enjoyed the rest at their belays as they climbed through and we waited each time to pull our ropes.

At La Brecha we continued abseiling. The good snow ice of the previous morning was now melting out big style and the ropes soon became heavy, wet and gritty. A final stimulating abseil over the bergschrund landed us back by our stashed ski poles and the rope was set for the walk back over the glacier. The bomber-hard snow we had enjoyed thirty-six hours previously now seemed to be bottomless snow soup. Heavy legs got us back to the Passo Superior. A look back up to Fitzroy saw the first clouds enveloping the mountain, as if to say 'show's over'. With a few gusts of the new breeze, we jumped inside our bunker, brewed up and slept the sleep of the dead.

Next morning, we packed up all our stashed kit as we decided our business with Passo Superior was done. The morning was grey, menacing and, of course, windy.

All smiles back down on the glacier, with Fitzroy looming up behind on the right

We hoped that all the climbers from the day before were safe, then we shambled down the glacier and into the forest for the long, but happy, walk back to town.

The following week had pretty terrible weather, but it was easy for us to sit it out. Other climbers not as lucky as us dragged their bottom lips around town in the daily routine of checking weather forecast, reading, bouldering, or the big treat … El Choco. This was the chocolateria, serving great coffee, pizza and, of course, everything chocolate. Housed in the oldest wooden building in town, this was the hangout of choice, and so a great meeting place.

Eventually, a sort of weather window appeared to give us hope. As with our first trip to Poincenot, the best part of a day was on offer, but with what was deemed by those in the know, right on the margin of comfortable winds. We decided on the east face of the Aguja St Exupery, via the Buscaini route. Buscaini was an Italian climber responsible for lots of exploratory climbing throughout Patagonia, and wrote a very comprehensive book about climbing in the region. His route, we hoped, offered sheltered climbing in steep corners that would be manageable in the westerly winds.

The approach was up a beautiful, steep valley, with a great glacial lake at its head. This left us with a waist-deep and very cold crossing of the river issuing from it, to access the approach slopes to our climb. At the edge of the glacier we bivvied on the rocks for warmth and waited to see what the morning would bring.

The alarm went off, and an eye was cast over the sky above. Stars were plenty, and the dark silhouettes of the peaks were cloud-free too. A roar of wind could be heard, but not felt, and so we started the approach. The climbing was great all the way in the corners. Some icy bulges required some wide bridging in our rock shoes and, as we left the shelter of the corners for the final few pitches, the constant roaring wind let rip. I think we crawled to the top, and hunkered behind the summit block. The view was wild. The higher summits of Poincenot and Fitzroy were disappearing quickly as the weather closed in around us. The Torres to the west were nowhere to be seen; just snow on the wind.

Only a few abseils down, and back in the corner system, things got back in hand. At the glacier everything had a distinctly Scottish feel. We remade the river crossing at dusk, and arrived at one of the old disused climbers' camps on the edge of the forest a short while later. These were the hangout for climbers in this range in the days before accurate internet weather forecasting changed everything. They allowed quick access to the peaks if the barometer gave an optimistic hint of rising pressure. Of course, there was no way of knowing how long for, and so being able to do what we'd achieved so far would be more a case of very good luck than a calculated plan. Inside the huts were ornate wooden carvings and other signs of climbers whittling away the days of bad weather. They were a perfect shelter for a night, but we reckoned it would be a real test of psyche to stay here in a constant state of readiness for weeks on end.

So the last part of our month in Patagonia was a relaxed mixture of rock-climbing, socializing and two shorter alpine climbs in two very tight weather windows. The first had a forecast of six hours of reasonably light winds. We decided on a quicker ice and mixed route of moderate difficulty on Aguja Guillamett. This peak is a little to the north of Fitzroy, and our chosen route meant a return to Passo Superior. This time no one else was there. While I don't necessarily like sharing routes with other people, sometimes their company reassures your decision-making!

The morning brought the promised calm weather and just the odd swirl of snow on light winds. The perfectly parallel and narrow Amy Couloir went quickly on good snow ice to the Brenner Ridge. The rock was really snowed-up and the wind was increasing. The last section up a steep snow slope was really exposed to the wind, making it, ironically, the crux. At the summit our 60-metre ropes were arcing in the wind between us, creating a sight I'll never forget. After some fairly challenging abseils, the walk back over the glacier was the last crux, and so every navigation trick in the book was deployed to see us reunited with the snowhole.

Our last climb was in the Torre Valley the day before we were to catch the bus out of El Chaltén. The Japanese camp was a great spot. Lots of climbers were enjoying predominantly shorter alpine rock routes and often at a much lower altitude than those from Passo Superior. Of course there were the mighty Torres themselves, but the lack of substantial good weather seemed to have ruled them out during our time. We climbed Cerro Mocho, a popular little satellite peak at the base of Cerro Torre. It gave us 500 metres of perfect, weathered granite as good as anywhere. The low-stress climbing, without packs and on dry, sunny rock, was the perfect conclusion to our lucky trip. We sat in the sun at the summit, and were surrounded by our climbs of the last month. The view of all the other possibilities surrounding us was amazing too. Perhaps if we came back, we'd coincide with good weather, long enough to climb this, or that – or maybe not.

ANOTHER WEEK, ANOTHER WALL

Jonathan Preston

I first met Aqil Chaudhry at the Etive Slabs during the summer of 1987. This was a pre-expedition meet and we were both members of a team going out to India in the autumn in order to attempt the first ascent of Changuch, a 6,300-metre peak in the Garhwal. We never got up that particular mountain, though we did make three other decent first ascents of peaks around the 6,000-metre mark. Later that year I joined him for a very successful venture on Mount Kenya, climbing a couple of good ice routes as well as a long rock route on the Diamond Buttress. We were a good combination and worked well together. After a fantastic 'hard rock' weekend the following May, ticking classics on the Ben and in Glencoe, we decided to go for broke and head for California in September.

Heading to Yosemite is many a climber's dream. Spectacular granite cliffs dominate the valley, with routes for every ability of climber. To be able to climb amongst these vast walls in generally good weather conditions allows a climber with a bit of time to progress to bigger and greater adventures, to learning about aid-climbing and to making multi-day ascents of the famous walls themselves, as Jonathan Preston discovered.

Yosemite – commonly known simply as The Valley – is a Mecca for rock-climbers. Composed of pristine golden granite, there is a plethora of over 3,000 short, medium, long and very, very long climbs of all different types and styles for the obsessive climber to enjoy. In June 1864 Abraham Lincoln signed the Yosemite Grant, deeding the valley to the state of California, the first recorded action by a government to set aside land for preservation as wilderness. In 1890 it became the world's second National Park after Yellowstone and is now owned by the Federal Government. Though errant bears still occasionally roam through the region, it is hardly a wilderness. A huge influx of tourists is managed by a resident staff of over 2,000, providing all the amenities of a small town.

As the bus from Merced lurched into the valley, I stared resolutely out of the right-hand window. Most people on board were craning their necks over towards the left-hand side in order to catch their first glimpse of El Capitan, the mighty 900-metre rock wall that dominates the view. I knew that if I saw it and felt

Half Dome stands proud
above the upper
Yosemite Valley

overwhelmed by the thought of climbing it, at that point I would never go near the thing during the course of our month-long stay. We had both managed to get an extended period of leave from our respective workplaces – Aqil as a site engineer in London and I at an outdoor centre in Scotland. We were keen to attempt some of the bigger routes, but first of all we had to get organized.

There is a fairly convoluted system regarding accommodation for climbers, rooted in the fact that there is only one 'walk-in' campsite, Sunnyside (originally known as Camp Four), which has basins and toilets but no showers, with six people sharing a site. Up until 15 September, there was supposed to be a seven-day camping limit; after that it was thirty days. The trick was to keep a low profile and hope that you wouldn't be recognized as you booked in for a second seven-day period.

We soon settled in and did a few straightforward climbs before embarking on our first bigger test – the east buttress of Middle Cathedral. This is a day route of eleven pitches that involves an early start. Being north facing, it is slightly cooler than the scorching temperatures elsewhere. Despite the fact that the base of the valley is at about 1,200 metres the heat in September is still oppressive. All went well, including a basic aid pitch and the descent off via the Kat Walk, although halfway up I glanced round from a belay and found myself looking straight at The Captain: an awe-inspiring sight – almost 1.5 kilometres of cliff, 600 metres high at one end at the south-east face, rising to 900 metres in height as the aspect changed at The Nose round to the south-west face. I had spent a bit of time climbing in the Verdon Gorge earlier in the year, trying to acquaint myself with the feeling of exposure that comes from hanging around on belays on a 600-metre wall of limestone, but surely this was a massive step up, being one and a half times the height.

With a few more reasonable day routes under our belt, we decided to try something bigger. The 'regular route' on the north-west face of Half Dome seemed like a good initiation. So far we had been climbing almost exclusively 'trad', i.e. placing and removing gear as we went and making all the moves 'free' without any aid. Though some of the big walls in Yosemite have now been freed, in the 1980s big routes were still aided to one degree or another. Todd Skinner and Paul Piana had recently climbed every pitch on the Salathé Wall without aid and this was a huge breakthrough.

Having not done much aid-climbing we set about doing some training and after finding a suitable boulder, I practised gaining height by stepping up into *étriers* clipped into leader-placed protection. Once on top I set up a hauling system to bring up a heavy sack. It wasn't going too well – I got the ropes into a bit of a tangle. Aqil, with his engineer's mind, is better than me at this sort of thing and gave me his best, most withering Axel Foleyesque look – he must have wondered what on earth he was letting himself in for – but with some subtle rearranging I soon got the hang of pulley systems and we felt ready for our first big wall.

Half Dome – originally known as South Dome – at 2,430 metres is one of the few true summits in the valley. It was first climbed by a Scotsman, George Anderson, in 1875, who drilled laboriously for weeks in order to anchor a handline to the top. His route is equipped with a cableway today and provides easy access to and from the summit. We needed to get to the foot of the north-west face and, after a strenuous approach walk, we slept out under the stars not far from the start of the 'regular route'. By the time we emerged in the morning, people were already climbing and we left a gap before starting up ourselves. The lower part of the route appeared devious at first, though it turned out to be quite straightforward.

At this point we hadn't quite sorted out our tactics and were trying to climb in traditional style, i.e. the leader setting off with a light sack and freeing or aiding the pitch before the second followed, again free-climbing as much as possible, or aiding but removing all the gear. The trouble was, the second got too tired climbing with a heavy sack and was then wilting on the next lead. We had hoped that this technique would be quicker, but soon reverted to standard big wall procedure whereby the leader leads on a single rope, trails a haul rope and brings up the sack while the second jumars and cleans the pitch. We made good progress and though the best sites at the Big Sandy Ledges were already taken we managed to make ourselves reasonably comfortable and settled down for our first night out on a big wall. The next day saw us moving up some intricate ground on the zig zags, peg-scarred cracks that our newly acquired Metolius tri cam units fitted into perfectly. This was solid A2 climbing, using nuts and cams – no pegs or bolts as used on the first five-day ascent in 1957, which was America's first-ever grade VI climb. The Thank God Ledge followed; an airy traverse left that thankfully avoids the capping overhangs (hence the name). A few more pitches and we were on top, enjoying one of the finest views in the Sierra Nevada.

Once safely back at Sunnyside a bit of serious R+R was in order. This involved taking the shuttle bus to Curry Village for a hot shower; multiple trips to the deli;

Looking down at the author topping out from Salathé Wall

general loafing around the campsite listening to the squawking of the Stellar's Jays and engaging in idle banter with fellow climbers. A cool, refreshing dip in the Merced River was another diversion; head kept above the water in order to avoid ingesting the dreaded Giardia protozoa. However, there is a limit as to how much pizza and ice cream a man can eat and after a few more outings on routes in the Serenity Crack area our thoughts were once again turning to greater things. From the summit of Half Dome a sculpted feature had really caught the eye. This was the impressive south face of Mount Watkins, a remote big wall in the upper reaches of the Tenaya Canyon. We didn't feel quite ready for the rigours of El Cap, but figured that Watkins would be a realistic step up from Half Dome.

The walk-in was both long and arduous, followed by a lot of fourth-class scrambling and occasional pitches that brought us up through trees to the base of the climb proper. This was first pioneered by Harding, Chouinard and Pratt in 1964 – a five-day epic in July heat. Their twenty-pitch route initially takes a circuitous line up, down and across to the commodious ledge of the Sheraton Watkins. This was too low down on the face for us for an overnight stop so we continued on steeply to the upper reaches of the wall and a constricted bivvy. We topped-out in good time the next day and started the long haul back to the roadhead, feeling reasonably pleased with ourselves. We had managed a pitch of A3 and even placed a Rurp (a Frost/Chouinard invention; a Realized Ultimate Reality Piton).

Although more low-level cragging kept us busy (Freewheelin', Quicksilver, Central Pillar of Frenzy and Mr Natural all being highlights), the route we both really wanted to do was The Nose on El Capitan. We felt ready for it. We were by now well versed in the art of basic aid-climbing and had also learnt some of the tricks of the trade, such as taping up properly and using tincture of benzoine to harden the fingertips. We went down to have a look at the start of The Nose and were astonished to find a line of haul bags neatly stacked at the base of the route. This was an elaborate queuing system and people were obviously prepared to wait for days in order to get on to the climb. We were bitterly disappointed, but as luck would have it, I had a copy of the Salathé Wall topo with me and although this route takes an opposing line up a different line; it starts just 30 metres away from The Nose. We walked along to check it out. No one on it — and no haul bags. It was a change of plan but logistically no different – requiring the same amount of food and water (two litres per person per day) and equipment: three sets of wires, two sets of cams, twenty quick-draws and numerous slings and karabiners. Both of these routes would go peg-free.

So, the next morning, bright and early, we caught a ride along to El Cap bridge and staggered up through the trees carrying supplies for three days and all the climbing gear. Ten pitches of superb climbing (often done in its own right as Freeblast) took us to the Mammoth Terraces and an abseil down to a comfortable night on the Heart Ledges.

The climbing was so good – mainly free, with the odd section of aid, often bolted – that it seemed a shame only to be climbing every other pitch. When seconding it was a case of jumaring (or jugging as the Americans call it) while cleaning the pitch and imagining what it would have been like to climb it. The next day involved some technically

Jonathan Prestn

Getting ready for a narrow ledge bivvy: Long Ledge on Salathé Wall

easier climbing but a lot of scary chimneying and off-width climbing including the 9-metre horizontal bomb bay of The Ear. An A2 pitch then brought us to The Alcove beneath another chimney and El Cap Spire – home for the night. We even had time to fix the next pitch before settling down to eat and rehydrate. The view was stupendous; the valley spread out before us; the huge ponderosa pine, incense cedar and giant sequoia trees looking like matchsticks way, way below. The Spire is, in fact, a free-standing pinnacle, worryingly detached on all sides from the main wall. I had a solid night's sleep however and felt in fine form the next day as sustained climbing took us up to The Roof – a 6-metre tiered overhang giving access to the 60-metre overhanging headwall which had been looming ominously above us for most of the way up. The headwall provided an exhilarating climax to the day, leapfrogging friends up the single crackline splitting the otherwise blank granite. We eventually flopped, exhausted, on to the totally inappropriately named Long Ledge.

It may have been just long enough to lie down on, but was so narrow that if you were to roll the wrong way you would be dangling in your harness nearly 900 metres

Jonathan aiding up a
steep leaning wall on
The Nose

above the void. The next day saw us finishing off the final three pitches to complete a memorable thirty-five-pitch route that many consider to be 'the finest rock climb in the world'.

Our time in Yosemite was coming to an end. We had had a fantastic spell, both in terms of the climbing and the weather, with barely a hint of a light shower throughout. I anticipated a few more days at Glacier Point Apron and the Cookie Cliff before we went our separate ways; Aqil to San Francisco and home, me to Colorado to visit an old Sheffield University pal completing his PhD in Boulder. But Aqil is made of sterner stuff and although time was a little tight, when the subject of The Nose came up we both began to wonder if there might just be a chance…. We hurried along to the base of the route – not a haul bag in sight. Frantic packing ensued: food and water for three or four days; bivvy gear; rack; ropes – we knew the routine by now.

Early the next morning we found two Spaniards already on the route and although we waited for them to get a few pitches up we soon overtook them and progressed up the Stoveleg Cracks – so called after the pegs that Bill Feuerer (The Dolt) made from the iron legs of a stove. We made it to Dolt Tower that night. No sign of the Spanish, who must have abseiled off.

The following day began in a bizarre fashion – a portent of what was to come … I awoke to see what I thought was a large rock hurtling towards us. Instinctively, I cowered into the rock face only to hear a 'wumph' as the BASE jumper's parachute opened. He glided down to the valley floor, no doubt to be picked up by friends and whisked away before the park rangers appeared. We continued on our way up; some reasonably straightforward ground to El Cap Tower. There was no one above or below us on the route at this point. Suddenly I heard a voice calling out 'Come any closer and you'll be ——— shot'. I stopped. Nothing happened. I moved on a little further. There it was again, more insistent this time: 'Come any closer and you'll be ——— shot'. Not wanting to get my head blown off by some nutter with a gun, I ground to a halt and waited. What happened next can only be described as surreal. Captain James T. Kirk of the *Starship Enterprise* appeared from around a corner, in full eighty-fifth century get-up (this was star date 8451.1 after all). In fact it was well-known American climber Dale Bard, doubling for

William Shatner enacting a scene from the opening sequence of the movie *Star Trek V The Final Frontier* in which Kirk, while ~~rock climbing~~ in Yosemite tries to solo The Nose only to fall off and be caught in mid-air by Spock whizzing to the rescue in a pair of jet boots. Massive ~~telephoto lens cameras were filming~~ him as he ostensibly soloed Boot Flake in the early morning light. He was actually being belayed by another old Yosemite hand, Werner Brown. They had jumared up fixed ropes in the dark: 'We prefer to commute', they said. We stayed out of shot while they finished their filming.

Afterwards they came over to chat and thank us for waiting. 'Hey man, what did you guys do in your previous lives to get a clear run at The Nose like this?' Dale drawled. There was no way I could possibly answer this so I shrugged, took my leave and continued on up. Pitch after classic pitch followed; the Texas Flake, Boot Flake; the King Swing, involving a huge pendulum; the Great Roof; the colour of the rock changing from off-white to brown to grey as we gained height. Bivvy sites at Camp 5 or even Camp 6 beckoned. At last, elated and worn out, we collapsed on to a ledge for what we hoped would be our last night out on a big wall for a while.

Dale Bard (as Captain Kirk) and Werner Brown on El Cap Tower

Jonathan Preston

The next day was hot, very hot and, despite a strong wind, we fried. It was hard going all the way to the top. This is where Warren Harding bolted through the night on the first ascent in 1958 (the final push after forty-five days of effort spread out over eighteen months; 675 pegs and 125 bolts placed in total). We were glad to finish by nightfall and settled down for one last bivvy, at the top of El Cap. It was a fitting end to a great four weeks. Dusk enveloped the valley, creating a mystical aura (though you could almost hear the beer being poured in Yosemite Lodge). Car lights twinkled silently on the distant freeway.

We were down in good time the following day and the morning after that I saw Aqil off on the early bus. Back at Sunnyside I was awoken by someone shaking the tent. It was a friend from Outward Bound Loch Eil, looking for a climbing partner. I made my excuses, saying that I felt a bit tired. 'A bit tired? What have you been up to?' I reeled off a list of routes. 'Ah, okay. In that case I can see that you might be a bit tired.' With that he left and I rolled over and went back to sleep.

El Capitan

A TRIP DOWN MEMORY LANE

Rob Collister

'Only on a wave of memory that ebbs and flows capriciously can I recapture … the impulses and emotions of those days' (Dorothy Pilley, *Climbing Days*).

In the summer of 1977 I had only recently qualified as a guide, having worked as an aspirant for Dougal Haston in Leysin the previous year. I was in full-time employment for the first time after several years of freedom as a climbing bum, and relieved to discover that the generous holidays of an LEA centre meant that I could still go to the Himalaya for a month.

I had also not long been a father and I have to admit that coming home subsequently to find my son and heir did not recognize me gave me considerable food for thought.

The middle of Zanskar was truly the back of beyond in the mid-1970s, yet this fascinating landscape lent itself to follow-your-nose exploring and mountain climbing, with much opportunity for new-routing and new peak-bagging. In this environment, however, the decisions made by you and your climbing companions were crucial, as Rob Collister discovered.

Be that as it may, I arranged to meet Geoff Cohen and Des Rubens in Srinagar towards the end of July. It was only on arrival in that city that I realized we had not agreed a time or place for a rendezvous. It was purely by chance that, walking over a bridge in the middle of town, I saw a dead cow, legs in the air, floating downstream. I paused to watch it long enough to catch the sound of a distinctly Scottish accent issuing from a nearby houseboat. Moments later, with some relief, I was reunited with the rest of the Scottish Zanskar Expedition. Two more even-tempered and good-natured companions one could not hope to find. Whether they would say the same about me is another matter, but I do not recall a single cross word or argument the entire trip. Geoff and I had been climbing together in Scotland, the Alps, and the Himalaya for the previous ten years. Des, I had met in Gilgit two years earlier, though we had not yet climbed together.

The pair of them had just spent a damp couple of weeks successfully climbing a peak of 5,800 metres, despite the monsoon, in the beautiful Wadwan Valley in Kashmir. Our choice of Zanskar for the second phase of their trip was based, largely, on the belief that its climate would be unaffected by the monsoon. In this we were to be disappointed, for while Zanskar as a whole might receive only around 8 centimetres of rain a year, the mountains straddling the watershed with Kishtwar

Water meadows in the Suru valley, which was followed on the walk in from Kargil to the Pensi La

Rock walls overlooking the Suru valley, Des Rubens in the foreground

Rob Collister

attract a great deal of orographic cloud and significant snowfall in the summer months. The other reason for our choice of venue, however, was simply the desire to explore, rather than climb a specific peak. This meant we could do without the expense of an official permit and a liaison officer; and while many expeditions had been to the west side of the Kishtwar Himal, the east side was *terra incognita* from a climbing point of view.

Muleteers crossing a river on the way to Padam

Like most Himalayan journeys this one started in a bus, a vehicle built for half the number of passengers it actually carried, and with seats designed for passengers significantly shorter than us. It took us from the forests and meadows of Kashmir over the Zoji La into a dry, arid Tibetan landscape, reaching the little town of Kargil as the sun set. A fortuitous meeting with the local bank manager led to a comfortable night in sleeping bags on the roof of his house. The morning found us clambering into the back of an open-topped truck which we thought we were sharing with sacks of rice, a goat and some chickens, until the engine started and we were joined by twenty other passengers. Three hours and some 50 kilometres later we reached the village of Panikar, the end of the driveable road. Here, in due course, we were joined by Hassan, an impassive ponyman with two mares, each accompanied by a foal, who had agreed to carry our bags for the four-day journey to the top of the Pensi La.

As so often happened, the distance travelled each day seemed remarkably short to sahibs impatient to reach the mountains. But the mares needed to suckle their foals at regular intervals and Hassan liked to spend his afternoons helping other ponymen shoe their animals. This process was a far cry from the quiet skill of a farrier in Europe. Instead, it was a social event relying heavily on the presence of

Rob Collister

A Zanskari wedding
party

excitable onlookers to lasso, wrestle to the ground and sit on each struggling beast, while nails were driven into its hooves. It was a sport much enjoyed by everyone but the horse.

There was much else to wonder at and enjoy on the walk-in. The dry, unpolluted air made for an extraordinary purity and clarity in the light, especially at each end of the day when the sun was low. There were fabled blue poppies, somehow surviving the fierce heat in the shade of undercut boulders. There were views of Nun and Kun, the twin 7,000-metre peaks of this region, and glimpses of rock walls reminiscent of Piz Badile. Above all, there were people, mostly Buddhist, in undyed, homespun woollen garments even in the height of summer, the women wearing colourful coral and turquoise jewellery and elaborate leather head-dresses.

There was the polite curiosity of the child monks who visited us one afternoon from Kingdom Gompa, their hill-top monastery, and the touching assumption of other children, playing with our ice axes, that they must be a form of plough. It felt a magical place, little touched by the twentieth century, quite unlike anywhere we had been before.

On the summit of the Pensi La, in a valedictory gesture, Hassan insisted on lighting a cow-dung fire to brew up a last cup of tea before he headed home. To reciprocate we cracked open our hill-food to offer him a Ritz biscuit. For the previous three days, emulating Shipton and Tilman, we had been living on *tsampa*.

This is flour made from roasted barley which needs only the addition of hot water to be edible, rather like couscous. With little in the way of vegetables or spices to enliven it, the *tsampa* had been heavy going and we were not sorry to move on up our mountain railing. Another urgent incentive to start eating was the weight of our packs. As we made a demanding traverse from the pass on to the dry ice of the Durung Drung Glacier, we were bowed under loads of at least 35 kilograms, even though we had done everything to reduce weight. The three of us were sharing a lightweight two-man tent; we had just the one 9 mm rope between us: hardware was restricted to a few nuts and pegs and some unsophisticated ice screws, and we did not have harnesses, improvising with tape slings for glacier travel and abseils. But we had food and fuel for three weeks and there is a limit to how little food you can survive on in the mountains. We were verging on the skeletal as it was when, much later, we finally reached the fleshpots of Padam.

As we bade farewell to Hassan and his little posse, I was suddenly aware that no one else in the whole world knew exactly where we were or where we were going; and Hassan, shaking his head mournfully, clearly believed we would never be seen again. We were not very sure ourselves where we were going. It was only a week or two before leaving the UK that I had been sent a Japanese sketch map that included the east side of the Kishtwar Himal, and it was only in Srinagar that we had decided to make for the Pensi La and the Durung Drung Glacier. There was a powerful sense of venturing into the unknown. Zanskar itself had only been opened to westerners two years earlier, for the first time since Partition, and we knew of no climbing at all in the region south of Nun Kun. It required a level of commitment, which we took for granted, but which is all but impossible today, when pressure from clients or loved ones obliges us to carry a satellite phone or radio or, at the very least, an emergency beacon, when venturing into the wild. I remember being excited rather than disturbed by the prospect of being so totally out on a limb. Should anything go wrong we would be very much on our own.

In the event, it did not take long for *something* to go wrong. A few hours' walk up the Durung Drung, where the dry glacier became snow covered, we cached some of our food by a prominent boulder to lighten our loads. Soon afterwards, we entered a crevasse zone and roped-up. After skirting a number of holes and cautiously crossing others I found myself confronted by an area where, despite probing, the edge of the crevasse was not obvious, nor even the direction in which it was running.

'Watch me here', I called out to Des, turning round and giving him, I thought, a moment in which to tighten up the rope. Then I took a step forward and found myself falling through space. Instead of the rope going taut, I fell about 6 metres and landed on my back with a splash in a pool of water. I did not appreciate the soaking at the time but the water almost certainly saved me from injury. I shouted but there was no reply, the sound of my voice swallowed up by glistening, dimpled walls of vertical ice. The only light came from the ragged hole I had made in the snow bridge above. It was dark, cold and wet and I was beginning to shiver. No one came to the edge and, suddenly, I felt very much alone. With numb fingers, I attached prusik loops to the rope and set about climbing up it. Luckily, I had spent the previous summer teaching clients this very skill. Ten minutes later I emerged, panting, to find Geoff and Des simply sitting on their rucksacks. Exhausted by heat and altitude they seemed totally uninterested in my plight.

Viewpoint Peak seen in the early morning from the Durung Drung glacier, climbed by the right-hand skyline

Remonstration about the slack in the rope elicited no response. Grumpily, and rather nervously now, I moved on to reach a place safe enough to camp, though still surrounded by crevasses. My priority was to dry my clothes while the sun was still high in the sky. To this day, I do not know quite why I was allowed to fall so far. Recently, climbing with Geoff in the Alps, I asked him about it, to discover that he has no recollection of the event whatsoever. On the other hand, I am reassured that my own vivid memory is not pure fabrication (and memory is known to play strange tricks sometimes) by a photo showing me standing outside the tent clad only in T-shirt, underpants and a pair of bright red overboots – the sum total of my spare clothing. It was only when I put on those overboots that I discovered, carefully written around the inside, the words 'Made with love in the Tyn y Waen Himalayan Equipment Works'. That made my heart lurch; though on this occasion I was probably missing Netti more than she was missing me. She spent one of the best summers on record driving around the Highlands from farm to farm, baby on the back seat, working as a locum for the vet in Fort William.

In all events, the next day Geoff languished in the tent, nursing a sore head, while Des and I attempted the steep ice face of a small peak overlooking our camp. Nowadays, a click of the mouse brings up numerous images of the Durung Drung Glacier taken by axolotl and mountain bikers crossing the Pensi La; on some of them this peak is visible on the true left bank, though much of the face is now rock. A promising start, scrunching over crisp, well-frozen snow, was brought to an abrupt halt by a huge uncrossable bergschrund, invisible from below, running the width of the face. Tails between our legs, we were back at camp by midday.

We fared better the following morning. Cloud lifted as we prepared and we made straight for the obvious col at the foot of the west ridge. This required axes, crampons and the rope for some awkward rock steps and a couple of abseils. On one side of the ridge the orange granitic rock was warm to the touch; on the other the cracks were full of ice and Dachstein mitts were swiftly pulled back on. By noon we were on top, enjoying spectacular views westward to the magnificent Sickle Moon, at 6,570 metres the dominant peak of the Kishtwar Himal, and north towards Nun Kun, savouring that special frisson that comes with knowing that, almost certainly, no one had ever been there before. With remarkable lack of imagination, we called it Viewpoint Peak, but it did reveal a feasible approach to another, higher peak, on the same watershed ridge. The sketch map showed it to be Pt 6560 and although it did not look as high as that, relative to Sickle Moon, it was an attractive objective.

Reaching it the next day was not straightforward. From the col of Viewpoint, carrying tent, food and fuel for five days, we down-climbed through steep snow, pitching with ice screw belays when it turned to ice, to reach a snow basin at the head of the Prul Glacier. Crossing this basin, just above a huge icefall, we set off up a rock spur which gave nearly 300 metres of wonderfully enjoyable rock-climbing, with plentiful holds on steep but solid granite.

The setting was as wild and remote as one could wish for, the gaping crevasses and fang-like pinnacles of the icefall snapping at our heels. At its top, the spur petered out into a snow slope too soggy and full of water under the afternoon sun to risk venturing on. Instead, we used our axes as mattocks to level an unpromising bank of shale into a platform. While pitching the tent, the bottom section of one of the poles dropped off and went tinkling forever down a nasty couloir flanking the spur. For the remainder of the trip that corner of the tent had to be propped up on a rock or a rucksack.

The next four days were frustrating. The weather was never really bad, but it snowed lightly, on and off, much of the time and the cloud would lift briefly, only to fall again when we tried to move up.

Geoff and Des climbing up the rock spur with the Prul Glacier below

Rob Collister

Geoff Cohen at the bivvy camp on Delusion Peak in a brief clearing of the weather

Leaving the top of the rock spur: the snout of the Prul Glacier and the Kiar Nullah valley far below

Rob Collister

After two days we decided to move camp to a safer and more comfortable site at the bottom of the spur. Geoff's report mentions an abseil down the wrong side of the spur which consumed a few hours. Since I have no memory of the incident, it seems fair to assume that I was responsible for this route-finding *faux pas*. On the fourth day, leaving Des in the tent feeling poorly, Geoff and I crossed back over to the Durung Drung, labouring through new snow, to fetch more food from the cache.

Finally, we awoke to a morning with pockets of blue sky and rapidly clearing mist below us. Leaving the tent behind, but carrying bivvy gear, we set off for the summit.

Back up the rock spur (not so pleasant plastered with snow), up the slopes above and into more mixed terrain of rock and ice, we gained height steadily to reach an upper cwm where we had originally hoped to camp. Above, a broad couloir of steep but firm, kickable *névé* brought us to the summit ridge. Almost simultaneously, the mist rolled in, the wind rose and the temperature plummeted. In a matter of minutes ice was forming on eyebrows and beards and we had progressed hurriedly from T-shirts to wearing everything we possessed. There was nowhere flat enough to call a bivvy site so we pressed on along a knife-edge of a ridge, snow and rock alternating, towards the feature we had called from afar the grand gendarme.

This called for some pitched climbing and on the far side of it, on a vague levelling, we stopped for the night. It was not a comfortable bivouac. Snow fell, light but persistent, most of the night, pressing the cold, clammy nylon of the Zdarsky sack against our faces and making it difficult to breathe. We all awoke from an uneasy doze with headaches.

Packing up was a stiff, cautious affair as we crammed wet sleeping bags into our sacks and struggled to put on frozen boots, terrified of dropping one. As we did so,

Packing up and putting on crampons after the first bivouac on the crest of the summit ridge

Rob Collister

Moving together on the summit ridge

the clouds parted to reveal Sickle Moon and a snow-smothered array of other, nameless, peaks. The clearing was brief but it was exhilarating while it lasted, making us acutely aware of the drops beneath us, a couple of hundred metres on one side, many more on the other. Then the mist rolled in again. We roped-up for a final steep step and, in no time, it seemed, we were on top. It was something of an anticlimax. There was nothing to be seen and nothing to be done except begin the descent.

My memory of the next couple of days is even hazier than usual, for a very good reason. Geoff and Des were wearing helmets, heavy, bulky, fibreglass things. In my determination to save weight, I had opted to leave mine at home. Predictably, as we pulled the rope down after the first abseil, it was on to my head that a boulder the size of a football landed, fair and square. I fell to my knees, feeling extremely groggy and almost certainly concussed. I could still put one foot in front of the other but I was in no state to think for myself or make decisions. The others shepherded me carefully down, pitching most of the way. We bivvied a second time just below the ridge and it took the whole of the next day to get back to the tent.

I remember next to nothing of that descent apart from feelings of embarrassment at my stupidity, and relief that I was in such capable hands. We were all glad, I think, to spend a day brewing up and recuperating while my head cleared. However, when it was still cloudy and snowing intermittently the morning after, we decided to call it a day. We still had some food left but the idea of further exploration was no longer appealing. Travelling through the land of Zanskar and on to Lahul and Kulu seemed much more attractive (and, in the event, did not disappoint).

Rob Collister

Setting out for
the summit

We called that second summit Delu-sion Peak, based on the fact that it was clearly nowhere near the height shown on the map – probably more like 6,000 metres than 6,560 metres. However, we did not actually feel deluded in the slightest. Since our first sight of it from Viewpoint we had had only tantalizing glimpses of the mountain, but it had been a demanding climb – serious rather than technically difficult, like one of the classic Zermatt ridges – and a peak to be proud of. We felt both pleased with ourselves for persisting, and privileged to have been allowed to climb it and return in one piece. It was time to go.

Rob Collister

Geoff brewing up at the first bivvy site

DIRAN

Adrian Burgess

One summer, with the arrival of a particular birthday, Adrian Burgess was determined not to let a mere number get to him – not only by doing battle with an alpine-style route on a Karakoram peak but also within a few weeks on returning to the USA be fighting fit to get back on the rock and sport climbing as hard a climb as he'd ever done, thus proving that, at fifty, one is not yet over the hill …

'Aid … we need to make a decision pretty soon,' Rob panted as he arrived at my stance on the 45-degree slope.

'It's okay, man. I've already made it. We'll turn around when we reach the top!'

We'd been climbing for nine hours and had another one to go, although we didn't know that at the time. The summit of Diran looked very close. This snowy and beautiful peak stands at 7,266 metres above the Hunza Valley in northern Pakistan.

I'd first seen photos of the mountain in the book *Himalaya Alpine-Style* by Andy Fanshawe. It had seemed that it would provide an enjoyable and safe acclimatization prior to attempting Nanga Parbat later in the season. However, when we arrived at the high, green pastures at around 3,650 metres I hardly recognized it as the snow plod it was supposed to be. Seracs and avalanche debris were everywhere. The whole north side of the mountain looked more like the Brenva Face of Mont Blanc – and I'd run a few gauntlets there.

We'd settled into watching and studying the life of the mountain from the comfortable grassy meadows at the base while brewing beer for our evening's pleasure. The route was obviously going to weave through masses of ice cliffs further to the west of the summit and then follow a ridgeline eastward for a long way to the little-climbed summit. Any direct route would clearly be suicidal as we could hear avalanches tearing down all over the place.

We were six climbers climbing as three separate ropes. My partner was Rob Ziegler, a 34-year-old American from Salt Lake City. Strongly built and fit as a butcher's dog, he'd climbed twice before in the Karakoram. Stevie and Laurence were a man-wife team and Laurence's biceps were as thick as my thighs. Then there were Chris and Jim, who had normal day jobs but enjoyed mountain vacations in distant lands.

There was a small snow dome at 4,560-metres where we could open up our lungs a bit, but nothing much to acclimatize on prior to our alpine-style ascent so, after

The north face and west ridge of Diran Peak

about a week when the weather looked good, we just set off. I'd told Rob that I'd rather gasp my way up the peak in good weather without acclimatization than try it in a storm when I was fitter.

We left our small snow platform on the edge of the glacier at 1 a.m. and waded up deep snow in the small pools of light cast by our headlamps. Suddenly the snow improved and we made better progress until, out of the gloom, reared an ugly 1.5-metre crown left by a slab avalanche. We dodged rightward out of its way, very aware that we could easily trigger another one. As darkness turned to grey we could see the horror show of a glacial bowling alley directly above us and scurried rightward beneath more ice cliffs.

'This is not at all what I'd hoped for'; I shook my head in disbelief. Almost running across hard slab towards a steep cliff I felt like a spider with a curled newspaper hovering above my head. Once up that steep bit, which I'd borrowed Rob's axe to climb, we were a bit safer, but the heat of the morning was changing the snow and old avalanche debris was everywhere.

'Let's find somewhere to stop if we can, because it's getting a bit dangerous around here.' We dumped our

Aid and Rob at base camp

sacks and began zigzagging around trying to find a safe place to spend the day. There were many small eyebrow seracs but nothing good or safe. Then, looking down, I spotted a big platform protected by a huge crevasse. It was actually the top of another serac which was calving away from the main face.

'If that decides to topple today then that's really bad juju', Rob surmised.

I preferred not to think about juju at all. It had to be one of the safest places on the lower flank of the face. After melting snow and drinking as much as we could we slept all day – luxury.

At 1 a.m. we were off again, moving around in the small pools of light offered by our headlamps. I tried to recall what I'd seen the day before so as to find a way around all the ice cliffs which loomed above us like the huge, dark bows of so many ships. First to the left, then right again. We were climbing together with a short rope, but it never got hard enough to have to belay. After three hours it started to get light just as we reached a large, snowy ledge which disappeared around to the right. Great – we could finally get out of the way of all the crumbling ice. Rob had set off up a 50-degree slope with me at his heels when I suddenly had a horrible sensation of climbing on a drum-skin.

'Rob. Stop. I think we're on wind slab because I can feel every step you make.' Descending slowly and being careful to step into the existing footholds, we arrived back at the ledge.

'Hell. We get out from under all the falling crap and then on to this.' I led off further right and up a steep wall which gradually eased in angle, and ran out all the rope.

'Okay, Rob. This is much safer.' Another few rope lengths and at 6 a.m. we climbed out on to a shallow col with a great campsite sheltered from the wind.

The small blue tent was dwarfed by all the great mountain scenery but we were thirsty and so set about melting water and preparing for another day in the tent. We thought we should be at around 6,100 metres but later figured out that we were only at 5,500 metres. That meant a very long final day and so it was just as well we didn't know. I remember thinking it was a long way down to the meadows and the coloured dots that were our tents.

'Rob, do you have a paper and something to write with?'

'Yes – why?'

'I want to write down a topo of our route today because if we fry our brains going to the top I won't be able to remember how to get back down.' That drew a curious look from my partner as he handed over the paper. 'Just while it's fresh in my mind. That's all.'

There's something very exhilarating, but also a bit scary, about being far out of reach of any help on a big mountain. Two people all alone. I'd felt that when on Dhaulagiri with my brother so many years before. You just can't let it get to you, though you can't ignore it. It's better to try to bask in it.

We left the tent and all the gear except for water and food bars, plus a spare pair of dark glasses. It was 1.45 a.m. The weather was clear. I had on my down suit. We moved together with a short rope. There were some crevasses and all was very dark. As we plodded on I couldn't help but reflect on how often I'd been up at this unearthly hour, busting a trail through snow. We traversed two small rises in the ridge and we weren't gaining much height. Two hours later we arrived at another

prominent col. There wasn't much to see but I think previous expeditions had arrived at this point from down below. The mountain had changed since, and it was much more dangerous now.

The world of seracs

I begin climbing, crab-like, slowly up the slope above. The snow was quite wind-scoured and up above, through the half-light, I could see a bright yellow object. 'Curious,' I thought. As we drew closer I realized I was looking at the body of a young man. He was curled in a foetal position and frozen to the slope. It was quite surreal as I stepped past him. I never said a word to Rob and neither he to me – the implications of our isolation were too obvious.

A broad ridge loomed ahead as we zigzagged up firm snow towards a band of seracs blocking the way. Out to our left the slope turned golden and the cliffs more menacing. I took a quick look up to the right and decided the snow was too loose and steep and I didn't fancy it at all.

This meant the only other way was to traverse beneath the cliffs and head for a weakness in the barrier above. We'd have to move quickly; ice could fall at any time. After three rope-lengths of looking over my shoulder we began to ascend. It was hard, perfect snow at 50 degrees, but the serac above looked really chossy and unstable. My lungs were bursting as I shouted down to Rob for us to climb together. Our escape came in the form of a 20-metre crack in the ice and I was back in the shade on the west side of the ridge.

'I'm not sure I want to go back down that way when the sun's been on it for a while,' I said to Rob. He nodded in agreement and took over the lead. We climbed together with a short rope along the ridge, which then merged into the final head-wall at the point where a lone rock tower stood sentinel-like. It was the only rock we had seen on the whole climb so far. The slope above was about 45 degrees and required exhausting step-kicking into various depths of snowy slab. Rob began to

On the last day,
Rakaposhi in the
background

run the rope out until he felt tired and then brought me up to him. Off he'd go again and we'd repeat it for around five pitches, then I'd take my turn. It was real leg-burning work and I noticed the pitches were becoming shorter as we struggled to keep going.

About that time Rob voiced his doubts about whether we'd make it. I didn't want to give it all up when we'd worked so hard. The sky was a clear blue, though a chilling wind howled from the right and I had my down hood held up in place by ski goggles. Ever so slowly I crept up to the left, passing an icy bulge on my right. The trick was to go really slowly but not to stop. My heart hammered in my chest and my legs felt heavy and almost wooden. Rob rejoined me and, without a word, I headed off to the highest point I could see and hoped it was the summit. It wasn't – there was another one above – but the slope did ease off a bit, although it stretched out in front of me, taunting and challenging me to give it all up.

'It can't keep going on like this,' I told myself. 'It has to finish soon.'

Rob's face looked quite gaunt as he joined me. I wondered what I must look like. I turned and began again. Then I could see that the summit was not the traditional pointed affair at all, but was big and flat. The snow was striated from the wind. I went to what I thought was the highest point and stopped and waved wearily back at Rob. When he joined me we hugged with strangled laughs. It was exactly noon.

The trouble with big, flat summits is that you cannot stand looking down at base camp and gloat on how far up you've climbed. There were big mountains off in the distance but we'd have to begin the descent before we could really sense any height.

As we plunged down the headwall Rob went first until the rope ran out and then I joined him. There were fifteen full pitches before we got back to the rock; and it had seemed a long way going up! Next, we avoided the dangerous serac traverse by going down the steep, crappy snow. It felt so much easier going down. Off came the rope and down we continued. At 4 p.m. I crawled into our tent and prepared a drink for us as Rob threw down his axe with a long exhalation of air: 'That was one long day!'

The next day we left at 4 a.m., first light. Five hours later we walked into base camp but not without having had a couple of scary close encounters with wet snow slides. One was huge: a big block of ice came off a cliff and hit the slope 100 metres to our right. This precipitated the biggest wet snow slide I've ever seen. A kilometre and a half down the slope it did begin to slow as the angle eased, but still it moved on slowly. The front of it must have been about 12 metres high and as heavy as concrete.

Fast-forward two months and, after leaving Nanga Parbat and been driven away by heavy stone fall, I arrived back in the USA on 8 September 2011. In two weeks' time, I would turn fifty. I am not one for having crises, but that is a big number. I hadn't rock-climbed all summer and was looking forward to a peaceful autumn on steep rock. I decided to set myself a challenge, I knew I couldn't achieve it by my birthday so my deadline was the end of September. I would climb the hardest route I had ever done to that time – I would red-point a 5.12a (French 7b).

Half an hour away from Salt Lake City is a quiet, shady canyon – American Fork Canyon. Here, there are multiple steep limestone cliffs famous for their steep-pocketed climbs. I began slowly, building up muscle endurance that I'd lost during my time in Pakistan. They were steep, gymnastic routes protected by bolts and required powerful, dynamic moves. I fell; I hung; I top-roped.

The last day of September arrived and I still hadn't quite managed to achieve my goal. A number of friends and I arrived at the base of a gently overhanging buttress. There were a couple of 5.11s to warm-up on and then the big moment arrived. I would try a route called Gordon's Route.

It began up a steep little corner to a sharp roof. I couldn't waste any energy because the next moves were big and powerful. I gripped a small undercut hold with my right hand, twisted my left hip into the rock and launched out leftward, around the roof to a big jug at full reach. I got it first time. My body was then horizontal. Next, I allowed my feet to come off the rock and pendulum leftward back into contact with the rock and a small flat hold. I was breathing heavily as I quickly moved one hand at a time up a flake then stood up on a small ledge. This was the only real rest on the climb and I intended to use it to get my heart-rate back down. I shook the blood back into one arm at a time while retaining a good hold with the other. I began to get to a point of diminishing returns and prepared to climb up a series of pockets in the overhanging wall. It was imperative that I kept one hip or another into the rock as it steepened and bulged above my head. It began with one long reach with feet side-stepping. I had learnt that, to maximize reach, I had to drop my head on to the opposite shoulder and that meant I couldn't see the hold I was going for. Fingers curled around the edge of another pocket, I pushed with both feet and pushed my hips into the rock while I reached for a two-finger pocket. I stuck it, but barely. My forearms ached and I began to have doubts that I could finish it. I had clipped four bolts since the rest and had one more to go, and then the anchors. I made one more move up to a better hold; shook my right hand to get the pain out of it; set my feet and carefully reached up to clip the bolt. I was at full reach and couldn't keep the body tension for long. The 'biner went in and I quickly clipped the rope. A quick dab of chalk for my hand and I reached for a pinch. I then set my feet beneath me and, with one last push in and up with the hips, I reached the final good handhold – except that it didn't feel that good. I was staring at the chains hanging right there. My body ached. I re-adjusted my position, grabbed a quick-draw, made the clip. Got the rope in and fell off.

When one is both an alpinist and a sport climber it's very important to choose carefully where to fall!

MY LAST THREE

Alan Hinkes, OBE

The great 8,000-metre peaks of the Himalaya and Karakoram represent a particular extreme of the Earth's landscape, both to climbers and to the general public alike; they are the highest points of altitude the human body can experience whilst the feet are still on the ground, while also enduring the associated extremes of lack of oxygen and cold. That there are only fourteen of these peaks has suggested a challenge that has only been achieved by a few, and only within the last thirty years.

Here, Alan Hinkes describes the pressures and challenges of surviving extreme altitude mountaineering in attaining his last three 8,000-metre summits.

I shuffled tentatively across the snow bridge that spanned the deep, dark crevasse, although all my senses were warning me that it would collapse. It gave way and I frantically threw myself forward at the steel-hard ice of the crevasse wall. Hearing a metallic crack, I thought my ice axe pick had snapped, then I felt the pain and realized I had broken my arm. Still, I had another arm and two legs, and had avoided falling to my death in the yawning hole. I felt lucky, pulled myself together and retreated painfully and slowly down to base camp. This incident was at 6,800 metres on the slopes of Kangchenjunga which, at 8,586 metres, is the world's third-highest mountain; I was climbing alone and descending after making a solo summit attempt. Kangch would have to wait for another day.

Climbing big mountains in the Himalaya is dangerous; there is no point in pretending otherwise. All the usual objective dangers of avalanche, rockfall and frostbite from the cold and bad weather are exacerbated and increased at these greater altitudes. However, I do not have a death wish! Climbing enhances my life and I climb to live, not to die. Staying alive has always been important to me. No mountain is worth a life – coming back is a success and the summit is only a bonus. Also, I do not think any mountain is worth a digit and I have managed to keep all my fingers and toes, avoiding frostbite on the highest mountains in the world.

Over a period of more than fifteen years I have made twenty-eight expeditions to the fourteen 8,000-metre peaks, pushing up into the 'death zone' many times. For some (good) reason I was willing to risk my life over and over on these highly

dangerous Himalayan and Karakoram giant peaks. Perhaps I like suffering and masochistic challenges, for there were many close shaves and near-death experiences. It might seem like madness to risk my life, but on the first of the biggest peaks it was pure adventure; a *frisson* with danger and possibly a youthful 'it won't happen to me'. Later I felt that I could minimize the risks using my skill, determination, stamina and experience. I was always prepared to back off, never classing a retreat to base camp or abandoning the climb as a failure; I could always return – the mountain was not going anywhere. Yet, after climbing and surviving on several 8,000-metre peaks there must have been a certain amount of cognitive dissonance as I pushed the risk factor to climb all fourteen of them.

I always aspired to the bigger mountains more than pure rock routes. My first 8,000-metre summit was in 1987 on the 8,047-metre Shisha Pangma. I climbed a new route alpine style up the big couloir on the north face. Although tempered by the frostbite and subsequent amputations of my climbing partner's toes, it was a successful start to my campaign. This was a Polish-organized expedition led by the great, legendary Jerzy (Jurek) Kukuczka who also climbed a new route. Whereas it was my first of these giant peaks, it was Jerzy's fourteenth and final one. We had a celebration at base camp for Jurek and his fabulous achievement of being just the second person after Reinhold Messner to climb all of the 8,000-metre peaks. I had no thoughts at that time of climbing all these elusive giants; I just wanted to climb more big mountains. As Ernest Hemingway said, 'There are only three true sports: bull-fighting, motor racing and mountain climbing. The rest are merely games.'

The author on Dhaulagiri summit

Alan Hinkes

Dhaulagiri viewed
across the Kali Gandaki
Valley from high up on
Annapurna

Lhotse south face, a 3,000-metre big wall was my next challenge, with Krzysztof Wielicki. I spent several nights crammed into a tiny bivouac tent with Krzysztof as we pushed the route out. Extremely bad weather stopped us getting to the top; even base camp was wiped out in an avalanche and we were lucky to survive.

None of these experiences put me off. I climbed K2, Everest, and several other of the giants before deciding to go for all fourteen.

In 2002, I headed for Annapurna, at 8,091 metres the tenth-highest and the least climbed of all the fourteen big ones – even though it was the very first of them to be climbed, by the French in 1950. Since then it has developed a reputation as a very dangerous mountain: before my ascent around a hundred people had climbed it, but nearly sixty had been killed. Statistically, I had a 60 per cent chance of getting killed as soon as I left base camp and set foot on the mountain!

To minimize my exposure to the risk of avalanches I made a lightweight, fast two-man ascent of a new route on the right-hand side of the north face. This was steeper and only marginally less avalanche-prone than the original French route up the centre of the face. It was the first British ascent for thirty-two years; the last two Brits on the top were two of my heroes, Don Whillans and Dougal Haston, back in 1970. I took the usual quick summit photo of me holding a picture of my daughter Fiona as the weather closed in. My sense of achievement on the summit was mixed with anxiety about the deteriorating conditions. The descent in often whiteout conditions and with fresh snowfall building up potential avalanches was

Alan Hinkes

scary and mentally taxing. Surprisingly for Annapurna there were no major tragedies, just the usual testing setbacks, such as base camp being flattened by katabatic winds, near misses on the mountain with loose rock and dodgy crevasse bridges and coping with the dangers of extreme altitude and cold.

Dhaulagiri, at 8,167 metres, was my penultimate giant – my thirteenth – but fortunately I am not particularly superstitious. In April 2004, I reached base camp just in time for a ten-day spell of bad weather. There is nothing you can do but wait in conditions like this, when high winds rip over the mountain and snow piles on to the slopes. I tend to listen to the BBC World Service on a short-wave radio, go for short walks around the camp and read. Again, I was planning to attempt a two-man lightweight push on the mountain, this time with Pasang Gelu, a good friend and climbing mate. Pasang lived in Kathmandu, but was originally from a village just below Lukla in the Solo Khumbu region of Nepal. I had known him for several years and when he was not climbing with me he usually made his living as a trek leader or climbing guide. He wanted to get more experience of the giant peaks so he could work with clients on the lucrative Everest climbs. I liked climbing with Pasang; he was easy-going, had a very generous nature and a genuine enthusiasm for the mountains. Tragically, on a later Japanese expedition to Dhaulagiri, Pasang was swept away in an avalanche.

The lower part of the route is often strafed by rocks as if in an artillery barrage as it traverses under a loose, unstable 800-metre-high rock face. I wore a helmet as

Jet stream winds over Dhaulagiri

Looking down from the Dhaulagiri summit ridge, swept bare of snow by jet stream winds – Pasang sets off back down

a futile gesture and protection against small stones. The eerie whiz and whirr of falling stones preys on your mind, wearing down your resilience. Further up, the glacier is very exposed to avalanches breaking off from higher on the mountain. Huge ice cliffs as big as the White Cliffs of Dover loom menacingly over the route, and when one of these seracs calves away it engulfs the whole valley; there would be little chance of escape. Avalanche debris is spread liberally over the glacier, including many ice blocks the size of a minibus. I was scared as I made my way higher on Dhaulagiri and I was aware that several well-known and experienced mountaineers had been killed in this area.

Thankfully, most of the snow was firm and the snow bridges held out over the huge crevasses. We had time to rest for a few hours before a two-day push up steeper icy slopes to the summit. Further up, while climbing brittle, hard, bare ice, we passed the tattered remains of tents on a narrow ledge and I noticed a body wrapped in tent fabric – a sad, lifeless messenger of the danger and perils that faced us getting to the summit and, more importantly, getting back down.

Pasang and I decided to leave our sleeping bags at 6,400 metres so we could move slightly faster with less weight and push on to the final bivouac. We didn't really have much time to miss them in our cramped, high altitude bivvy at 7,500 metres as we squeezed together on a tiny ledge hacked out of the ice. It was bitterly cold and I knew we would freeze to death if we had to spend more than a few hours there.

Most of the prior night was spent melting snow for drinking water before struggling out into the pitch darkness at 3 a.m. It was -25 °C and after an hour of climbing my toes were going numb, breathing was adding load. I contemplated returning to the bivouac. Finding a flat rocky ledge I managed to massage some life back into my toes and feet, which took more than half an hour of painstaking effort. It was now daylight and we were now on the upper ice field, with a thick bulging glacier smeared over the glacier. The slope was hard packed avalanche-prone wind slab with patches of soft snow. My first gut-feeling was that it was extremely unstable and that there was a 50 per cent chance it would crack and slide. I always remind myself, no mountain is worth a life, returning is a success and the summit is only a bonus.

There are times when you have to push the risk level more, so I dug a small inspection trench and reassessed the slope. Somehow I persuaded myself there was only a 10 per cent chance it would slide. I also persuaded Pasang that the slope was safer than first impressions suggested and we climbed on, oddly acceptant of the 10 per cent chance of getting killed.

Around midday we emerged out of a steep couloir on to the bare, rocky summit ridge at 8,100 metres. Jet-stream winds at 200 kilometres per hour had stripped the summit ridge clear of snow, exposing grey-brown bedrock. As if to quash any rising sense of triumph, there was a body laid flat on the rock. I gazed at the well-preserved, still-clothed corpse. He was wearing his crampons and just lying there on his back as if sunbathing or resting and about to get up and climb on. It was certainly a grim, stark reminder of the seriousness of our situation. Just the two of us on the mountain at 8,100 metres; we were alone and no one could help us. The summit was a rocky scramble over barren ground, crampons scraping like fingernails on a school classroom blackboard, to a bleak and unwelcoming final lump of wind-scoured grey-brown rock.

I did not want to linger in this desolate, inhospitable place. I gazed across the Kali Gandaki to Annapurna, where I had stood on top two years earlier, got a quick summit photo and video clip and set off down.

Passing the body again, we descended the couloir to the avalanche-prone summit slopes. The drop to base camp was a dizzying 3,000 metres and the avalanche potential, which I had accepted on the way up, was a 10 per cent chance it might release, heightening my anxiety and fear levels. I was really scared, but there was no choice; we had to continue down. Two hours later, as we reached the bivouac at 7,500 metres, a storm broke; violent wind and snow battered our tiny tent and most of the night was spent clinging to the poles to stop it being blown away.

It took two more harrowing days of effort to struggle down to base camp where we could finally relax with milk, tea, eggs, chips and chapatis.

Dhaulagiri was done; only Kangchenjunga, at 8,586 metres my final giant, was left. The year 2005 was the fiftieth anniversary of the first ascent by a British expedition: in 1955 Joe Brown, George Band, Tony Streather and Norman Hardie got to the top via the south-west face.

My plan was for a two-man, lightweight alpine-style ascent of a new line on the south-west face. My good friend Pasang Gelu was again joining me for this climb; we had climbed well together on Dhaulagiri. Kangch is approached by a twelve-day arduous trek to base camp. In 2005 the mountain was plastered in snow and bad weather prevailed for most of the season. We were holed up in camp for over a month before we could make a summit bid. Spending a month in base camp might be good for acclimatizing, but it can severely debilitate and weaken you, both physically and mentally.

It was nearly the end of May when we finally left camp and we had the mountain to ourselves, just the two of us on this vast peak. In contrast, further west in Nepal, Everest would have perhaps 300 people attempting it. In many ways it was quite a daunting prospect, just Pasang and me against the notorious third-highest mountain in the world. We had a big challenge; our excitement was tempered with a spoonful of trepidation bordering on fear.

Having been on Kangch before (in 2000, when I broke my arm falling into a crevasse), I knew a lot about the route. By 29 May we had struggled and battled our way up to 7,400 metres where we scraped a narrow ledge out of the ice and snow slope for the bivouac tent. This left us with some 1,200 metres to climb to the top, which is a big push. By comparison, on K2 the shoulder is at almost 8,000 metres leaving 600 metres to climb to the top and, from the South Col on Everest, there is only 800 metres to climb to the summit.

On 30 May we had intended to leave at midnight, but the time slipped to 1.30 a.m. because of faffing around in the minuscule bivouac shelter. At first there was some steep climbing over a bergschrund and I fixed some 6 mm cord, which I had found left over from an Indian expedition, as a back-rope. This would help on the descent as climbing down this steep ground when exhausted would be dangerous – although it did slow down our ascent.

Luckily the weather remained stable for most of the day – some wind, some cloud and a temperature about -20 °C; not too bad for a peak of this size.

By now I had resolved that I was going to keep going until dark, which is 7.30 p.m., even though I knew midday would be a more sensible turnaround time. This was to be my last 8,000-metre mountain and I could not bear to think about descending without bagging the summit. I was prepared to accept a higher-than-usual risk and cut down my margin of safety.

The terrain became more mixed; snow, ice and rock, with some tricky steep rock sections. This was real climbing at well over 8,000 metres. In places over steep, vertical rock steps I fixed more short sections of 6 mm cord. This definitely slowed our ascent, but I knew it would be essential for safety.

By late afternoon Pasang had turned back and I was left alone to climb on to the summit. Just below the top was a steep rock wall. I scrambled up this in the dusk and collapsed on a flat spot just below the summit. It was nearly dark and cloud was swirling and boiling around me. I felt anxious, but took a few photos and video clips at arm's length before clambering through the gloom to the very top, a snow mound. One more step, I thought, and I would stride from Nepal into India/Sikkim. Suddenly I was scared; I was shaking like a leaf in the wind and hyperventilating. 'Shit, this is serious,' I thought. The reality of my situation had hit me – I was alone at 8,600 metres in the dark at night in a snowstorm, descending from the third-highest summit in the world. No rescue team, no helicopter, could help me. This was the Death Zone and I could die. I was having a panic attack as my mind faced the reality of the situation. To get down I had to pull myself together and take control. Somehow I did. Life then became so simple – get on with the descent and down to

safety, or die – nothing else mattered. Though I was scared, I was also elated; this was for real and I savoured the reality of the situation. Realistically, I expected to be swept away in an avalanche as it was now snowing heavily, making it even more difficult to find my descent route. Somehow I found an inner strength to carry on, drawing on all my reserves of stamina and experience. It was torture, the -30 °C cold gnawing at my life and freezing my toes and fingers. Eventually I caught up with Pasang, who was descending very slowly, and we continued down to the bivouac at 7,500 metres; it had been an epic, non-stop push for nearly twenty-six hours. We collapsed into the bivvy at 3 a.m. We were spent, dehydrated, withered with cold, but alive.

It took another one and a half days to reach base camp, finally staggering in for tea, eggs, chips and *dhal bhat*. It was the best feeling to be safely back down in base camp; better than the feeling on the summit. Kangchenjunga, my final 8,000-metre peak, was bagged. I had climbed all fourteen of the giant peaks, and now I was free – finished with near-death experiences, free just to enjoy the hills …

Kangchenjunga base camp

HAGSHU; ONE THAT GOT AWAY

John Barry

The fascination of a beautiful peak, in a wild and remote setting, viewed from afar on a previous expedition, is the source of many a subsequent foray into the mountains. Can the peak ever meet expectation? Perhaps this truly depends on what one's expectations are in the first place, as John Barry discovered on his return to Zanskar.

Stories are supposed to have beginnings, middles and an end. So, to the best of my diminishing recall, here's The Beginning.

In nineteen-ninety-something the *Alpine Journal* published a black and white photo by Stephen Venables of a mountain in Zanskar. She was a beauty, and virgin. She was called Hagshu.

I showed the photo to four mates. They, much taken, convened at the pub that same evening for a planning conference and, thirty seconds later, had decided to go; had it all figured; all over bar the shouting. The shouting went on for some time after closing, grew several decibels more vehement and, insofar as any remember, met with rather less accord. As these things do.

They went to climb Hagshu: they never came back. Damndest thing you ever heard of.

We mounted searches and found signatures at the police post at Machail; and later a diary; bits of a tent; a lock of hair; scraps of clothing; a broken campsite – but nothing conclusive and never enough to hazard a narrative, or plausible explanation. But what was sure was that they'd disappeared.

It was on a search that I saw Hagshu for the first time. This is no ordinary hill – it's about the best-looking bit of vertical geography on this planet: Ama Dablam, Alpamayo, Thamserku, Matterhorn; contenders all, but no cigar. Hagshu is the mirror-on-the-wall fairest; and unclimbed by any of a half-dozen possible lines – or was then. What I saw, from a smartish potential base camp, rendered Venables's photo pedestrian. Here it was, now in glorious full-spectrum colour: a vision of savage splendour; a shimmering edifice; a wee stotter. And there and then I thought, maybe even said, 'Gotta have a go'. And by that face – right there, in the middle straight on up the hey diddle diddle. Morbid perhaps, to call the disappearance of mates a beginning, but that's the start of this tale.

So began a pilgrimage; a mini-series of adventures, misadventures, scrapes and

escapes and escapades, attempts, essays, forays, failures and the laps, stnd trips one would credit.

And so, The Middle. The solipsism intrinsic of it was me — an ungrammatical me — with some mates. We had given it several goes; ardent suitors/fantasists/dreamers that we were. Typhus did for us one go. Or typhoid. I forget. And who cares; it was the end of the trip. On another we ran out of gas, or maybe guts — mostly the same thing.

This go was the best — we got it on. Except we didn't, quite. But nearly — sort of. It went something like this. I don't recall the year, but it was Heathrow to Delhi by Aeroflot — remember them? Via, as they always did, Moscow — easily the most dangerous part of the entire trip.

The team was what might politely be termed eclectic. Let's hear it for Smiler — pathological optimist, Pollyanna and Pangloss, all rolled, somewhat untidily, into one. Nicest man you ever did meet and, as the soubriquet hints, Smiler smiled — a lot. Near as damn it, a pretty much permanent, all-but-360-degree latitudinal grin circumnavigated his head in a wrap-round, enamel-plated wonder of the universe: the physical evidence of the Nirvana of near-permanent optimism that the smile's owner inhabited; a smile so wide that you wondered if there had, at some stage, been a surgical intervention. But no surgeon could have wrought this blinding Colgate of physiognomy. And all this was weatherproof. Indeed, close to universal proof against all circumstances and all human misfortune.

A good man to have on a rainy day. The verbal manifestation of this pathology was a vocabulary of fantastic, of surreal, optimism, albeit of limited scope and

Thalay in the distance, first viewed during the search-party trip variety. As far as Smiler was concerned, all humanity, all existence, everything in the human register, could be captured in two phrases, which did universal office for all of mankind's existential and lexical needs. The first was 'Grite' (for 'Great' – he's a Brummie), which was pretty much standard; covered 90 per cent of everything and would certainly embrace mere inconveniences like flood, pestilence, contagion, pandemic, plague, disease, avalanche or sundry cluster-fuck. An impressive span, I think you'll agree. If things were better than that, like if it wasn't raining or he wasn't broke, then it was 'Fockin' Grite'. The sophist or pedant might describe this as a simplistic view of the universe: a limited take on the complexities of the human condition. The generous might argue that to smile in permanent defiance of all reason is a gift to humanity and – yep – Smiler is a gift to humanity.

Then there was Jan. Jan the Crow – don't ask; an old Marine mate and fellow traveller in more madness and scrapes than you could shake a fist, stick, cudgel, blow-pipe, boomerang, spear, pistol, rifle, 105 mm howitzer or anti-aircraft missile at (and Jan had up-close-and-personal acquaintance with all of that arsenal). He is possessed of what is probably the finest criminal mind in Europe. Had he been Russian he'd be a billionaire oligarch; he'd have owned a Premier League club – or all of them; he'd be paying barristers zillions to sort out his byzantine affairs and affaires … but he was Devonian, so it was Plymouth Argyle Saturdays and Diamond Lill's evenings. Baddest twinkling-eyed man you ever did meet. Also hard as nails. Also as kindly and as generous as Christmas. So far as I can judge the history of it, he won the Falklands all but single-handed, returning be-medalled and be-trophied, the grandest of which trophies was a brand-new Mercedes Jeep that Jan liberated from some Argentinian general in Stanley the day after the surrender – with a cheeky, 'General, I am the victor; you the vanquished. Out – you won't be needing this anymore.'

There was a four-hour delay to our flight, time which we invested in an excursion to the bar. All the other passengers seemed to have beaten us to it – as well as the crew. The passengers were drunk – all of them. So, too, the crew – all of the crew. The bar went Wild East; went Vladivostok; went Korsakov; went Kamchatka in less time than it takes to order '*Tri vodka, pazhelsta*'. This is what it must have been like when all those dodgy billion dollar gas and utility deals were going down the other side of Siberia. Booze flowed freely and was consumed apace.

At intervals, seemingly for the single sin of not being Russian, we were variously threatened with beatings, knifings, throat-slittings and buggery or, if I am to be terminologically consistent, buggeries. This continued on the plane. To go to the loo was to invite a collective howl of Anglophobic invective and to run the gauntlet of a dozen, terrifyingly explicit gestures. Few of the cameos needed translation. A throat-slitting is easily conveyed: no interlocution necessary. Same goes for evisceration; there's not much to be lost in translation. As for the buggeries, little – rather too little for my taste – was left to the imagination. Picky, I realize. Nor was there succour to be found in the cabin staff; to ask for a coffee was to earn a torrent of abuse and to get no coffee.

Somehow we got to Delhi alive; unbeaten, unknifed, unthroatslit and, mercifully, unbuggered, a fate to which, as one, the team, professed ignorance – at least of the receiving end.

Next day was Delhi to Jammu by train, then on to fabled Srinagar, ignoring, as

John E...

always, dire FCO warnings. Then, by a hitched, Leh-bound truck, over the Zoji-la to Kargil and thence south to Zanskar. The campsite paradise

Two lorry-top days later we rolled into Zanskar, a place as wild, remote, beautiful, and brutally hospitable as anywhere on Earth. We jumped off in Abring, leaving the Sikh driver and his mate balancing a primus and an enormous pressure cooker on their knees. On top of the pressure cooker, a large rock overrode the release-valve; no effete, Western safety-culture nonsense for these boys. They bounced on down to Padum cooking breakfast – a movable, if precarious, feast – while we scouted round for some likely lads to porter. After some time we had, by sign and histrionics, recruited a couple of very likely lads, and a yak and some ponies. (A liaison officer may have been handy, but we were unofficial, illegal and skimping.)

Nearby, a Genghis-lookalike farmer toiled to till a barren, drystone-walled field. He and we apprehended each other with quizzical regard: we contemplating survival on the vertical – a thing, a game, of utter irrelevance, because we could: he contemplating a hard-scrabble struggle on the horizontal – a thing, no game, of existential imperative because he had no choice. Not for the first time the metaphysics of mountaineering sat uneasily on Western conscience – the philosophical bollocks of it all.

It had started to snow and it was late. We'd go tomorrow. We asked the farmer if he'd mind if we pitched our tent by a wall that afforded some shelter from the

John Barry

Hagshu captivates the
whole journey to
beneath its face

storm. He insisted that we slept inside, in his parlour, by his fire. We spread our
cushioned mats on the mud floor, a little humbled and slightly embarrassed by our
host's hospitality as we nestled into our riches of soft pile and luxuriant down. Come
morning, we found ourselves alone in the house, to discover the entire family, hubby,
missus and a couple of kids, outside in the yard in a snowstorm all huddled under
the same yak skin and a foot of snow. It seemed they had wanted to give us Westerners some privacy. I tried to imagine the roles reversed in, say, Snowdonia or The
Lakes – and struggled.

Next day, first parade, we loaded-up, saddled-up, booted-up and headed-up to re-
find that potential base camp that I'd spotted on a search. We ambled under cobalt
skies and alongside a silver stream and talked of bear and of snow leopard.

Towards the end of the second day we found it. *Potential!* Check 'idyll' in the
Thesaurus – Paradise, Avalon, Elysium, Nirvana, Shangri La – this camp was all
and more. Add any superlative that takes your fancy – and you won't come close.
This was heavenly, veriest: grass; sky; mountains; a stream; big hills. If Heaven itself
is half as fine I'd better start minding my manners. This was a place to dwell; to
spend time; to spend your last time. And in no time we had our camp – two tents
and a tarp in our very own Elysium. And there, up the road apiece, was Hagshu. At
dawn she was luminescent; by day golden; by dusk luminous. If you had commis-
sioned Rodin to do you a mountain this is what you'd have got – but only if he was
on form. She wore a come-hither look. The faecal wasteland that is Everest wears
an only-if-you-can-afford-me-and-can-stand-the-stink look; K2, an if-you've-got-

John Barry

the balls look. Where Everest acquiesces, Hagshu winks; where K2 threatens, Hagshu beckons, flaunts – bit of a tart of a hill. And whereas Everest exacts its toll in treasure, and K2 in blood, all Hagshu wants is a flirt, and a two-step. If you can step the measure you get to climb. When folk ask, 'Why do you climb?' I show them a picture of Hagshu and of that base camp. If that doesn't do it, doesn't explain, then there's no point: nothing will. Hagshu, as Jan's Janner has it, is 'Proper job'.

But maybe not a *great* hill. To be a great hill a mountain must, perhaps, inspire fear; awe; must still the soul; quicken the heart. Everest is not a great hill, except in the narrow sense of dimension. K2 is – it holds the cards and knows it. Inspires fear and knows it; has you grasping – and gasping – for excuses. Everest has you grasping for your bus pass. No one goes to K2 lightly; you go as a cortège. The world goes to Everest as the world goes on holiday. You do Everest; K2 does you. To stand at Concordia and gaze at K2 is to look into your soul and to ask 'do I have it?' and to doubt that you do. To stand at Tangboche and gaze at Everest is to be a tourist. But to stand at our little base camp was to be privileged. Our pristine, unspoilt little beauty up the road stirred *frisson* rather than fear. Nor any soul here for many miles.

A couple of days and a reconnaissance later we assembled, loins girded, tooled-up, psyched, at the foot of the north face under an unavoidable, slightly overhanging and doubt-fuelling bergschrund, geometrically central and plumb-bound on a line that would have met with Signor Comici's or any surveyor's approval; slap-bang on the isosceles median from bottom to top. The first 10 metres – okay, make that a bit less – consumed all but about two of my entire stock of calories, but by the use

– somehow – of three axes, I got – somehow – on to the face proper. Some start. Ten or so metres out of a thousand and I'm already knackered.

From here we went arrow-straight and summit-direct, bang to the hey-diddle-diddle of it. There can be few things finer than having an unclimbed Himalayan face to yourself. The not knowing what's round the corner, not knowing whether the next metre never mind the next thousand are *possible*; not knowing whether *you* can climb the next metre – not the same thing; not knowing where the next breather lies, or belay waits; not knowing whether this is madness; whether this is, indeed, your last time: all that accumulating uncertainty draining, drip, drip, your well of courage. I love that timeless moment when you are out-front and trying to hold the line, and the 'holding infinity in the palm of your hand and eternity in an hour'. You are Vitruvian man. Four-square and spread-eagled and grasping at the furthest corners of a world of a *graffito impasto* of snow on rock; a spanning of all the universe, or the only bit of it that matters to you – that small section to your immediate front; the here, now and for the next however long or far. Anything more than a fraction below your feet is history; done, dispensed with; and anything more than a fraction above your reach is future, maybe even tomorrow – and you hope you *have* a tomorrow. And, framed and bounded by the span of your spread-eagling, the world – your world – climbs with you, move by move, inch by inch, while below Zanskar waits and whispers, 'That a man's reach should exceed his grasp – or what's a heaven for?'

The freedom: no rules, deadlines, queues; no traffic to dodgem; MOT to fail; car tax to expire; speed cameras to cheat; lies to tell police; breathalyse-able-beers to forgo, or – and wonderfully ironic this – any 'elf an' safety to trip over: just you, your mates, a mountain and the next move, and maybe a heathen prayer to the gods of hills, just in case – a sort of retrospective, almost-certainly-too-late, insurance.

We fought the hard yards; cruised the easy ones; grabbed, galloped, gambolled, gavotted and gambled – and won. Made mighty height. Pitch followed pitch with little drama beyond the sheer, unalloyed, naked, 100 per cent proof exhilaration of it all. Sure, we got lucky but, this day, we were good. We were shining

Little drama that is, except maybe this: towards the end of the day I was bringing up Smiler. The pitch had been a full rope-length and about Scottish V with next to no gear – a mind-concentrator; a soul-searcher. Smiler seemed – I couldn't see him – to be making good progress. Then, all of a sudden, the rope went tight – about Smiler plus big-hill-paraphernalia tight. The belay was good (or I wouldn't be telling you this) and all held fast. A little later, as he pulled over on to the stance, all teeth and perma-grin, I waited for some comment, some remark, word, perhaps, of a slip – after all, a fall on a Himalayan north face is not exactly the quotidian stuff of a weekend's cragging and would surely at least earn a token acknowledgement? I examined his face for some betrayal, and in the absence of word or expression, asked: 'You come off, mate?'

There was a pause, and as the smile widened to an aperture-dazzling blinder, the inevitable – you guessed it – 'Took a flyer mite … Fockin' grite!'

It was now dark and past bivvy time. There was a buttress like the bows of a battleship. It offered possibilities, not much more. We plundered those possibilities, arranging ourselves about the prow, Smiler and I either side, and an uncomplaining

Jan (personal code, 'never, over whippe") bent round the bow like a ship's fender. Nowhere was the ledge more than half a metre wide, but pegged and pitoned we were safe, if not comfy. Blithely balancing with the stove, we had a cuppa. Then sleep, sort of.

Dawn. More stove acrobatics and more tea. Did we procrastinate? You bet; bravado had gone absent; badinage had bolted; there was a collective funk. We procrastinated for several cuppas more and then, tea-fortified and courage collectively screwed to a sticking place, we got to it for Day 2. Lines of faith were followed and faith finds good fortune. (Amazing, though, how tortuous a direct line can be.)

No banter at all now; there was work to be done. I led; Jan led; Smiler led; we led all three; a mutualization of funk.

But if we had no banter we had gusto. And gusto's sometimes worth a foot; and a foot is sometimes the difference between up and down; done or dead. The force was with us again and we were going like a train. Hagshu – she doesn't lie. We got lucky every pitch: couloir led to corner, led to snow slope, led to pitch of mixed, led to buttress, led to couloir. I won't claim it was seamless, but it *went*. Sometimes it went all Tommy Cooper-ish: 'jus'-like-that', and sometimes it went with only a liberal dab of gusto; but always it *went*; always there was a hold, an unlocking move that worked, a slice of rock that surrendered, an axe-compliant chunk of ice, an accommodating splodge of snow; and always a belay and something, if only vestigial, to tie to. You can call it high-mountain savvy – or you can call it luck.

'Round there, mate.'
'Traverse right, mate.'
'Over there by the crack, mate.'
'Fuck that!'
'Cracked it! Fockin' grite!'
'I'm knackered. 'Bout time we bivvied.'
'Don't look great bivvy ground.'
'There's always one.'
'Well you find the bugger. Smart-arse.'
'This'll do.'

It can only be Smiler

John Barry

The author, showing the strain

Cut for an hour and get a feet-over-the-edge ledge, and a peg and a nut and a screw for a three-abreast-ish, beggars-can't, needs-must bivvy. Eat something. Guzzle tea. Ponder the stars and the madness beyond and think of – jeez what is it exactly that you think of? And sleep, sort of.

A snowflake! There are times when, to be woken by a snowflake's lover-like nose-tweak would be – well – the sweetest awakening imaginable. But here it fell some way short of a cuddle. I half-woke from a half-sleep. It was snowing lightly. I dozed. Now it was snowing heavily. I dozed. Now it was heaving down in torrents of spindrift avalanches, channelled slap through our bivvy site by some monstrous conspiracy of fate, weather and geology – windy too. Spent the rest of the night shedding increasing accretions of snow. Words between us were few; each lost in his own unspoken, and by the code, unspeakable anxiety. Anyway what was there to say? Grim for one is grim for all.

Some semi-conscious, huddling time later, a starless black night dawned a reluctant day of undifferentiated grey. I dug for the stove and, against all odds, got it going. The night before, a star-spangled Zanskar had been far below us; now it was nowhere to be seen. I was aware of Jan stirring: the ritual shedding of snow, the punching outwards from the inside of a still zippered bivvy bag. Snow in a sleeping bag is a wet bag, and a wet bag is white-flag time. There was a tentative unzipping, a hand carefully brushing, a nose sniffing – and Jan appeared on the end of the nose.

A council of war ensued. Plenty of fuel; and fuel is water and water is life. Some food – but you can go hungry as long as you don't go thirsty. Let's sit it out until tomorrow. There followed a long doing-nothing day and the hopeless piling of hope on hope. And then into a second night, morale sustained by brew and biscuit.

Avalanche! Smiler, who like us all, is cocooned and over-the-head-zipped in his bivvy bag, is swept off our half ledge by all-invading snow; in a spluttering, thrashing Dervish-desperate dance. Banshee yells jerk us from our half-sleep. There's no sign of Smiler, but inchoate exhortation tells us he is somewhere below. We find him in a torch beam and drag him up by the anchor ropes, still fully mummified; get him head-out, dust him off, administer encouragement and a biccie and restore him, worryingly damp, badly shaken and re-zippered, to his bivvy-spot. He's unhappy and sore. At last he also's smiling.

By the next morning all hope was fled. I woke – if, that is, I had slept – to a continuing maelstrom.

I was dozing off into it again, when Jan rolled over and from the depths of his bag began that mountaineer's reveille ritual. At last a face appeared cowled monk-like but in full buvvy bag. He smiled thinly, of scanning the horizon – which was as far as your hand could reach. The situation asked for few words. There was no longer any hope of up; and not much of down. It was hard to see how things could be worse. While I struggled for something semi-heroic to say, fumbled for words that might pass into posterity as something less than abjectly craven, Jan, with shrugged insouciance, an interminable dramatic pause, and with the affected resignation of a man about to down the first pint of a summer's evening at the local, uttered a spectacularly laconic, incongruent, insanely chirpy and faux-philosophical, 'Yer Matey … S'nodda *bad* ol' loif.'

Where he found the spirit is – well – an enduring mystery and source of wonder. Zeno and his Stoic mates might have approved.

Retreat was the unspoken and unsolicited call. We packed like desperate men and set up an abseil. I went first. At times like this it takes less courage to be the messenger. As I prepared to step into the void, I remembered the words of mock encouragement of a sergeant instructor on my first night jump, twenty years back, when learning how to parachute from Her Majesty's aeroplanes: 'Gentlemen; night jumps. Piece of duff. Like jumping from nothing into fuck-all.'

We knew that today fuck-all was Zanskar somewhere beneath, but it could have as well been the moon – though here at least we had gravity on our side.

We threw the ropes to wind and void. We could see little beyond their first few metres. Where had they gone? Where would they take us? Would there be a stance at their end? Or anywhere in between? Or an anchor? This time; next time; every time? And what if …?

Then we abseiled – from nothing into … How many times – ten, fifteen? Who's counting? We'd know when we were down – it would be flat. Into the breach – once you can handle, but ten times and you're running low on guts. But we were absurdly, beyond-faith, beyond-deserving, lucky. Abseil after abseil the ropes came compliantly down on first summons and without snag. And every time we found anchors to suit our dwindling hardware – or a spike would volunteer – or something. Once, twice, fifteen; and fifteen equals miracle. Could it be there *is* a God?

Some time towards evening we sensed ourselves on the lip of the bergschrund, the spot from which we'd set out in blithesome hope three days earlier. Now there was no anchor – or none that, in our beaten state, we could think to conjure – and our supply of hardware was exhausted. We remembered it was 10 metres, or was it 5? We chucked our sacks over and, on hearing no report, prayed for deep, forgiving, new snow and, on a count of one-two-three-and-all-together-now, we jumped – into and on to Zanskar. The landing was neck-deep and soft; never have three men been so happy to be buried alive! We laughed like madmen. And Smiler said – well you know what Smiler said. For once it was spot-on.

John Barry

Hagshu awaits

So we got down – obviously – this ain't posthumous – and trudged back to base camp for a final night in a now blizzard-besieged paradise, but paradise still – and all those other synonyms.

Down to the road, as we passed through Abring, the same farmer toiled. And I thought … because he must … because we can.… The absurdity, the idiocy of it all; the sheer, unutterable daftness. I couldn't recall who it was said that life is a great cosmic joke played on itself, but he had a point.

At the road, a single half-cocked thumb stopped the first truck – this is a hitch-hiker's galaxy – and we clambered atop and roared off towards Srinagar, beer, a bath and bordel. I was still lost in the magical realism of it; trying to make some sense of it as we settled into the rooftop-box and hunkered down for the twenty-hour trip across the magic that is Zanskar, and was maybe about to get twaddle-bound, when Jan ushered in sense – of a sort: 'Seemateitoldee – s'noddabadoloif.' (Which may be transliterated as, 'See, mate, I told you – it's not a bad old life.')

That's The Middle. The End? Someone will. Someone may have. If not, it belongs now to the boldest – which ain't me any longer. A couple of grand, thirty seconds planning – and some balls. Four should be enough; two scrotas' worth. Stand at the foot, look up, count to three and go. Go straight and do right by her. She never lied to us. And she let us off.

As Jerry Lee nearly sang, 'Hagshu, you broke my heart, you broke my will; but what a thrill.'

And, as he did say, 'Great balls of fire!'

SOME THOUGHTS ON RISK AND MOUNTAINS

Victor Saunders

Although we are professionals, most of us mountain guides are also lovers of our environment and thus, in a pure sense, true amateurs. In my opinion there is no better office to work in; I feel extremely lucky that my passion is also my job. Yet the activity that I love does not come without risk. If we are too timid, we impoverish the life we are given: if we are too bold, we make an early entry into the next. In a sense it is the decision-making process which makes climbing so captivating. In this short chapter I want to discuss our attitude to risk and our decisions around it.

When I began climbing, some decades ago, we talked of objective

Using as a theme the public and popular aspiration to summit Mount Everest, Victor Saunders discusses and attempts to quantify some of the particular objective risks climbers face when ascending the Khumbu Icefall. In doing so, he addresses the human factors that can contribute to how decisions are made in the pressurized circumstances of high mountain environments.

versus subjective risks. Emphasis on this duality has been replaced to some extent by focusing more on the human factors. After all, without humans there is no danger. As they say: 'If a serac that falls where no one can hear or see it … is it still wrong?' Of the three stories below, two concern decisions about objective risks, and one, although it looks more like a narrative about human behaviour, is more particularly about the difficulty of making good decisions under stressful circumstances.

My starting point here is that in the mountains, decisions about risk appear to be very complex, and this can, in turn, lead to poor decisions. So, how to improve the process? When we make decisions we are prone to a flow of misinformation, biases and heuristic devices which mask what is essentially a very simple but hard-to-answer question: what is the probability of an event that carries with it grave consequences?

This takes me to my first tale, which relates to Mount Everest in the climbing season of 2009. The Khumbu Icefall is well-known for being one of the more complex stages of the South Col route on the Nepali side of Everest. Here, the Khumbu Glacier tumbles steeply down from the Western Cwm to not far above base camp. It is a constantly but slowly changing maze of accessible terrain and

thinking that there was something wrong with the temperature. Definitely, over the last few years, the route has been pushing us further and further left; to the West Ridge. In 2012 we were within 25 metres of the West Ridge, with no protecting crevasse. These were warning signs to us. There was something not right this year. There was a gut feeling that said 'this is not working'. We were extremely lucky this year that there was no big accident.[3] Most people who had been there in previous years would agree – they felt that the chances of a big accident were higher than usual in 2012.

There was a near miss on the Lhotse Face on 16 May. When it was empty, part of lower Camp 3 was destroyed by a serac early in the morning. Two Sherpas were injured and needed rescuing. There were between twelve and eighteen tents destroyed – fortunately, they were empty. Had the avalanche fallen a day later there would have been in excess of twenty fatalities, most of them from the Indian Army who had placed their tents directly under a leaning serac, right in harm's way. This was a foreshadow of the tragedy that would take place on Manaslu just six months later, yet on this occasion the climbers escaped. One can only hope they learnt the relevant lesson.

There were also several major avalanches in the Khumbu Icefall, each one taking out 200 metres or more of the route. One was in the afternoon; at least two were very early in the morning. There may well have been more than these three, which are just the ones I saw evidence of. Each one covered a smaller area than the 2009 avalanche.

Being seracs, one could not predict when they would fall, but it was certain that they would fall within the climbing period. Most Chamonix-based guides felt that, if this had been Mont Blanc, the route would have been closed for the season.

Given a few assumptions, the calculation was easy to make. The chances of being caught in the Khumbu Icefall by serac fall were at least as great as in 2009 (and yes, the rest of the mountain, and the other risks, would add to that number). In the event, despite all the other fatalities on Everest in the 2012 season, no one was actually killed in the Icefall. However, this clearly does not invalidate the calculation. The probability of being caught in just that one element of risk, the Icefall, was in excess of 1.1% per person. But Himex had a very large team, with over a hundred members, including Sherpas. One in five people on the mountain would have been with Himex. If there were to be random injuries, Himex had an exceptionally high chance of hosting a victim.

So, Russell decided to remove his entire team from the mountain. Himex was the only team to take that hard decision and yet none of the remaining teams had anything but praise for it. As François Marsigny said at the time: 'To be a guide is to be able to say no!'

So why did the rest of the teams stay? Some stayed because of that attitude to risk that we can call the fatalistic approach: 'It is either going to happen to me, or not.' This is horribly common. One person I asked said the chance of an accident was 50/50. When I asked what he meant by this he replied, 'Either you get away with it or you don't; it is 50/50.' I shan't embarrass him by naming him – let us just agree we can very clearly reject this risible 'reasoning'.

So, other than the 50/50 approach, what have we got? How about gut feeling? Intuition is sometimes described as the summation of subliminal observations which the sub-conscious mind has processed but not passed on to the conscious mind. This may well be so, but is it always right to listen to it? If we have the feeling that our intuition is right it is generally because the occasions when the intuition matched the observed world are easier to remember than all the times there is no correspondence. This is a fairly obvious flaw with intuitive decisions.

But are there circumstances when intuition can be trusted? In one of the cases above, where intuition had a role in decision-making, the events feared did not materialise. This may not mean that the intuitive feelings are invalid: perhaps they can be used as a basis for more conscious analysis.

According to some experts, intuition can only be trusted in those circumstances where it is backed up by expert training and the feedback is close in time. It cannot be trusted where the feedback from the training is not there and the decision is remote.[4] From a guiding point of view, this suggests that it is a useful tool in tactics – but not for strategy, when calculation is safer. The accepted wisdom suggests that intuitive decisions have to be the result of practice and training, to come easily.

One reason we may turn to intuition is that it saves us time in hurried situations (and effort, if having to work at the calculation is hard). We often prefer to replace a difficult question with one that is easy to answer at the time. Here, by way of example, is another story from Everest, which illustrates how intuition failed in a situation where it should not have.

On 20 May 2012 there was a strong wind at Camp 4 on Everest, and only one group was able to make it to the summit that day. A team from an American commercial outfit walked past three bodies and at 8,400 metres, below the balcony, they passed a Korean who was delirious and trying to eat snow. They passed him both on the way up and on the way down.[5] Let us try to imagine how the team felt at this time. The weather was awful; they had tunnel vision; they were focused on reaching the top. They were hypoxic, so they were unable to think clearly enough to analyse the situation. Probably this was their reasoning: 'To attempt to rescue the man would cost us the summit.' This pressure would have led to the justification of their behaviour: 'He is not going to survive anyway.' Maybe they also moralized that any climber who was in trouble has only himself or herself to blame.

All of this is perfectly understandable: many, if not most, people faced with the same parameters would come to the same decision. But had the team primed themselves with a few alternative decisions, had plans B and C in the back pocket; if they had discussed what their reaction would be in such circumstances, they might have come to different conclusions. I wonder whether the guides had primed themselves with the difficult question: 'How will I and my clients feel about this afterwards?'

If they had asked this question, they might have come to a different decision. When the group passed the Korean on the way down, he was still alive and moving at that stage. It would seem that the intuitive decision mechanism failed them. Perhaps they asked themselves the wrong question. The correct question was not how likely the man was to survive the rescue, but how they would feel about themselves afterwards. Intuition did not work for them: I wonder whether the climbers feel that their summit, on that day, has been devalued.

Other than the risible 50/50 approach and unreliable intuition, there would also have been some teams (not many, but my own was amongst them) that thought

Hypoxic, exhausted and it's time to make decisions

about the numbers. These teams were generally much smaller than Russell's. For them, the chances of a random injury to the team would have been less: a team of ten members including Sherpas would have had ten times less chance of hosting a victim than Himex. Their perception of risk in relation to team size was a significant factor in deciding to stay.

So, to conclude, while consequences are fairly easy to define, calculating probabilities remains one of the most important, difficult and overlooked tools in our armoury of risk management.

We have basic statistics for climbers, summits and mortality for many of our mountains before we set foot on the route. And, as shown above, it is possible in some circumstances to put numbers to the probability of an element of the risk. This suggests that there is always a numerical probability of an event occurring; it is just that we do not always have the time or energy to estimate it. Even when it is easy to measure past events it seems hard to calculate future probabilities. Part of the reason for this is that, not only do we lack a clear way of measuring the level of risk, we also often fail to perceive and act on the different degrees of risk that we can see.

Consider, for instance, a simple financial model. Where there is increasing risk there are also bigger returns, compensating for the risk of losses: safe investments have lower returns. But when aggregated, all investments show a similar overall rate of return. In the mountains, this would be analogous to there being the same rate of fatalities for all avalanche danger levels. Yet we know there is a higher incidence rate in the middle of the avalanche danger scale. This shows very clearly that we are unable to correlate our perceived risk to actual risk.

When we take a particular course of action, we accept a level of risk; a probability that the accident will occur. This is true for all the stories above; it is true whether we are aware of it or not. By this rationale there is no such thing as luck, just a series of bets on the eventual outcome.

Accordingly, if the probability of an accident is one in a thousand, and we are that one, we have not been unlucky – we have simply been the natural result of that bet; a statistic. Someone else would have been that statistic anyway. That person was also not unlucky. And if it was us, neither would we have been. Nine hundred and ninety-nine times we would have been safe, a result of the same probability; not lucky. To think otherwise is to accept fatalism, which we have already rejected. This means that although it is difficult to count the numbers, to measure the risk, we should nevertheless try.

In summary, it is my simple belief that we should set aside fatalism. We should treat intuition with a healthy suspicion and we should try to calculate the risk we take, where possible. We should try to develop convincing ways of measuring

Victor Saunders

elements of risk which we simply guess at this time. And we should understand the qualitative difference in elements of risk, even if we cannot put numbers to them.

The Western Cwm from Camp 3

References

1 Recorded on interview 15 October 2012.
2 Interestingly, the chances of a 60-year-old in the UK not reaching their sixty-first birthday is also 1.1%. Perhaps when you compare the risk of being avalanched in the Khumbu (a beautiful place with amazing views and great weather) to the chances of not surviving 365 more miserable days in the UK (weather, suburban landscape and income taxes) you might well consider the Khumbu risk not so bad after all.
3 Recorded on interview 15 October 2012.
4 David Kahneman, *Thinking Fast and Slow*, p. 236 *et seq*.
5 Notes from a conversation with an American guide on 22 May 2012, at Camp 2. See also Leanne Shuttleworth's blog which was redacted within twenty-four hours. Fortunately the *Daily Mail* copied some of the blog before it was erased, here is an extract:

'There were casualties from the day before which was tragic and horrendous. There were quite a few bodies attached to the fixed lines and we had to walk round them. There were a couple who were still alive. Our Sherpa helped one of the people but a couple were so far gone they didn't even know we were there. It was the most horrendous thing to see.'

GLOSSARY

Ab

To abseil (*German*); the controlled descent of a cliff or steep slope using a rope. Also known as rappelling, or to rap (*French*).

Abolokov thread

A belay anchor made in good ice, where two holes are drilled into the ice, which interconnect at the ends to form a 'V'-like channel. A cord is then threaded through this hole and tied to make a loop.

Adze

The shovel part of a climbing axe. Alternatively, the axe may have a hammer end instead of an adze.

Aid-climbing

A style of climbing in which standing on or pulling oneself up via devices attached to fixed or placed protection is used to make upward progress. The term contrasts with free climbing, in which progress is made by holding on to and stepping on natural features of the rock.

Alpine style

Where the swifter, self-contained style of climbing routes in the Alps is taken to the Greater Ranges and big walls (as opposed to expedition style).

Approach shoes

A hybrid form of footwear with some characteristics common to both hiking and rock-climbing shoes.

Ascender

A mechanical device that grips on to a rope, aiding a climber to climb the rope or to haul kit. Also called jumars.

BASE jumping

An activity where participants jump from fixed objects and use a parachute to break their fall. 'BASE' is an acronym that stands for four categories of fixed objects from which one can jump: buildings, antennas, spans (bridges) and earth.

Bat-hooking

A system used in aid-climbing; shallow, drilled holes that can be hooked.

Belay

A belay is the location of the anchor used by climbers at the start and finish of a pitch of climbing.

Belaying

There are a variety of techniques that climbers use to exert friction on a climbing rope so that if they fall, they do not fall very far. A climbing partner typically applies friction at the other end of the rope whenever the climber is not moving, and removes the friction from the rope whenever the climber needs more rope to continue.

Bergschrund

A continual crevasse that forms at the point where the moving glacier pulls away from the steeper, stagnant mountain. Often a significant obstacle, even on the simplest of alpine ascents.

Camming device

A popular form of climbing protection whereby spring-loaded cams are forced out against the walls of a crack when a load is applied via the stem of the device. These work particularly well in parallel-sided cracks. Although the device seems easy to operate, it still requires a reasonable amount of practice to make a good placement.

Chocks

A general term for climbing protection that consists of metal wedges or differing sizes, trapped on wire, to be wedged in cracks. Also called 'nuts' and 'wires'. Hexes, or hollow hexcentric tubes of metal, offer climbing protection for wider cracks.

Chock-stone

A jammed rock inside a crack, around which a sling or rope can be tied.

Chossy

A mountainside where the rock is particularly loose and rubbly.

Classic abseil

An abseil where a rope is descended without the use of climbing equipment such as a harness and a metal friction device. Instead, friction is obtained by wrapping the rope around the person in a particular way in order to control the rate of descent safely, if not especially comfortably.

Coire (Cwm)

Welsh (*Gaelic*) word for a high mountain feature that has an amphitheatre-like valley head, formed by glaciation.

Crevasse

A deep crack in an ice sheet or glacier which forms as a result of the constant movement of a glacier over or around a feature in the underlying bedrock. As such, they can both open up and close.

Crux

The significant obstacle on a climb.

Dachstein mitts

Traditional heavy-duty woollen mitts, made well oversized and then boiled to shrink to a tough, thick woollen felt. As used by Scottish winter climbers, Alpinists and Himalayan expeditioners for over fifty years. Not waterproof, but when used in snow they are very effective at keeping hands warm.

Dhal baat

A traditional Nepali staple food consisting of steamed rice and cooked lentil soup.

EBs

The climbing shoe of the 1970s into the early 1980s, introduced by Frenchman Edouard Bourdonneau.

Étrier

A specially manufactured sling used in aid-climbing to allow a climber to step up higher on a piece of protection.

'Feed one's rats, to'

To get one's required fix of climbing adventure.

Friends

The brand name of the first camming devices to be developed.

Grand gendarme

A significant tower and obstacle found on an alpine ridge.

Gripped, to be

'Being gripped' is a phrase used in climbing particularly when one is a bit nervous and is gripping on too tightly to the rock. Generally suggests some state of anxiety.

Hand jam

A climbing move that succeeds by the climber holding their thumb across their hand to jam it in a similarly sized crack.

Hemp rope

Hemp was the material used for climbing ropes up until fifty years ago. Subsequently, new materials were developed that increased a rope's dynamic properties and durability, and therefore improved the safety of climbers greatly.

Hobnailed boots
Boots with hobnails inserted into the soles, usually installed in a regular pattern over the sole. Used since antiquity for inexpensive durable footwear.

Hypoxic
When the body is deprived of oxygen supply. Generalized hypoxia occurs in healthy people when they ascend to high altitude, where it causes altitude sickness which can lead to potentially fatal complications.

Jug
A very good handhold when climbing.

Jumaring
A system used in aid-climbing; the process of climbing a rope with mechanical ascenders.

Karabiner
A metal loop with a spring-loaded gate used to quickly and reversibly connect elements in climbing protection systems. A *snap link* karabiner allows for a rope to be easily clipped in and out, whilst a *screw-gate* has a rotating barrel that enables the gate to be locked.

Lay-backing
A style of climbing where, using the edge of a surface, a crack or an arête, one pulls sideways with both hands whilst pushing one's feet off the wall, relying on friction or small holds for your feet.

Météo
Weather forecast (French).

Mixed
Mixed winter climbing; climbing a frozen mountain, whether that be on snowed-up rock, frozen vegetation or with iced-up cracks.

Moac
The original purpose-made climbing protection in the form of metal wedges of differing sizes.

Névé
A type of snow which has been partially melted, refrozen and compacted, yet precedes the form of ice.

Off-width
In climbing this refers to crack features, which are wider than hand-jamming width and therefore a climber has to develop a range of jamming techniques with their arms, legs and body to succeed in climbing them. Often these cracks are difficult to protect unless one owns particularly large camming devices.

Pitch
A climbing pitch is the section climbed between two belays.

Protection
The equipment needed in trad climbing to place into the rock or ice, to protect the climbing team; to be removed again afterwards.

Prusik loops
A prusik knot is a friction hitch or knot used to put a loop of cord around a rope, which is used to grip a tensioned rope to enable it to be climbed, to aid in a rescue situation and to protect an abseil.

Pumped, to be
With the onset of lactic acid build-up in overworked muscles, such as the forearms of climbers, muscles become pumped: over-tight, and no longer operating as required. Often a difficult situation to solve when one is still trying to hang on to the chosen climb.

Quick-draw
Two snap-link karabiners connected by a very short loop of climbing sling. Used to connect the climber's rope to their protection whilst leading. Also called an extender.

Rack
This is the climber's collection of protection, such as wires, camming devices and quick-draws, and would include other equipment such as ice screws and pegs for winter conditions.

Rap

From the French *rappel*; another term for abseilling.

Rimaye

The French term for bergschrund.

RP

A small nut or wire used for rock climbing protection, named after Roland Pauligk.

Runners

From the term *running belays*; climbing protection placed by a leader to protect the ascent of a climb before climbers reach the end of a pitch.

Rurp

A Realized Ultimate Reality Piton. One of a number of differently shaped and sized pitons/pegs to be hammered into parallel cracks. Other pitons are knifeblades, lost arrows, angles and bongs.

Serac

An ice cliff where a glacier pushes itself over a significant drop, to fall as blocks of ice in a random, unpredictable fashion.

Skin-up

When ski-touring, in ascent, skins are stuck to the base of the skis to facilitate uphill skinning.

Soloing

To climb a route without ropes or climbing protection.

Sport climbing

A form of rock-climbing that differs from *traditional* rock-climbing in that it relies on permanent anchors such as bolts fixed to the rock for protection, rather than the leader placing removable protection. The style of ascent can differ in that sport climbers may then fall off more often in relative safety and practise routes that are harder than they might normally attempt when placing runners themselves.

Swing lead

Where two climbers take it in turns to lead a series of pitches on a climbing route.

Topo

A popular style of diagrammatic guidebook.

Torquing

The twisting part of a climbing axe, usually the pick, in a crack to gain purchase.

Verglas

A thin sheen of ice covering rock.

Wind slab

Wind slab is a cohesive slab of snow that is wind-deposited on to an underlying weak layer. Wind slabs consist of snow crystals broken into small particles and packed together by the wind and are created on leeward (downwind) slopes.

Zawn

A deep and narrow sea-inlet cut by erosion into sea-cliffs, and with steep or vertical side-walls.

CLIMBING GRADES

Climbing grades give a reasonable forewarning of the difficulty that can be expected on a route. As with anything concerning numbers and the aspirations of human beings, they can become the focal point of one's endeavours, but they can be the greatest motivating factor for improving on one's performance that is summed up very simply by the grade of the hardest climb you can do. Can I climb any harder?

On rock-climbs, which have different rock types promoting differing climbing styles, there is much variety and the grade is still only a guideline that adds to a route description, enabling a climbing team to make the best choices for their day of rock-climbing.

As a climber ventures into winter and alpine environments, much can be learnt about the nature of possible climbs by looking at the way they are graded, or categorized. Ice and snow climbs are described separately from buttress climbs. Within the space of two categories one can move from mountaineering terrain to definite grading levels climbs and to testing climbs of a committing nature.

Tennis Shoe, Hard Severe 4b, a classic of the Idwal Slabs, Ogwen, North Wales where the grade given doesn't perhaps allow for the polished nature of the holds now to be found on this route ...

Mal Creasey

Rock-climbing

The British grading system is for *traditional* runner-protected climbs. The adjectival grade gives an overall impression of the difficulty of the climb, taking into account factors such as how serious it is, how physically sustained it is and how technically difficult the climbing is. The addition of a technical grade gives an indication of the single hardest move on any given pitch. The grade can also suggest, at each level of difficulty, whether a route is typically a well-protected steady climb, is particularly bold with easier moves, or is technically a tough climb but safe, such as an overhanging crack. Describing climbing difficulty has come a long way from the purely descriptive terms of VDiff and Very Severe, yet it is these climbs that still make up a big part of the essence of British rock-climbing.

Bolted *sport climbs* tend to be given a single grade and, although each country can have its own grading system, typically in the UK the French system is used. A single grade is still used if a climb does have some traditional protection (such as in the USA), but there would not be anything to suggest whether the route was sustained or was a one-move-wonder.

The grading systems are as follows.

		UK	French	American
M	Moderate			
D	Difficult		F2	5.2
VD	Very Difficult		F2, F3	5.3, 5.4
S	Severe	4a, 4b	F3	5.5, 5.6
HS	Hard Severe	4a, 4b, 4c	F4	5.6, 5.7
VS	Very Severe	4b, 4c, 5a	F4+	5.8
HVS	Hard Very Severe	4c, 5a, 5b	F5, F5+	5.9, 5.10a
E1	Extremely Severe	5a, 5b, 5c	F6a	5.10b
E2		5a, 5b, 5c, 6a	F6a+, F6b	5.10c/d
E3		5b, 5c, 6a	F6b+	5.11a
E4		5b, 5c, 6a, 6b	F6c, F6c+	5.11b/c
E5		5c, 6a, 6b, 6c	F7a, F7a+, F7b	5.11d, 5.12a/b
E6		6a, 6b, 6c	F7b+, F7c, F7c+	5.12c/d, 5.13a
E7		6b, 6c, 7a	F8a, F8a+	5.13b/c
E8		6c, 7a	F8b, F8b+	5.13d, 5.14a

Alun Richardson

Sea-cliff climbing is all that's great about trad. climbing in Britain. Here at Blind Bay, next to Mother Carey's Kitchen, Trevor Messiah is climbing Aristocrat, E5 6b, belayed by Matt Spenceley

Graeme Ettle on Postman Pat, VII 7, Creag Meagaidh

Bruce Goodlad

Adam Wainwright on pitch 5 of Anzac, VI 6, on the Black Ladders, during its first ascent

Chris Parkin

Winter Climbing

As for UK rock-climbing grades, winter climbs also have a two-tiered grading system. For each overall grade there is an average technical grade, which would not normally vary more than two grades above or below the average. From the balance of the two grades the nature of the route can be determined.

In this way A V 4 would be a serious ice route, whereas a V 5 would be a tough ice route with adequate protection. A V 6 would be a classic mixed route and V 7 would suggest a technically difficult but relatively well-protected mixed route. Each route has the same overall difficulty of being Grade V, but they have different levels of technical difficulty and seriousness, which also indicates the difference between climbing ice and mixed routes.

Basic definitions of the overall grades are as follows:

Grade I
Simple snow slopes with possible corniced exits

Grade II
Gullies with individual or minor pitches
High-angled snow with difficult cornices
Ridges and easier buttress routes

Grade III 3,4,5
Gullies containing ice or mixed pitches up to 75 degrees, normally with one substantial pitch or several lesser ones
Buttress climbs with the beginnings of technical difficulty for short sections

Grade IV 3,4,5,6
Gullies and icefalls with sections of 75 degrees to near-vertical ice
Buttresses with reasonably technical sections

Grade V 4,5,6,7
Vertical ice for longer sections
Steeper buttresses with technical difficulties

Grade VI 5,6,7
Long sections of vertical and near-vertical ice with fewer resting places
Vertical buttresses with technical difficulty

Grade VII 6,7,8
Thin vertical ice, fragile freestanding pillars and icicles
Steeper buttresses with high technical difficulty

Grade VIII 7,8,9 ...
Extremely serious vertical and overhanging, very thin ice for long pitches
Very sustained and technical buttresses for long pitches

Hannah Burrows-Smith

The final section of the Forcan Ridge, Grade II, looking on towards the Saddle, Glen Shiel

Alpine Climbing

For routes of an alpine nature, whether in the European Alps or elsewhere, the French adjectival system is used (or a comparative one in the German language). These are overall grades that reflect the length, commitment and technical difficulty of a climb based on 'normal' summer conditions. The allocated grade for a route reflects a mixture of these three elements, so a short, safe climb with some steep rock pitches, and a serious snow/ice route with no special difficulty, may both have the same grade of AD.

Traversing the Aiguille Tour Noir, PD+, Argentière Glacier basin

Mal Creasey

To give more information, each grade is sub-divided by the mathematical notations '+' (superior) and '-' (inferior).

F – Facile

[faded text, largely illegible] ... on snow ice up to 40 degrees where the rope must be good; easy rock scrambles without serious exposure or technical difficulty.

PD – Peu Difficile

Consisting of steeper glacier transitional short exposed snow slopes up to 45–50 degrees; narrow ridge crests without special technical difficulty; long rock scrambles and shorter rock routes with occasional pitches of grade II/II+.

AD – *Assez Difficile*

Snow and ice ascents with angles up to 55 degrees; sustained narrow snow arêtes requiring good balance and crampon technique; complex rock ridges requiring good scrambling techniques in ascent, descent and traverse; rock routes with pitches up to III/III+ and occasional moves of IV, and where abseils may be required.

D – *Difficile*

Steep face climbs on snow and ice up to 60 degrees, with possible mixed climbing on icy rock; seriously exposed and delicate snow ridges of considerable length; major rock or mixed ridge climbs featuring rock pitches up to IV+ with occasional short sections of V.

TD – *Trés Difficile*

Long snow and ice routes with complex route-finding or technical difficulty and pitches up to 75 degrees in angle; rock and mixed ridges and faces with sustained difficulties of IV, V and occasionally VI.

ED – *Extrêmement Difficile*

Major face or couloir climbs with snow/ice pitches up to 90 degrees and/or long serious mixed sections, often with considerable objective danger; sustained rock face and buttress routes with many pitches of V and VI.

Rob Jarvis climbing on the lower walls of the Dru's north face, TD

Hannah Burrows-Smith

The grading of rock-climbing pitches on routes is given in the normal UIAA grading system and these are added to the adjectival grade where needed. These equate to the UK rock grades as shown.

The nature of alpine climbing can be further understood as one has to imagine climbing a particular grade in big boots, carrying a rucksack and at altitude – much tougher than in rock shoes, carrying a chalk bag and at sea level!

I	Easy	Simple scrambling
II	Moderate/Difficult	Short pitches of Moderate or Difficult standard
III	Very Difficult	Longer, more sustained pitches of V-Diff/ Severe
IV	Severe/Hard Severe	Steeper, sometimes strenuous, passages, up to Mild VS 4a
V	Very Severe/HVS	Long, sustained run-outs with moves of UK 4c/5a
VI	HVS/Extremely Severe	Major pitches with difficulties of UK 5a/5b

Martin Moran

On the Dent Blanche south ridge, AD

Aid Climbing

Aid climbing naturally has its own grading system, which largely comes down to how good the protection is.

To ascend a face with a multitude of cracks, but which is still too hard for most climbers to climb free (or traditionally, with one's own hands), is one thing. Here there is a methodical approach that is based on there being some good gear to rely up on, for runners and for belays – to allow a steady progression of climbers and all their kit to ascend a face during one day, or over a number of days.

The following aiding techniques are used to find the potential of many barer walls, to discover where it is possible for a human being to hang their weight and somehow make upward progress.

A0   Pulling on solid *in situ* gear – as many a traditional climber might do, on occasion.

A1   *Easy aid:* using gear placements that are straightforward to place and are solid. Aiding equipment generally required. No risk of any piece of protection pulling out. Safe falls.

A2   *Moderate aid:* gear placements solid but possibly awkward and strenuous to place. Short sections of tenuous placements above good protection. Low fall danger.

A2+   As above, with possibly several tenuous moves in a row, although still above good protection. A 5- to 8-metre fall potential but with little danger of hitting anything. Route-finding abilities may be required.

A3   *Hard aid:* involves many tenuous placements in a row above good gear. Generally solid placements (which could hold a fall) found within a pitch. Long fall potential, up to 15 metres, but generally safe from serious danger. Usually takes two to three hours to complete a pitch.

A3+   Similar to A3 but with more dangerous fall potential. Tenuous and marginal gear placements of specific aiding protection. Gear that might take bodyweight but not a fall. May include easier A4 moves but is not hard enough to be rated as such. Time required to ascend a pitch exceeds three hours.

A4:   *Serious aid:* lots of danger. A 20- to 30-metre fall potential common, with uncertain landings far below. These leads generally take many hours to complete and require the climber to endure long periods of uncertainty and fear, often requiring a ballet-like efficiency of movement in order not to upset the tenuous integrity of marginal placements.

Aid-climbing on Mount Watkins, Yosemite